Minority Governance in and beyond Europe

Minority Governance in and beyond Europe

Celebrating 10 Years of the European Yearbook of Minority Issues

Edited by

Tove H. Malloy and Joseph Marko

EURAC research

EUROPÄISCHE AKADEMIE

ACCADEMIA EUROPEA

EUROPEAN ACADEMY

BOZEN - BOLZANO

EUROPEAN CENTRE FOR MINORITY ISSUES

TUTA SUB AEGIDE PALLAS · 1683 ·

BRILL
NIJHOFF

LEIDEN | BOSTON

Library of Congress Control Number: 2014954490

ISBN 978-90-04-27648-2 (paperback)
ISBN 978-90-04-27649-9 (e-book)

This book is printed on acid-free paper.

Table of Contents

Tove Malloy and Joseph Marko

Foreword

On behalf of the editorial team, we are pleased and honored to present the special jubilee volume of the *European Yearbook of Minority Issues*. This volume is dedicated to the issuance of ten *Yearbooks* and is designed to emphasize and reflect its major achievements during the last decade.

The European Yearbook of Minority Issues was launched in the early 2000s as a unique multidisciplinary periodical with the view to provide a critical and timely review of contemporary developments in minority-related problems in Europe and beyond. Looking back, we believe that the *Yearbook*, as had been envisaged from its outset, has been combining analysis, commentary and documentation in relation to conflict management, international legal developments and domestic legislation affecting ethnic and national minorities.

The idea behind this jubilee volume is to celebrate the anniversary by issuing a collection of emblematic articles from the previous volumes, which are still relevant to date. The *Yearbook* authors have made many important contributions both to the theoretical understanding of minority issues and to the analysis of domestic and international legal and political developments. For a variety of reasons, the *Yearbook* has a limited audience, and the publishing team therefore wished to launch a volume, which would be easily accessible for scholars, students and policy-makers engaging in minority-related activities and interested in valuable insights concerning multiethnicity and cultural pluralism in Europe.

The choice the editors were to make was not an easy one, and the selection of 10 articles does not mean that all other contributions to the *Yearbook* do not deserve the same degree of attention. The editors exempted more than 250 excellently written academic articles that were published in the *Yearbook* during these last years. For obvious reasons, in this instance, the preference was given to theoretical articles and articles that address lasting normative and institutional developments at the pan-European level. Hence, the jubilee volume offers an academic lens that sharpens the reader's understanding where more academic thinking and political will is needed to advance the minority rights protection regime in Europe in the future and to continue the European path of integration. This volume gathers contributions dealing with several key fields in minority protection, namely, the theory and practical implications of power-sharing;

the dichotomy of 'old' and 'new' minorities; definitions of human rights violations; public institutions for minority protection and countering discrimination; theoretical reflections on minority activism; political participation of minorities; justifications of minority protection; the evolution of language rights; minorities and the evolution of EU law; and Roma issues within the European Union. There is no doubt that this compilation cannot cover all significant—be this fundamental or topical—issues pertinent to minorities, but we hope that it will serve as a valuable contribution to the most demanded scholarly literature in this thematic area.

The article by Carmen Kettley "Power-Sharing and Ethnic Conflict: The Consociational-Integrative Dichotomy and Beyond" (Vol. 1) addresses the issues of institutional design in fragmented societies, which have become central for the recent debates around democracy theory and conflict regulation. The author points out that the broad and multi-layered notion of power-sharing coined by Timothy Sisk is perceived as an overarching term for two basic approaches: consociationalism and the so-called integrative approach. The former implies a complex policy and institutional design which includes so-called grand coalitions of different segments which serve as the given society's constituent elements; segmental autonomy; veto power of the segments; and the principle of proportionality which concerns representation and resource distribution. The model, often closely associated with its pioneer Arend Lijphart, is subject to criticism for the exaggeration of the role played by elites and negligence of segregation patterns in societies at large. The integrative approach put forward by Donald Horowitz envisages incentives for the creation of institutions and public movements transcending ethnic dividing lines. In addition, this approach evokes criticism because it ultimately contributes to institutionalization of ethnic divisions, but it can also lead to majoritarian rule in disguise. Carmen Kettley argues that the scholars should look at power-sharing from a broader perspective without confining it to either of the basic approaches. Instead, researchers shall take into account the entire multiplicity of the existing power-sharing arrangements, pay due attention to exogenous factors, such as involvement of international organizations that create incentives for interethnic cooperation, and integrate human and minority rights polices into the analytical framework.

Asbjørn Eide's article "The Rights of 'Old' versus 'New' Minorities" (Vol. 2) concerns the distinction between so-called 'old' and 'new' (or migrant) minorities, which has become topical among scholars and practitioners in the recent years. Although empirical evidence does not suggest any clear dividing line between the two categories, political considerations and common wisdom back this dichotomy. Besides, it can be grounded in political philosophy in the sense that if 'old' minorities are the groups whose residence precede the given state's independence, then they must be regarded as a part of the initial social contract, while the groups having arrived later are not. Asbjørn Eide suggests looking at the issue from a legal standpoint and summarizes the approaches embedded in the modern international instruments pertinent to minority protection. He argues that minority protection ought to be regarded as a derivative of the human rights law, or a way to adjust the general human rights approach to the specific minority context. In this perspective, general human rights, such as the liberty of assembly and association, the right to free expression and so forth apply to all without distinctions on the grounds of ethnicity. What really matters is citizenship, because the so-called participatory rights stipulated in several international instruments can be legitimately restricted on the grounds of citizenship. However, the latter concerns the division between 'old' and 'immigrant' minorities indirectly. Asbjørn Eide also points out that there is no universal consensus of the scope and content of the so-called positive obligations of states, particularly with regard to culture and language, and nothing obstructs preferences for 'old' or 'traditional' minorities.

William A. Schabas focused on the recent developments around the trials in the International Criminal Tribunal for the former Yugoslavia (ICTY) in his article "'Ethnic Cleansing' and Genocide: Similarities and Distinctions" (Vol. 3). In 2004, the ICTY Appeal Chamber concluded with some reservations that the crime of genocide had been committed on the territory of Bosnia and Herzegovina, and this decision prompted reexamination of where a dividing line between 'genocide' and 'ethnic cleansing' can be drawn. While 'genocide' is a clearly defined legal notion which has become a part of international human rights law, 'ethnic cleansing', which means persecution on ethnic grounds aiming at physical relocation of certain ethnicities, remains a journalistic term, although widely applicable in the vocabulary of international organizations. The author describes the recent controversies stemming from the narrow legal definition embedded in the UN Convention on Genocide of 1948 (implying that genocide is a crime committed with direct intent to physically exterminate a national, ethnic or religious group) and the need to adequately qualify the crimes against humanity committed during the recent armed conflicts which in fact amount to genocide. The case of *Krstic*, central for the author's analysis, which concerned the mass extermination of Muslim Bosnian men in Srebrenica, gave rise to legal arguments both in favor of and against the qualification of this crime as genocide. The ICTY ruling and the legal reasoning behind it did not clarify the distinction between genocide and ethnic cleansing, and the issue remains highly relevant.

The article by Andrea Krizsán "Ombudsmen and Similar Institutions for Protection against Racial and Ethnic Discrimination" (Vol. 4) analyses the operational patterns and potential opportunities of the relatively new institutions. The recent change in the international and EU law as well as in domestic legislations brought about the need to have independent public institutions for countering discrimination on a multiplicity of grounds. Among the new organizations forms are ombudsmen on racial and ethnic discrimination, of which many follow the working scheme introduced by Sweden that pioneered this development. Andrea Krizsán observes the existing models and lists the opportunities the institution of ombudsmen offers. Being a multi-functional body with a broad mandate, on discrimination issues, an ombudsman can consult individual victims; he or she may represent public interest in a court of justice where private action may be inefficient or too burdensome for an individual; he or she may have more capacities for conducting monitoring and collecting information than any civil society actor can have; ombudsmen can carry out effective awareness raising campaigns targeting both the general public and the civil servant; the institution can coordinate action of other public institutions in charge of anti-discrimination and so forth. In general, the institution in question needs further development and analysis.

David Smallbone's article "Ethnic Minority Entrepreneurship, Diversity and Competiveness" (Vol. 5) concerns minority businesses and their potential input to social integration. The case-study addresses entrepreneurs of minority origin in the UK, particularly in London. The statistic data available show that people of minority origin who engage in business usually run small enterprises which are in their large part oriented at customers belonging to the same group or networks connecting them to their co-ethnics or countries of origin. However, minority businesses demonstrate a variety of patterns, and in many circumstances they transcend ethnic and racial boundaries and serve as a device for integration. This integrative effect multiplies when minority businesses bring input to the local communities' development or increase their attractiveness for tourism; positive outcomes can be also achieved through governmental supplier policies which are in their early stage in the UK and elsewhere in Europe.

Rainer Hofmann's article, "Political Participation of Minorities" (Vol. 6), is the annotated version of the first Annual Minority Rights Lecture held on 30 November 2006 at the Institute for Minority Rights in Bozen/Bolzano. The lecture elaborated on political participation practices as established by the Advisory Committee under the Council of Europe Framework Convention on National Minorities (FCNM), Article 15. While the necessity for effective political participation of minorities is widely accepted by the Council of Europe member states, it remains a major challenge to define to whom and under which conditions these rights shall apply as well as how they shall be implemented. An inclusive approach, as supported by the Advisory Committee and the HCNM, would favour the application of the FCNM, albeit on a differentiated right-to-right basis, to members of "old minorities" as well as "new minorities". As regards the application of Article 15 of the FCNM, the political participation of national minorities is based on individual and group rights, namely, the freedom of association, electoral rights such as the right to vote and the right to run for offices during elections, electoral mechanisms that safeguard the rights of minorities as well as consultation mechanisms and bodies such as binding co-decision procedures or *stricto sensu*. However, Hofmann underlines that the bottleneck for political participation of "new minorities" remains the possession of the citizenship that guarantees for all political rights to the individual. Political participation of "new minorities" as a collective body remains widely restricted to consultative mechanisms *stricto sensu* embedded in the governance systems of the Council of Europe member states.

"Shifts in the Multiple Justifications of Minority Protection", authored by Sia Spiliopoulou Åkermark (Vol. 7), resumes the historical justifications for the existence of minority rights as international obligations of states. There are four raisons d´etre for minority rights, namely, peace and security, human dignity, protection of culture(s) and cultural diversity, democratic participation and democratic pluralism. These have evolved over time and are interconnected and mutually reinforcing. Minority rights as a guarantee for peace and security go back to the establishment of minority rights provisions of interstate peace treaties, in particular the post-World War I Paris Peace Treaties, as well as unilateral declarations of the states before the League of Nations that, at the same time, created the international dimensioning of today's minority rights regime. The League of Nations, as the first international body that safeguarded the rights of minorities, fostered the internationalization of minority rights and the more recent bilateralism of minority rights, as well as the establishment of the HCNM, both of which are a continuance for this international trend. More recently, under the FCNM, minority rights became explicitly embraced under the umbrella of international human rights law. The most recent development is the interpretation of minority rights as an inherent part of democratic participation based on citizenship rights that secure rights to the individual member of a minority group on the one hand and the representation of group interests on the other hand. These four justifications for minority rights shall be taken into account during the interpretation and implementation of legal norms to guarantee for minority protection its constant relevance and its potential for development.

Roberta Medda-Windischer's article "The European Convention on Human Rights and Language Rights: Is the Glass Half Empty or Half Full?" (Vol. 8) elaborates on the safeguarding of language rights under the prohibition of discrimination enshrined in Article 14 ECHR. It rules out the discrimination on the ground of language and of belonging to a national minority, in conjunction with the enjoyment of other provisions defined in the Convention. Medda-Windischer's contribution provides a timely overview of the evolution of case law and the interpretation of Article 14 by the Strasbourg Court regarding the use of minority languages in judicial proceedings as a prerequisite for effective participation in public life as well as political representation, of minority languages in the educational sector and in the media as well as of identity-related issues that *inter alia* regard the use of the minority language in the name-giving of persons and topography. Medda-Windischer demonstrates how the interpretation of the ECHR and its protocols in the jurisprudence of the Court became the main mechanism that fostered the applicability of the ECHR for safeguarding the rights of minority groups and in particular their language rights. Nevertheless, the case law also makes evident that the Court followed a conservative approach in regard to the protection and the advancement of the language rights regime in administration, in subnational assemblies as well as in the use of one's name in the form of the minority language. Also, the author finds that the Court remains hesitant in regard to the application of positive discrimination measures that could vent the rights of minorities and the use of their languages.

"Defining the Indefinable: A Definition of 'Minority' in EU Law" by Gulara Guliyeva (Vol. 9) is an avant-garde contribution of how the European Union may develop a wide framework definition of the term minority. In 1993, the European Union made the protection of minorities conditional in the frame of the Copenhagen accession criteria, thereby creating a double standard for the protection of minorities in the "new" and "old" EU member states. Also, Article 2 TEU states that minority rights are an inherent part of the EU's identity and Article 21(1) of the EU Charter of Fundamental Rights guarantees for equality and non-discrimination *inter alia* for members of a national minority, the European Union, and in particular, the European Court of Justice, remained silent on defining the concept of minority in the light of EU law. Guliyeva assesses various defining elements of minorities by drawing from the CCPR, the FCNM and member state practices thereby keeping an eye on the multifacetedness of minority groups in Europe. She elaborates on a wide needs-based minority concept that backs away from the established "labelling" of minority groups and argues that the needs-based approach creates flexibility and an inclusive approach for appropriate state action that assures minorities, be they "new" or "old", be included under the minority rights umbrella.

Peter Vermeersch's contribution, "The European Union and the Roma: An Analysis of Recent Institutional and Policy Developments" (Vol. 10), provides an overview of how the European Union institutions have responded to the "Roma issue" thereby elaborating on the increasing Europeanization of the various problems that Roma encounter in today's Europe. Vermeersch underlines the significance of the institutional developments, in particular, the Racial Equality Directive 2000/43/EC, the Copenhagen accession criteria, the Charter of Fundamental Rights and their reporting systems as well as the social inclusion agenda as part of the EU's 2020 agenda that helped to bring the situation of Roma to the attention of policy makers on the European and on the national level. At the same time, various European initiatives were implemented as responses to the rising xenophobia and populism *vis-à-vis* Roma in the member states of the European Union. Vermeersch underlines the consolidation of the "European Roma Summits" that function as a platform for the change of information and advisory boards between policy makers, Roma representatives and the wider advocacy community and the European Commission's Communication COM(2011)17 that calls for active dialogue with the Roma on the national and the European level. Furthermore, the European Union has been keen in promoting social inclusion on the local level with the help of EU funds. Nevertheless, despite the rise in awareness and responsiveness on the European level, Vermeersch warns that the Europeanisation of the "Roma issue" may curb the attention of the local, regional and national authorities who shall remain the main responsible actors for accommodating the Roma.

We are extremely grateful to a large number of individuals who have contributed to this volume; first and foremost the contributors to this volume. Special thanks are extended to all the general editors of the *Yearbook* since its inception Arie Bloed, Rainer Hofmann, Josef Marko, James Mayall, John

Packer, Sia Spiliopoulou Åkermark, Hanna Suchocka, Marc Weller, Francesco Palermo, Ilze Brands-Kehris, Petra Roter and Markku Suksi. We thank Ugo Caruso, Maren Meyer and Alexander Osipov, the co-managing editors from EURAC and ECMI, who have completed this volume. We are also grateful to our copy editors, Melanie Bonsall and Katherine Nobbs, for their careful work. As always, a particular debt is owed to Lindy Melman of Martinus Nijhoff Publishers.

Dr. Tove Malloy,
Director, the European Centre for Minority Issues, ECMI

Prof. Dr. Joseph Marko,
Head of Institute, the Institute for Minority Rights at the European Academy of Bozen/Bolzano EURAC

*Carmen Kettley**

Power-Sharing and Ethnic Conflict: The Consociational-Integrative Dichotomy and Beyond**

> We no longer lack basic data on ethnicity. We lack explanation – principles by which to classify cases, depictions of the structure and texture of group relations, an understanding of patterns of conflict-explanation that would hold cross-culturally. There is, in the main, too much knowledge and not enough understanding, too much evidence chasing after too few categories.
>
> *Donald Horowitz*[1]

I. Introduction

Power-sharing has become a fashionable theme in the study of institutional design for multiethnic societies since the end of the Cold War. It has evolved out of an equally fashionable debate on the applicability of the most advocated models of institutional design in fragmented societies: the consociational democracy theory and the integrative model of ethnic conflict regulation. Both models have become *the* main approaches to power-sharing, although much too often the concept of power sharing itself is either erroneously identified with consociationalism only, or limited to defining an all-inclusive power-sharing executive.

However, in order for research on power-sharing to advance, it needs to depart from explanations and normative prescriptions based on a single "grand logic".[2] The complex nature of ethnic conflict and its destabilizing potential have revealed that unidimensional or dichotomous approaches to institutional design often fail to provide adequate explanations of more recent patterns of power-sharing in countries experiencing various degrees of ethnic unrest. This paper

* The author is a PhD student in International Relations at the Centre of International Studies, University of Cambridge, UK and a member of Wolfson College, Cambridge, UK.

** An earlier version of this paper was presented at the Annual Convention of the Association for the Study of Nationalities (ASN), Columbia University, New York, 4-7 April 2001.

1 Donald Horowitz, *Ethnic Groups in Conflict* (Berkeley, 1985), xi.

2 Bernard Hoffman and Robert Stockwell, "Institutional Design in Plural Societies: Mitigating Ethnic Conflict and Fostering Stable Democracy", paper prepared for the University of Messina Conference on The Political Economy of Institutional Development, 14-17 September 2000, at http:// www.democ.uci.edu/democ/papers/stock.htm#N_1_.

Minority Governance in and beyond Europe, ISBN 978-90-04-27648-2. pp. 1-21.

argues that power-sharing includes both consociational and integrative principles but represents more than the sum of the two models. Elite cooperation, electoral devices and autonomous powers may be initially sufficient to achieve political stability in ethnically divided societies. The question that arises, however, is whether this limited set of regulatory measures alone can ensure long-term political stability and a self-sustainable multiethnic polity. Any observer of the evolution of communal disputes throughout the world during the past decade would notice that ethnic conflict represents a process, the dynamics of which are influenced by both internal and external factors sometimes unrelated to the conflict itself. Hence, power-sharing should be seen as a flexible strategy, able to adapt to changing circumstances. Therefore, my contention is that productive research programmes on power-sharing need to integrate analyses of other determinants that are critical to the design and, ultimately, the success of any power-sharing project. Such determinants include, but are not limited to, the legal framework, the relationship between elites and the groups they represent, the dynamics of party politics, political culture, economic development and the complex role of exogenous factors.

The purpose of this paper is to indicate the possibilities for elevating the debate on power-sharing beyond the confines of the consociational-integrative divide. An in-depth critique of the consociational and integrative approaches to power-sharing is beyond the scope of this paper. However, the analysis below includes a brief overview of the most controversial issues raised by each approach. This overview aims to highlight the limitations as well as the contributions of consociational and integrative principles to expanding the meaning and the applicability of power-sharing, both as a concept and as a means of interethnic accommodation.

II. Political and Academic Responses to Ethnic Conflict

A. Political Responses

The salience and complexity of ethnic conflict, in particular of self-determination disputes, have constantly been acknowledged in recent years by both scholars and politicians. However, there is little agreement on what are the best political, social and legal means to balance the interests of minorities and majorities in multiethnic societies.

The option generally preferred by states is a system based on the liberal principles of equality and non-discrimination and on the operationalization of the individual rights discourse. Minorities claim that the liberal solution does not offer sufficient guarantees, in particular linguistic rights, for the preservation of ethnic identity. They request collective rights and autonomy in order to control their cultural reproduction.[3] Moreover, the content of the terms 'autonomy' and 'collective rights' remains highly controversial, hence difficult to negotiate, as there is little agreement on what concrete meanings should be ascribed to these terms.

3 George Schöpflin, *Nations, Identity, Power* (London, 2000), 7, 65, 233.

Unlike secession and coercive practices, autonomy is seen as a less costly and less threatening mechanism of ethnic conflict management. Given its flexibility, both as a concept and as a tool, autonomy can be conveniently tailored to each specific case to which it is applied. It provides multiple possibilities from minimum competence to a broad range of powers short of full independence.[4] However, autonomy remains largely a political concept and it is unlikely that it will acquire the status of a 'right' in international law in the foreseeable future. It has therefore been argued that more emphasis should be placed on political participation and specific autonomous powers for minorities and on policies conducive to a genuine implementation of human rights norms.[5]

However, larger ethnic groups do not always limit their claims to autonomy. Provided that they do not agitate for secession, such groups also seek power, demanding some degree of control over the state itself. The more numerous minorities tend to organize themselves politically and to participate in regular electoral processes. By acting as political contenders, minorities do not limit their claims to individual participation in public life, but also seek organized access to central decision-making power. That is, minority groups seek to share power with the dominant majority.

B. Academic Responses

The issue of political stability in ethnically divided societies has generated a multitude of competing research programmes. There is little consensus, however, within the academic community as to which approach to ethnic conflict management would ensure greater chances for social peace and political stability. The theoretical frameworks proposed vary, ranging from the incompatibility theory of conflict regulation[6] and the control approach[7] to the conflict management approach[8] and

4 See Ruth Lapidoth, *Autonomy: Flexible Solutions to Ethnic Conflict* (Washington, 1996). See also Hurst Hannum, *Autonomy. Sovereignty and Self-Determination: The Accommodation of Conflicting Rights* (Philadelphia, 1996).

5 Patrick Thornberry, "Images of Autonomy and Individual and Collective Rights in International Instruments on the Rights of Minorities", in Markku Suksi (ed.), *Autonomy: Applications and Implications* (The Hague, 1996), 121-4.

6 Michael G. Smith, "Pluralism, Violence and the Modern State", in Ali Kazancigil (ed.), *The State in Global Perspective* (Paris, 1986); John S. Furnival, "Colonial Policy and Practice", in John Stone (ed.), *Race. Ethnicity and Social Change* (London, 1977); and John S. Furnival, *The Netherlands India: A Study ofPlural Economy* (Amsterdam, 1986). See also Alvin Rabushka and Kenneth Schepsle, "Political Entrepreneurship and Patterns of Democratic Instability in Plural Societies", 12(4) *Race* (1971), 462, 467, 470; and Rabushka and Schepsle, *Politics in Plural Societies: A Theory of Democratic Instability* (Columbus, Ohio, 1972).

7 Ian Lustick, "Stability in Deeply Divided Societies: Consociationalism versus Control", 31 *World Politics* (1979), 325-44.

8 See John Burton, *Conflict: Resolution and Provention* (New York, 1990); and id., "Unfinished Business in Conflict Resolution", in John Burton and Frank Dukes

the power sharing approach.[9] From the perspective of institutional design, it has been agreed that the most feasible options for solving interethnic disputes remain policies that accommodate the demands of minority groups within the political institutions of the existing states.

During the Cold War era, political science developed two major normative models of political engineering for fragmented societies: the consociational theory and the integrative model of ethnic conflict regulation. These approaches to conflict management have become the most frequently advocated theoretical models of system design for fragmented societies. Consociational democracy theory and the integrative approach were originally developed in order to explain the types of institutional design in 'deviant' cases of fragmented, albeit stable, societies in Western Europe. It was also hoped that either model could assist the nation-building processes of plural[10] or deeply divided[11] societies in the new independent states formed as a consequence of decolonization.

In the post-Cold War era, consociationalism and integrative theory remain the most popular theoretical models of institutional design for multiethnic societies provided by political science. As both theoretical positions claimed universality in their application, the assumption was that either consociationalism or the integrative approach could be conveniently applied to Central and Eastern Europe and elsewhere, without these models requiring major alterations. Consequently, regions like Central and Eastern Europe were included in the 'basket' of plural/fragmented/deeply divided societies together with Switzerland, Belgium, Malaysia, Lebanon and South Africa. However, as has been acknowledged by Sisk:

> Which approach will contribute to success is highly dependent on the structure of ethnic relations, the specific patterns of ethnic politics in a given community, the historical development of a given conflict, the relationship between

---

(eds.), *Conflict: Readings in Management and Resolution* (London, 1990), 328-36.

9 See Arend Lijphart, *Democracy in Plural Societies: A Comparative Exploration* (New Haven, 1977); Horowitz, *Ethnic Groups in Conflict;* and Timothy Sisk, *Power Sharing and International Mediation in Ethnic Conflict* (New York, 1996).

10 The term 'plural society' was originally defined by Harry Eckstein as a society "where political divisions follow very closely, and especially concern lines of objective social differentiation, especially those particularly salient in a society". See Harry Eckstein, *Division and Cohesion in Democracy: A Study of Norway* (Princeton, 1966), 34. Building on Eckstein's definition, Lijphart calls such divisions 'segmental cleavages', thus defining a plural society as "a society divided by 'segmental cleavages' ... that may be of a religious, ideological, linguistic, regional, cultural, racial, or ethnic nature". See Lijphart, *Democracy in Plural Societies ...*, 3-4.

11 Horowitz indicates that deeply divided societies are those societies where "ethnic affiliations are powerful, permeative, passionate and pervasive". See Horowitz, *Ethnic Groups in Conflict*, 12. In addition, Sisk argues that "the hallmark of a deeply divided society ... is the presence of separate organisations that permeate and divide every aspect of society on the basis of identity". See Sisk, *Power Sharing ...*, 15.

> the ethnic group and the state, the attitudes and the skills of political leaders, and the ability of the groups in conflict to agree on the core principles of the political system.[12]

Despite this acknowledgement, or perhaps because of it, no further steps have been taken to test these models against the patterns of ethnic conflict in more recent instances of communal conflict. For example, recent practice in some Central and Eastern European countries indicates the emergence of specific patterns of institutional design and minority practices that have not been considered to date by traditional approaches. In particular, power-sharing arrangements in Romania, Slovakia or Bulgaria have been established in constitutional, political and social circumstances which, traditionally, are considered unfavourable to power-sharing. Specifically, traditional approaches to power-sharing tend to dismiss a unitary form of state organization, unbalanced group size and lack of a tradition of elite cooperation as factors conducive to power-sharing.

While consociationalism and the integrative model suggest that they are mutually exclusive, both approaches to power-sharing are based on the same fundamental assumption: that political stability in fragmented societies can be achieved and maintained through some form of joint decision-making. Hence, although each approach proposes different institutions and mechanisms for achieving political stability, they agree that the main vehicle to achieve such stability is power-sharing. In an attempt to unify consociationalism and the integrative model in a single conceptual framework, both approaches were incorporated by Sisk into the broader concept of power-sharing, which has become the theoretical umbrella for tackling conflict resolution in fragmented societies throughout the world.[13] However, Sisk's debate on power-sharing remains centred on the consociational-integrative dichotomy. As will be explained below the advancement of the intellectual inquiry in the area of interethnic accommodation requires expanding the analysis of power-sharing beyond the traditional debates regarding the applicability of one theoretical model or the other.

III. The Consociational-Integrative Debate: Its Origins and the Current Controversies

A. The Incompatibility Approach and Coercive Conflict Management Strategies

Traditionally, the focus of political thought has been on how to attain stability in a culturally homogeneous society. The conventional wisdom in political thinking has been, for centuries, the belief that people of different cultures cannot live together peacefully in the same state. This thinking is based upon the assumption that their traditions, languages and laws create differences that are so great as to

12 Sisk, *Power Sharing* ..., 48.

13 Ibid., 3-9.

make these peoples incompatible with one another. This belief was, perhaps, best exemplified in John Stuart Mill's frequently quoted statement on culturally heterogeneous societies: "Among a people without fellow-feeling, especially if they read and speak different languages, the united public opinion, necessary for the working of representative government, cannot exist."[14]

Mill's pessimistic assumption retains a great deal of significance today, as it continues to be used to justify both oppression and secession in many societies torn by ethnic or religious conflict. The failure of many post-colonial states to achieve political stability has been considered an obvious example of the impossibility of ethnically fragmented societies to conduct a successful state-building and nation-building process. Mill's fatalism has inspired generations of political philosophers and scientists in their pessimistic perspective on political engineering in fragmented societies. Thus, Claude argues, since human beings have a low potential to cope with human diversity, contacts between different cultural groups normally lead to the domination by the larger group.[15] Further, Walzer adopts the Hobbesian postulate on controlling the Leviathan by arguing that "politics follow nationality wherever politics is free"[16] therefore the most likely outcome of contacts between "incompatible" groups is tyranny by the dominant group.[17]

The works of both Furnival and Smith represent, perhaps, the most influential expressions of the incompatibility approach.[18] They offer, respectively, an economic and an anthropological account of the prospects for stability in fragmented societies. Thus, by confining interethnic relations to economic interests, Furnival believes that in fragmented societies unrestrained competition for the control of the state and for access to resources leads to uncontrollable social fragmentation and no sense of common belonging since cultural diversity inhibits any attempt at social cohesion. This generates a bleak prospect for political stability, since such a lack of social cohesion leads to incoherent and inefficient governance. Therefore, stability can only be achieved and maintained by the intervention of an external force, that is a colonial power.[19]

The incompatibility approach could be sustained by the many examples of state failure and widespread ethnic conflict after the Second World War. Indeed, the end of colonialism did not just mean the emergence of new states but also the emergence of weak states, most of them ethnically heterogeneous. As the focus of

14 John Stuart Mill, *Utilitarianism: On Liberty and Considerations on Representative Government* (London, 1972), 361.

15 See Inis L. Claude, *National Minorities: An International Problem* (Greenwood, 1969), 1. See also Richard A. Schemerhorn. *Comparative Ethnic Relations* (Chicago, 1978), 68.

16 Michael Walzer *et al.*, *The Politics of Ethnicity* (Cambridge, MA, 1982), 6.

17 For a more detailed analysis of the incompatibility approach, see Stephen Ryan, *Ethnic Conflict and International Relations* (Aldershot, 1995), 29-43.

18 Furnival, "Colonial Policy and Practice"; Smith, "Pluralism. Violence and the Modern State".

19 Furnival, *Netherlands India ...*, 450-59.

Western scholars and policy makers alike was on how to achieve political stability by means of homogenization, they applied the normative prescriptions advanced by the incompatibility approach to the new post-colonial states. Homogenization strategies were based on the assumption that ethnic fragmentation was to be overcome by the assimilation of smaller groups into the larger nation. Interethnic accommodation was not considered a significant determinant of political stability. When communal violence began to break out, in virtually every post-colonial state, in the absence of any alternative explanation, traditional incompatibility rhetoric was used by post-colonial governments to design coercive homogenization policies against rebellious minorities. However, as Schöpflin has correctly argued: "Individuals may assimilate, usually if they migrate, but whole communities will not, because a community that has become aware of itself as a bearer of moral values will not abandon this status."[20]

The coercive nature of the political strategies that were developed from the incompatibility approach did not bring the political stability, though, that policy makers and scholars anticipated. Empirical evidence overwhelmingly demonstrates that secession, assimilation, control or genocide are neither realistic nor legal or moral responses to ethnic conflict. The evolution of ethnic conflict in Central and Eastern Europe during the 1990s represents a relevant test of the feasibility of coercive strategies of conflict regulation.

Thus, secession involves the territorial separation of an ethnic group resulting in the formation of a new independent state or in unification with a kin-state. However, secession often faces insurmountable practical difficulties and significant legal constraints under international law. For example, the current ethnic make-up of Central and Eastern European states leaves virtually little room for secession as a means of ethnic conflict resolution. Although they vary in size, Eastern European minorities remain overwhelmingly outnumbered by their dominant majorities. Also, minority populations are often mixed with other groups, and hardly form homogenous territorial units. This makes the prospects of these minorities establishing their own independent states or uniting with a kin-state highly unfeasible. Moreover, following the bloodshed that accompanied the dissolution of Yugoslavia, the international community reaffirmed its commitment to discouraging secessionist movements even in cases where secession, as an expression of the right to self-determination, appears to be the only realistic solution.[21] In Feith and Smith's words: "The UN recognises the right of all peoples to self-determination. But where a 'people' is a 'minority' the UN seeks only to 'protect' it."[22] Most notably, the international community's rejection of the secessionist

20 Schöpflin, *Nations, Identity, Power*, 232-3.

21 See e.g. Denisa Kostovicova, "Albanian Schooling in Kosovo 1992-1998: Liberty Imprisoned", in K. Drezov, B. Gokay and D. Kostovicova (eds.), *Myths, Conflict and War*, Southeast Europe Series (Keele, 1999).

22 Herb Feith and Alan Smith, "Self-Determination in the 1990s: Equipping the UN to Resolve Ethno-National Conflicts", in Kumar Rupensighe (ed.), *Conflict Transformation* (New York, 1995), 153.

claims of the Kosovar Albanians leaves little doubt that self-determination may be negotiable for 'peoples', for example Slovaks, Croats, and/or Slovenians, but is not available to minorities. Further, forced assimilation, genocide and population transfer are not only immoral options but they are also banned by international law. Finally, hegemonic control has the potential to lead to political dictatorship and is incompatible with the commitment of the post-communist states to democracy and the protection of human rights.

It follows that the most productive options remain policies that accommodate the grievances of minority groups within the political institutions of the existing states. However, there is little agreement on the best political and legal means to balance the interests of minorities and majorities.

B. The Consociational Democracy Theory: The Institutionalization of Ethnic Fragmentation

Towards the end of the 1960s, it became evident that the academic debate on political stability in fragmented societies represented more than an intellectual exercise.[23] Traditional 'remedies' based on the incompatibility approach could not sustain the nation-building processes in new post-colonial countries. In addition, the majoritarian electoral system was criticized for increasing social fragmentation and accused of encouraging the exclusion of ethnic groups from participation in central decision-making. There was therefore a need for a novel theoretical approach to political stability that would consider "systems in which political groups like to settle their conflicts by negotiated agreements among all the relevant actors, the majority principle being applicable to fairly limited domains only".[24]

The initial boost, and challenge, to the study of political stability in fragmented societies was provided by the launch of the consociational democracy approach. This approach addressed the possibility of designing a type of cooperative political system similar to the one initially envisaged by both Lembruch and Lijphart in the late 1960s. Consociationalism substantiated and justified its approach to political stability in fragmented societies by referring to the destabilizing effect of social segmentation on such societies. Fragmentation was believed to be generated by overlapping cleavages,[25] a lack of mobility amongst particular segments of society, a lack of floating voters[26] and by strict group differentiation. Arend Lijphart's approach, explained for the first time in his article

23 Kenneth D. McRae, "Theories of Power-Sharing and Conflict Management", in Joseph Montville (ed.), *Conflict and Peacemaking in Multiethnic Societies* (New York, 1991), 93.

24 Gerhard Lembruch, "A Non-Competitive Pattern of Conflict Management in Liberal Democracies: The Case of Switzerland, Austria and Lebanon", in Kenneth D. McRae (ed.), *Consociational Democracy* (Toronto, 1974), 91.

25 Lijphart, "Consociational Democracy", 21(2) *World Politics* (1969), 207-11.

26 Lembruch, *Non-Competitive Pattern ...*, 91.

"Consociational Democracy", published in *World Politics* in 1969,[27] represented a paradigm shift in the study of fragmented societies.

"Consociational democracy means government by elite cartel designed to turn democracy with a fragmented political culture into a stable democracy."[28] This definition was later operationalized by Lijphart in his 1977 study *Democracy in Plural Societies: A Comparative Exploration*,[29] which has become the classic text on consociationalism. Lijphart defines the four characteristics of consociational democracy as: grand coalition, segmental autonomy, proportionality, and mutual veto. All of these characteristics, Lijphart argues, must be present if a political system is to qualify as a consociational democracy.[30] However, this theoretical premise raises doubts regarding the extent to which consociationalism is applicable to the diversity of fragmented societies worldwide. In addition, each individual characteristic of consociationalism, as promoted by Lijphart, raises important theoretical and practical problems in itself.

1. Grand Coalition and the Proportionality Principle

An essential characteristic of consociationalism is the inclusion of representatives of all segments of society in the decision-making process by the creation of a power-sharing executive. This inclusion is also to be achieved by the formation of grand post-electoral coalitions, by proportionality in the electoral system and in the distribution of public offices and resources. Apart from differences in emphasis, most advocates of the consociational approach share the same core idea: that democratic stability is endangered by majoritarianism but is achieved at the elite level by non-majoritarian mechanisms for conflict resolution. These mechanisms should be institutionally anchored in all-inclusive governing coalitions. Proportional representation, therefore, is the electoral system that allows for the formation of such grand coalitions. A grand coalition, as envisaged by Lijphart, seeks to ensure a fair representation of all social segments. The consociational formula for a power-sharing executive seeks to involve representatives of all mobilized groups in a country and suggests that no democratic opposition is necessary to balance the government's actions. A question that consociational theory leaves unanswered, though, is by what mechanisms a power-sharing government can be made accountable to the electorate.

2. Segmental Autonomy

Another mechanism proposed by consociationalism is to assign to the elites of each group a large degree of control over its own affairs either through territorial or institutional mechanisms. Such segmental autonomy would have the function of keeping groups separate from each other, since less interaction among differ-

27 Lijphart, "Consociational Democracy ...", 207-25.

28 Ibid., 216.

29 Lijphart, *Democracy in Plural Societies*, 25-52.

30 Ibid.

ent segments has the potential to reduce conflict.[31] The consociationalists' plea for social separation raises fears of segmental autonomy becoming a strong incentive for secession.[32] Lijphart argues that there is no empirical evidence to suggest that federalism encourages separatism more than a unitary system.[33]

However, the difficulty with the consociational proposition for segmental autonomy does not rest with the idea of autonomy itself. Rather, it is related to the basic belief of consociationalism that increased contact between ethnic groups is potentially dangerous. Thus, whilst elite cooperation is crucial to political stability the 'segments' should remain in relative isolation as "good social fences make good political neighbours".[34] It is therefore questionable whether segmental isolation does contribute to long-term political stability and ultimately to the survival of the state itself. Segmental isolation need not be dismissed at all stages of conflict management. Such a formula may be necessary at an early stage of the peace process, especially in the case of violent conflicts, but it is doubtful whether long-term segmental isolation could help maintain a minimal will of the 'segments' to live in the same state.

3. Mutual Veto

The mechanism of a mutual veto is regarded as an important consociational device for protecting minorities against the abuses of the majority. The potential of the mutual veto for fostering political stability has been constantly questioned on the grounds that it generates immobility in the decision-making process. The consociationalists' response to this challenge is that even non-decisions are preferable to bad decisions.[35] However, such an assertion merely compounds the controversy about whether consociationalism can ensure long-term political stability whilst allowing political life the necessary dynamics that ensure progress.

4. Methodological Issues

Methodological inconsistencies add to the difficulties in interpreting consociational reasoning and challenge its validity as a coherent theory.[36] Thus, for example, the criteria by which multiethnic, plural, deeply divided or fragmented societies can be identified remain vague. Lijphart's response to these criticisms is that the

---

31 See Quincy Wright, "The Nature of Conflict", 4 *Western Political Quarterly* (1951), 192-211; Lijphart, "Consociational Democracy", 219.

32 Nordlinger, *Conflict Regulation* ... , 32.

33 See Arend Lijphart, "Power Sharing and Group Autonomy in the 1990s and the 21st Century" (1999), at http://www.nd.edu/~kellogg/pdfs/Lijphart.pdf.

34 Lijphart, "Consociational Democracy", 219.

35 See Lijphart, *Democracy in Plural Societies* ..., 36-8; Nordlinger, *Conflict Regulation* ..., 24-6.

36 For a useful critique of Lijphart's methodology and terminological inconsistencies, see also Rudy Andeweg, "Consociational Democracy", *Annual Review of Political Science* (2000), 509-36; and Ian Lustick, "Lijphart, Lakatos, and Consociationalism", 59 *World Politics* (1997), 88-177.

size of groups, their electoral strength and the overlapping of segmental boundaries with political boundaries indicate whether a society is plural, deeply divided or fragmented, although he leaves these terms unexplained.[37] Furthermore, "[O] n the basis of which criterion can one say that some division is *not* a cleavage and that a cleavage is *not* segmental?"[38] In other words, the question that arises is: to what extent does the existence of politically organized minorities, and of ethnic voting patterns, indicate that a society is so badly divided that it requires consociational treatment, in particular segmental isolation, in order to survive?

Answering such questions in view of the enormous diversity of ethnic conflicts makes the application of consociationalism to the complexity of ethnic relations even more difficult. It is important to note here that initially, consociational theorists believed that the presence of ethnic conflict in a society would inhibit the applicability of mechanisms associated with a consociational democracy. Thus, Barry argues that the question "may not be how the country is to be run but whether there should be a country at all".[39] Indeed, the consociational approach was originally designed to apply to religious and ideological conflicts. However, consociationalism was later embraced by scholars of ethnic conflict with no change to its core assumptions. Such an adoption raises doubts about the relevance of consociational theory, as a universal panacea, to the diversity of multiethnic societies and the complex challenges they face at the beginning of the twenty-first century.

5. The Role of Elites

Perhaps the most controversial aspect of consociational theory remains the issue of elite cooperation and the relationship between elites and masses. Consociationalism sees the behaviour of elites as the essential element of a stable democracy. The central argument of consociationalism is that elite cooperation can successfully overcome the flaws of traditional decision-making by the majority. Thus, elites seek to accommodate political conflicts through compromise or amicable agreement. For consociationalists this can be achieved by the "depoliticization" of a given conflict, for example by defining the conflict as "technical", economic or legal, rather than as an ideological, ethnic or religious conflict,[40] or by avoiding discussion of the conflict at all.[41]

Further, it is suggested that elite cooperation is necessary and sufficient for containing conflict and maintaining political stability. According to Nordlinger, "elites alone can initiate, work *out* and implement conflict regulating practices,

37 Arend Lijphart, "Consociational Theory: Problems and Prospects", 13 *Comparative Politics (1981)*, 355-9.

38 Marcel van Schendelen, "The Views of Arend Lijphart and Collected Criticisms", 19 *Acta Politica* (1984), 31 (emphasis in the original).

39 Brian Barry, "Review Article: Political Accommodation and Consociational Democracy", 5 *British Journal of Political Science* (1975), 503.

40 See e.g. Arend Lijphart, *The Politics of Accommodation: Pluralism and Democracy* in *the Netherlands* (Berkeley, 1975), 129-30.

41 Nordlinger, *Conflict Regulation* ..., 24-6.

therefore they alone can make direct and positive contributions to regulating outcomes."[42] However, by assuming the deference of the masses to their leaders, consociationalists ignore an important reality. That is, in deeply divided societies 'social apartheid' is often caused by the same elites who are expected by the advocates of consociationalism to cooperate.[43]

Moreover, consociationalism ignores the role that the masses have in creating or destroying a stable society as there are numerous examples of masses revolting against their cooperating leaders. The relationship between social segmentation and elite cooperation appears to be of minimal importance to consociationalism, since elites are assumed to cooperate and the masses are expected to support their leaders' political strategies. Consequently, no mechanism of controlling elites' behaviour is considered necessary. This assumption raises the question of whether a consociational political system can be referred to as a consociational *democracy,* since the masses are excluded from any real influence in the decision-making process.

6. Consociationalism in Action: Empirical Controversies

Traditional theoretical approaches to power-sharing have evolved out of a rather narrow interpretation of questionable cases. That is, the construction of the classic normative prescriptions for power-sharing was based on past and temporary instances of consociationalism or integrative practices. Many of these have either collapsed, renewing ethnic conflict (Lebanon, Nigeria), or have been transformed into liberal democracies proper (The Netherlands, Austria). The potential of consociational and integrative models to stand the test of time therefore remains controversial. In addition, the existing theoretical frameworks for institutional design in multiethnic societies have been based on a Western understanding of cultural diversity. However, these models claim to hold universal validity, irrespective of the region or type of conflict they are applied to.

Lijphart's original interpretation of Dutch consociationalism has been questioned on the grounds that Dutch society was never as fragmented as Lijphart suggested. Moreover, religious and class cleavages in Dutch society were actually cross-cutting and the risk of political instability was relatively minor. Likewise, Barry argues that Switzerland was never a plural society in Lijphart's terms, and that the Federal Council is not really a grand coalition because its members do not primarily act as representatives of subcultures.[44] Moreover, Daadler wonders

42 Ibid., 73.

43 George Tsebelis, "Elite Interaction and Constitution Building in Consociational Democracies", 2(1) *Journal of Theoretical Politics* (1990), 5-29. See also Richard Rose, "Northern Ireland: The Irreducible Conflict", in Joseph Montville (ed.), *Conflict and Peacemaking in Multiethnic Societies* (New York, 1991), 148; Horowitz, *Ethnic Groups in Conflict,* 568-76; id., *A Democratic South Africa? Constitutional Engineering in a Divided Society* (Berkeley, 1991), 137-45.

44 Barry, "Review Article ...", 502.

whether Switzerland ever fitted the consociational model at all, as it never had the depth of segmentation that the model stipulates.[45]

Similarly, arguments that South Africa, India or the Lebanon were consociational democracies at some moment in their history have added more doubts about the validity of consociational theory as a whole. This is because its theoretical construction is largely based on past and temporary cases of consociationalism.[46] Today, most of these countries retain no significant consociational elements in their political systems.

Furthermore, the traditional consociational scheme in more recent cases, such as Northern Ireland, has also been altered. The power-sharing system prescribed by the Good Friday Agreement, whilst providing incentives for executive power-sharing and segmental autonomy, does not require parties to have a formal coalition agreement as prescribed by consociational theory. Likewise, the power-sharing system in Northern Ireland does not follow the party-list proportional representation (PR) voting system advocated by consociationalism. Rather, the parties decided that the single transferable vote (STV) system better served their interests. This is because it was believed that it would encourage voters to give second preferences to pro-Agreement parties.[47] Finally, the survival of the Good Friday Agreement would have been impossible without the support of large segments of the population, although the difficulties encountered by its implementation reveal once more that elite cooperation needs to be accompanied by intergroup reconciliation for political stability to be achieved and maintained.

Against all the odds, Lijphart and his supporters remain dedicated to searching for evidence of consociational elements in every fragmented society, past or present, that appears to approximate Lijphart's prescriptions. Thus, consociational aspects of political engineering have been identified in India,[48] Columbia,[49] and the European Union.[50] However, the quest of the consociational scholars to identify elements of consociationalism in their recent investigations is inconsistent with Lijphart's original claim that consociationalism can only operate, as a political system, if all of its four defining characteristics are present. Such inconsistency has led his critics to argue that Lijphart is attempting to 'create' case studies for the purpose of validating his theory. In Halpern's words, "[t]he empirical inconsisten-

45 Hans Daadler, "The Consociational Democracy Theme", 26 *World Politics* (1974), 604-21.

46 Ibid., 618.

47 Brendan O'Leary, *The Nature of the Agreement,* text to accompany the 9th John Whyte Memorial Lecture, 26 November 1998, at www.incore.ulst.ac.uk/home/publication/conference/oleary.html.

48 Arend Lijphart, "The Puzzle of the Indian Democracy: A Consociational Interpretation", 90 *American Political Science Review* (1996), 258-68.

49 Robert H. Dix, "Consociational Democracy: The Case of Columbia", 12 *Comparative Politics* (1980), 303-21.

50 Matthew J. Gabel, "The Endurance of Supranational Governance: A Consociational Interpretation of the European Union", 30 *Comparative Politics* (1998), 463, 475.

cies within the consociational universe, and the debates engendered by them, are largely unresolvable since ... the disordered universe does not emanate from the cases but from the construction of the model."[51]

Nevertheless, consociationalism constantly claims universality of applicability to culturally fragmented societies. For most plural societies, Lijphart argues, the choice should be "between consociational democracy and no democracy at all".[52] However, consociationalism neglects the great diversity of cases and the peculiarities of each political, legal and social context to which it attempts to apply its universal model.

Lijphart has made attempts to broaden the theory by introducing the concept of consensus democracy.[53] This refers to a form of political engineering characterized by institutional devices that broaden involvement in decision-making. The concept of consensus democracy, advocated by Lijphart, claims to provide a softer option for political systems that cannot fulfil all the four criteria for consociational engineering. Similarly, Lijphart sees the consensus approach as tailored to 'divided' or 'semi-plural' societies rather than to deeply divided/plural societies, although he leaves the meanings of all of these terms unexplained. In order to distinguish between the consociational and the consensus model, Lijphart claims that "consociationalism is the stronger medicine: while consensus government provides many incentives for broad power-sharing, consociationalism requires it".[54] Hence, consensus democracy is seen as a "kinder, gentler" type of democracy, which would respond to claims for democratic quality, as it is not bound by a rigid combination of criteria for achieving stability.[55] However, consensus democracy has not replaced consociational democracy as the debate on consociationalism continues – independently from the debate on consensus democracy.[56]

B. The Integrative Approach: The Institutionalization of Multiculturalism

As a response to the rigidity of the normative prescriptions of consociational democracy theory Donald Horowitz has developed an alternative approach to ethnic conflict regulation, labelled by most scholars the "integrative approach".[57]

---

51 Sue M. Halpern, "The Disorderly Universe of Consociational Democracy", 9 *Western European Politics* (1986), 182.

52 Lijphart, *Democracy in Plural Societies ...*, 238.

53 Id., *Democracies: Patterns of Majoritarian and Consensus Government in 21 Countries* (New Haven, Conn., 1984). See also id., Patterns of Democracy: Government Forms and Performance in Thirty-Six Countries (New Haven, Conn., 1999).

54 Id., "Democratic Political Systems: Types, Cases, Causes, and Consequences", 1 *Journal of Theoretical Politics* (1989), 41.

55 Id., *Patterns of Democracy ...*, 275-301. For a more detailed criticism of Lijphart's consensus model, see also Andeweg, "Consociational Democracy", 512-4.

56 Andeweg, "Consociational Democracy", 513.

57 Horowitz, *Ethnic Groups in Conflict*, 563-684.

Unlike consociationalism, which assumes elite cooperation and relies on minority veto for protecting minorities' interests, the integrative approach relies on incentives for intergroup cooperation, in particular electoral systems that encourage the formation of pre-election pacts among candidates or political parties across ethnic lines. From the perspective of the integrative approach, the key to intergroup cooperation is to foster a political organization that cross-cuts ethnic loyalties.[58]

Thus, Horowitz's approach seeks to enhance minorities' influence in majority decision-making by the creation of incentives for moderation by political elites on contentious ethnic issues.[59] Rather than constructing a model of accommodation that sees ethnic groups as separate 'pillars', Horowitz's model proposes the creation of pre-election coalitions between ethnic parties and, ideally, the creation of larger multiethnic parties that transcend ethnic interests. For example, Horowitz emphasizes the role of economic and regional factors in generating social cleavages that crosscut ethnic loyalties. The idea of the United States as a cultural and ethnic 'melting pot' is often used to substantiate Horowitz's ideal of non-ascriptive, integrative political systems.

In order to transform a deeply divided society into a stable, and integrated, multiethnic polity, Horowitz proposes five mechanisms of conflict reduction.[60] Firstly, the devolution of the state's territorial powers, which would "proliferate points of power so as to take the heat off a single local point";[61] secondly, devolution of power on ethnic criteria for the purpose of encouraging intraethnic competition at the local level; thirdly, the creation of electoral systems that would encourage pre-election coalitions through the process of vote polling; fourthly, policies to encourage alternative social alignments such as those based upon social class or territory; and finally, a reduction of the disparities between groups through a fair distribution of resources.

The difficulties in validating Horowitz's integrative approach are, in some respects, similar to those identified by the critics of consociationalism. For example, both Lijphart and Horowitz propose federalism as a means of ensuring an adequate degree of autonomy for nondominant groups, in the belief that federalism generates better system support by the masses. The scope of the federalism proposed by Horowitz differs from the scope of Lijphart's model of segmental isolation. Although Horowitz acknowledges that "there is little more than dogma available about the utility of federalism",[62] he remains confident that federalism ensures a useful dispersion of powers to specific conflict zones. Such dispersion would transfer the heat of the conflict from the centre to local conflict areas. At the local level, intraethnic competition would help reduce interethnic competition, thus allowing the central government to work. However, much too often

58 Ibid., 596.

59 Ibid., 291-443.

60 Ibid., 597-680.

61 Ibid., 598.

62 Ibid., 602.

conflicts are fuelled by the centre and, in turn, local disputes often multiply inevitably reaching the centre and, in extreme cases, spreading across national borders. The disastrous dissolution of Yugoslavia is, perhaps, the most obvious example of the potentially lethal combination of such conflict dynamics. In addition, contrary to the conventional wisdom that federalism is a more flexible tool for cultural accommodation, recent research has shown that unitary states receive greater system support by their citizens than federal states.[63] According to Derbyshire and Derbyshire, federal states account for only 24 out of the 192 recognized states, although many other instances of decentralization have been recorded.[64]

The essence of the integrative model is the idea of integrating minority elites into the larger political fabric of the state by encouraging the formation of multiethnic parties rather than multiethnic coalitions.[65] Critics of the integrative approach argue that Horowitz's model is essentially majoritarian. Thus, whilst integrative mechanisms encourage majority representatives to develop a moderate, minority-friendly attitude, nondominant groups remain excluded from the exercise of real decision-making power.[66] To Horowitz, the PR system is not necessarily the only electoral mechanism that ensures the effective participation of minorities in the political decision-making process. On the contrary, Horowitz doubts the merits of the PR list-system in fostering interethnic cooperation as he believes that PR enhances ethnic divisions rather than reducing them. Instead, he favours alternative voting as a more effective mechanism to induce moderation among ethnic contenders. In addition, Horowitz argues that the majoritarian system should not be excluded from the range of options available to reducing conflict. He contends that "[i]t is not the Westminster system that causes the problem in such societies, but the Westminster system coupled with ethnically based parties."[67]

IV. The Power-Sharing Approach: Main Limitations and the Current Theoretical Debate

Both, the consociational and integrative approach to ethnic conflict seek to promote power-sharing executives that are broadly inclusive of all ethnic groups in a multiethnic society. Advocates of these approaches remain divided, however, over

63 See Pippa Norris, "Designing Democracies: Institutional Arrangements and System Support", paper presented at the Workshop on Confidence in Democratic Institutions in Comparative Perspective, 25-27 August 1997, Washington DC.

64 Dennis Derbyshire and Ian Derbyshire, *Political Systems of the World* (New York, 1996).

65 Horowitz, *Ethnic Groups in Conflict*, 629-50.

66 Sisk, *Power Sharing* ..., 44.

67 Donald Horowitz, "Ethnic Conflict Management for Policymakers", in Joseph Montville (ed,), *Conflict and Peacemaking in Multiethnic Societies* (New York, 1991), 116.

how such coalitions should be shaped and which specific institutions and mechanisms ensure a greater chance of success for political stability.

The first significant breakthrough in the consociational-integrative debate is represented by Timothy Sisk's attempt to unify the consociational and the integrative approaches under the conceptual umbrella of power-sharing. Power-sharing, Sisk argues, encompasses both approaches, as different institutions and mechanisms of managing ethnic conflict can be assembled and implemented in diverse ways.[68] Sisk defines power-sharing political systems "as those that foster governing coalitions inclusive of most, if not all, major mobilised ethnic groups in society".[69] Furthermore, Sisk emphasizes the international dimension of power-sharing in the contemporary world by highlighting the role of international mediation in achieving and maintaining political stability in ethnically divided societies.[70] Sisk's contribution to the research on power-sharing is pathbreaking in several respects.

Firstly, power-sharing is directly related to the existence, or the creation, of a democratic system of government within which modern interpretations of the principles of self-determination and democracy can be constructively interpreted and combined. Secondly, this new approach emphasizes the importance of human rights and of judicial mechanisms for ensuring an effective protection of minorities: "One important conflict-regulating practice often ignored by power-sharing theorists, or at least downplayed, is the role of human rights (particularly the careful balance between individual and group rights) and the role of judicial institutions in ethnic conflict mitigation."[71] Thirdly, Sisk correctly argues that patterns of cooperation should be encouraged not only at the elite level but that such patterns should influence and penetrate all aspects of society.[72]

V. Conclusion

Despite their limitations, and unlike incompatibility theories, both models demonstrate that the existence of a stable multiethnic state is possible and that severe disputes and outbreak of violence do not represent "a tragedy of necessity".[73] Most importantly, both approaches acknowledge the crucial importance of the political participation of minorities through power-sharing arrangements. Finally, the consociational and the integrative prescriptions for stability in fragmented societies need not be dismissed. Questioning the validity and the applicability of these models does not entail invalidating their basic ideas: that elite behaviour, electoral systems, autonomy arrangements, and institutional mechanisms of conflict

---

68 Sisk, *Power Sharing* ..., 6.

69 Ibid., 4.

70 Ibid., 77-80.

71 Ibid., 66-8.

72 Ibid., 82-5.

73 Ryan, *Ethnic Conflict and International Relations*, 49.

regulation have an essential contribution to make to the success of power-sharing design and implementation.

However, much of the debate on system design in multiethnic societies is channelled through the consociational-integrative divide. This has become a false and unproductive dichotomy. Each one of the strategies of accommodation outlined above may be effective and constructive when considering the particular ethnic environments that shape minority-majority interactions. It would be conceptually unrealistic and practically unproductive if one strategy or another were used in its pure form. Such a position would entail disregarding useful elements of other options for system design and conflict management. Explanatory and political resources for interpreting and managing ethnic conflicts would consequently be reduced.

Sisk's emphasis on the multiple facets of power-sharing reveals the need to take the discussion on conflict-regulating practices one step further. Constructive research on power-sharing needs to acknowledge that ethnic conflict is a highly complex phenomenon. Multiethnic societies provide an overwhelming diversity of conflicting interests as well as common purposes, hence very diverse social and political patterns of conflict and conflict management. Such multiple aspects of analysis require a new complex vision that, nevertheless, could provide a more coherent yet flexible theoretical framework for policy makers.

Yet, the conceptual foundation of the current power-sharing debate is clearly not sufficiently reflective of contemporary practice.[74] Indeed, practical instances of power-sharing in recent years have revealed not only that the most diverse combinations of elements of these two models have been utilized but also that other factors have a critical influence upon the success of power-sharing arrangements. These factors include most notably, democracy and the rule of law, the protection of basic human rights and economic development. Recent practice has also demonstrated that such arrangements are more complex in real life than either the consociational or the integrative models suggest, as they do not rely on a single theoretical prescription. Although the current literature provides an abundance of critical analyses of these two models, little intellectual inquiry has been devoted to elevating the debate on interethnic accommodation beyond the consociational-integrative dichotomy. It has become evident that the debate around a limited set of variables – decision rules, territorial divisions of power and electoral devices – has become unproductive.

Steiner argued that one way to explore interethnic accommodation beyond the confines of consociationalism is to narrow the focus of analysis from entire countries to specific issues within a country.[75] Such a methodological shift would

---

74 See Carmen Kettley, James Sullivan and Jessie Fyfe, "Resolving Self-Determination Disputes Through Complex Power-Sharing Arrangements: A Background Paper for Debate" (Cambridge, 2001), prepared for the 1st workshop of the project Resolving Self-Determination Disputes Through Complex Power-Sharing Arrangements.

75 Jurg Steiner, "Research Strategies Beyond Consociational Democracy", 43 *Journal of Politics* (1981) 1241-50.

provide a better understanding of the impact of cultural identities upon the decision-making process. This, in turn, would generate a more realistic picture of the actual degree of segmentation in the society to be stabilized.

Indeed, an in-depth knowledge and analysis of specific issues in a particular country is a critical aspect of any productive analysis of power-sharing. However, my contention is that Steiner's issue-centred approach de-emphasizes the complex economic, legal, political and social contexts in which specific ethnic relations develop. For example, economic development, political culture and the dynamics of party politics are often ignored, yet they are important variables, especially in transition countries where democracy remains 'work in progress'. It is important to note that such countries, most notably in Central and Eastern Europe, are facing multiple tasks that would place an enormous strain on any political system.[76] Thus, transition countries have to face simultaneously the burdens of economic reform and the pressures of the world market, the reconstruction of civil society, and the consolidation of a new political system based on values which are novel to most people in these countries.

Consequently, ethnicity is only one of the challenges these states are confronted with. As Mayall correctly argues, "there is a real need for an improved capacity of diagnosis and dealing with the symptoms."[77] Indeed, an identification of the real issues in each individual case is crucial to designing an adequate institutional framework for interethnic accommodation. A summary diagnosis of interethnic relations could lead to the construction of theoretical frameworks of questionable validity with potentially dangerous practical consequences. Therefore, it appears to be more worthwhile to identify the conditions that are favourable to power-sharing *in a given context,* rather than to attempt a generalization of past cases where consociationalist or integrative formulae are claimed to have been employed. Generalizations should emerge out of in-depth, context-sensitive analyses of case studies and may then provide the intellectual foundation for the construction of productive power-sharing research programmes.

Power-sharing is not a purpose in itself but a means to achieve the greater goal of political stability and, ultimately, social peace in ethnically divided societies. If this purpose is to be addressed productively, additional issues need to be incorporated and analyzed.

---

76 For a valuable account of the challenges of transition in Central and Eastern Europe, see Pippa Norris, "Ballots not Bullets: Testing Consociational Theories of Ethnic Conflict, Electoral Systems and Democratisation", paper presented at the Institutional Conference of International Design, Conflict Management and Democracy in the Late Twentieth Century, Kellog Institute, University of Notre Dame, 9-11 December 1999. See also Juan Linz and Alfred Stepan, *Problems of Democratic Transition and Consolidation* (Baltimore/London, 1996),434-57.

77 James Mayall, "Sovereignty and Self-Determination in the New Europe", in Hugh Miall (ed.), *Minority Rights in Europe: The Scope for a Transnational Regime* (London, 1994), 13.

Firstly, a distinction should be made between power-sharing regimes and power-sharing arrangements. A power-sharing regime indicates a system of government that is essential to the existence of a multiethnic polity. It represents the ultimate institutionalization of ethnicity. Power-sharing arrangements refer to political engineering and institutional adjustments to an existent political system, which promote an effective political participation of numerically smaller minorities in the political decision-making. This distinction is particularly important for those unitary states where the dominant group overwhelmingly outnumbers minority groups.

Secondly, the impact of exogenous factors upon domestic political order should be assessed. International intervention has recently become a common feature of domestic power-sharing arrangements, as ethnic conflict is often internationalized by involving kin-states, regional institutions and the international community as a whole. As Sisk has convincingly argued, the timing, purpose and extent of international intervention are of special importance for the effectiveness of such intervention.[78] It is also important to note that the foreign policy interests of these countries have shaped the political will of domestic governments and have directly altered the domestic legal framework. In addition, the dynamics of the relationship between kin-state and host-state is often an important factor in conflict escalation and/or de-escalation.

Thirdly, the debates on minority rights and political engineering should be integrated into power-sharing analysis. Whilst both law and political science address the complexity of ethnic conflict, they tend to develop parallel prescriptions to ethnic conflict management. This means that theoretical discourses on rights and policies do not intersect. One aspect that is often ignored in political analyses is that the existence of a legal framework for the protection of human rights is of crucial importance for any endeavour to accommodate the conflicting interests of minorities and majorities. In addition, a minority rights system is needed to ensure the protection of smaller minorities that are not part of specific power-sharing arrangements. The traditional models of institutional design, proposed by political science, are based on a limited set of rigid prescriptions, in particular a formal power-sharing executive and federalism. These models largely ignore the crucial importance of the rule of law, the protection of human rights and economic development in sustaining power-sharing arrangements. Similarly, current legal research on ethnic conflict retains a narrow focus on the detailed codification of minority rights and autonomy. It has a tendency to ignore the actual problems related to the implementation of international standards and the role of political processes as determinants of effective minority policies. As Hannum has correctly noted, "[i]n many states, a new partnership must be created between minorities and the majority and it may be too late for that partnership to be founded solely on a few minority schools and newspapers."[79]

78 Sisk, *Power Sharing* ..., 80-1.

79 Hannum, *Autonomy, Sovereignty and Self-Determination* ..., 73.

Power-sharing is a product of political science. Hence, analyses of power-sharing tend to limit their focus to political institutions and processes. However, policies and institutions are not established in a regulatory vacuum, nor are they immune to limitations of a legal nature. Governments, electoral systems and territorial arrangements are established within legal frameworks that are shaped by both domestic and international laws. The type of state, the domestic constitutional order and the role of the judiciary have a critical impact upon the limits and the utility of institutional arrangements in a specific country. Institutional design that ignores the role of the law in shaping and sustaining political institutions and processes is unproductive.

The relationship between politics and law is one of interdependence. Politics implies the existence of the law, in the same way as the law is, to a large extent, politics.[80] Thus, politics creates the law that, in turn, controls political action. Institutional design for multiethnic societies is largely a matter of how politics and law are combined. One important aspect of the relationship between law and politics is that some basic constitutional principles generally survive political processes. Constitutional norms that shape the type of state and territorial arrangements tend to outlive changes of political regimes in many countries, sometimes despite historic revolutionary changes. Therefore, such fundamental norms are long-term indicators of the possibilities, and the limitations, of macro-political decision-making. This is particularly the case in the highly sensitive area of interethnic relations. Eastern Europe represents a remarkable example of the diversity of ways in which law and politics interact and how such interactions can have dramatic consequences for interethnic relations. I therefore argue that current theoretical approaches to power-sharing require significant adjustments in order to advance theory and to inform policy.

Finally, the consequences of power-sharing should be assessed. It is important to emphasize that power-sharing institutionalizes ethnicity. Whilst the current trend in scholarly work, and international law and politics, is to celebrate multiculturalism and to promote a detailed institutionalization of ethnic differences, such practices can have both beneficial and dangerous consequences. It is therefore important for both theorists and policy makers to carefully assess how political stability, in a given society, can be best achieved and maintained.[81] The options for such stability include a power-sharing system of government, area-specific power-sharing arrangements and various forms of autonomy, or simply an effective legal framework for the protection of minorities. Decisions for one option or another must be based on consideration of the specific environment in which interethnic relations develop.

80 Louis Henkin, *International Law: Politics, Values and Functions,* 216(4) Recueil des cours (1989), 251.

81 Sisk, *Power Sharing* ... , 8.

*Asbjørn Eide**

The Rights of 'Old' versus 'New' Minorities

I. Problem Description

International minority rights law is law in the making. Important developments took place during the last decade of the twentieth century, but many issues remain vague and uncharted. In the long-standing efforts by the international community to develop international protection of minority rights, it has been impossible to agree on a definition of 'minority'. One of the stumbling blocks has been the disagreement on whether so-called 'new' minorities should be included, and if so, whether they should have the same rights as the 'old' minorities.

The purpose of this paper is to address that issue *de lege ferenda* (how the law should be, i.e. to which extent should minority protection extend to new minorities?). A second, related question is by which criteria we should separate the 'old' from the 'new'. I shall use as illustration the provisions of the United Nations Declaration of the Rights of Persons belonging to National or Ethnic, Religious and Linguistic Minorities (UNDeclMin).

As a basis for a meaningful discussion of the first question we would have to examine the justifications for minority protection, in order to make a reasoned assessment as to whether new minorities should be included, and if so, how far that protection should go. The second question – by what criteria we should dis-

* Senior fellow and former Director, Norwegian Centre for Human Rights, Oslo; Guest Professor, University of Gothenburg, Sweden; Chairman, UN Working Group on Minorities; Member, Advisory Committee under the Framework Convention for the Protection of National Minorities.

Minority Governance in and beyond Europe, ISBN 978-90-04-27648-2. pp. 23-38.

tinguish old from new minorities – is not easy to answer. I start with a very general working distinction, but will later show that there has to be considerable flexibility in its application. Provisionally, the distinction will be as follows: Old minorities are composed of persons who lived, or whose ancestors lived, in the country or a part of it before the state became independent or before the boundaries were drawn in the way they are now. New minorities are composed of persons who have come in after the state became independent. To be a minority, the old as well as the new must be numerically inferior to the dominant majority in the country, and share common ethnic, religious or linguistic features which they want to preserve.

There has rarely been a clear articulation of the reasons behind the claim for a distinction between the rights of old versus those of new minorities. It seems to be based on some conception of the need to respect the cultural and ethnic elements in the social contract. In the building of a nation, all the different groups already living there should be respected and their cultural practices and languages should be taken into account. Regarding groups of persons who immigrate after the state has been established and its present borders have been drawn, however, there seems to be a broad assumption that since they have decided to immigrate of their own free will, they should generally accept the cultural and linguistic make-up of the country in which they now want to settle. As will be pointed out below, however, it is difficult to sustain a clear-cut division when fully taking into account contemporary human rights law.

II. Justifications for Minority Protection

I suggest that there are fundamentally three major considerations which sustain the evolution of international minority law. The first is to ensure full enjoyment of human rights for everyone, including persons belonging to groups which otherwise might face exclusion or discrimination in society. The second is to ensure the preservation and evolution of cultural pluralism or diversity in society. A combination of these two considerations points also to the need to ensure respect for the identity of individuals belonging to minorities, to prevent the humiliation of individuals caused by negative stereotyping of any given minority. The third purpose is to preserve or strengthen peace and security, nationally and regionally.[1]

The first set of justifications sees minority protection essentially as an extension of human rights. When the foundation of modern international human rights was laid with the adoption of the Universal Declaration of Human Rights (UDHR) in 1948, the majority of the members of the UN were opposed to the inclusion of special provisions on minority protection. One of the main arguments was that there was no longer a need for such provisions: If the 'ordinary'

1 Athanasia S. Akermark suggests a similar categorization which largely coincides with the one given above. Her three justifications for minority protection are: (1) peace and security, (2) human dignity, and (3) culture. See Athanasia S. *Akermark, justiftcations of Minorities in International Law* (Uppsala, 1997), 67 and 68-85.

human rights of everyone were respected, the needs of the minorities would also be respected.[2]

There is considerable truth in that argument: Properly implemented, 'ordinary' human rights would cover many, if not all the needs of minorities. International minority rights law may help to strengthen that protection, precisely because without it, minorities are vulnerable to human rights violations. International minority rights can also help clarify some uncertainties that might otherwise exist. To illustrate: The freedom of expression and information also includes the freedom to express oneself and to be informed in one's own minority language. If anyone tried to argue against that interpretation of the right to freedom of expression, it has been made clear by relevant minority rights law that minorities can use their own language in their exercise of the freedom of expression, but it should not have been necessary.

The preservation of cultural pluralism is a purpose which does not necessarily follow from ordinary human rights law, and which therefore finds its main strength in minority protection provisions. The support for that purpose may be somewhat less strong than the support for human rights in general: There are those who feel strongly that linguistic pluralism is a positive feature, and others who do not worry that a small number of languages are gradually replacing many local languages.

The purpose of preserving and strengthening international and local peace can be very important in some contexts and much less relevant in others. Early minority protection in Europe emerged out of peace settlements following wars and violence, initially related to religion and later to the formation of nation-states, where ethnonations came to be divided by state borders. This sometimes caused very serious kin-state/home-state conflicts and contributed to the outbreak of World War II. The function of the OSCE High Commissioner on National Minorities is primarily to prevent international conflicts arising from grievances by minorities which have a kin-state in the neighbourhood.

Domestic peace can also be seriously jeopardized by neglect of minority rights. The UNDeclMin makes it clear in its preamble that one of the purposes is to protect domestic peace: 'Considering that the promotion and protection of the rights of persons belonging to national or ethnic, religious and linguistic minorities contribute to the political and social stability of States in which they live ...'.

International or domestic peace is threatened not only when certain minority rights are violated, but also when an ethnic group considers itself a nation without a state (the Tamils of Sri Lanka, the Kurds in Turkey and elsewhere) or wants to break out of the country to join a neighbouring state (the Armenians in Nagorno-Karabakh). These are issues that cannot be dealt with by human rights, not even by existing minority rights.

2 I have analyzed in some length the positions on this matter during the drafting. See Asbjørn Eide, 'The Non-inclusion of Minority Rights: Resolution 217C (III)" in Gudmundur Alfredsson and Asbjørn Eide (eds.), *The Universal Declaration of Human Rights: A Common Standard of Achievement* (The Hague, 1999), 701-23.

III. Application of the Justifications to the Old Versus New Dichotomy

The core question to be faced is whether the different justifications for minority protection are equally applicable to the new as well as to the old minorities.

The Human Rights Committee (HRC) in its General Comment on Article 27 of the International Covenant on Civil and Political Rights (CCPR) has expressed the most authoritative view:[3]

> Article 27 confers rights on persons belonging to minorities which 'exist' in a State party. Given the nature and scope of the rights envisaged under that article, it is not relevant to determine the degree of permanence that the term 'exist' connotes. Those rights simply are that individuals belonging to those minorities should not be denied the right, in community with members of their group, to enjoy their own culture, to practice their religion and speak their language. Just as they need not be nationals or citizens, they need not be permanent residents. Thus, migrant workers or even visitors in a State party constituting such minorities are entitled not to be denied the exercise of those rights. As any other individual in the territory of the State party, they would, also for this purpose, have the general rights, for example, to freedom of association, of assembly, and of expression. The existence of an ethnic, religious or linguistic minority in a given State party does not depend upon a decision by that State party but requires to be established by objective criteria.

The HRC was on solid grounds legally speaking. In conformity with Article 2 of the Covenant, states parties are under an obligation to respect and ensure all the rights therein, including Article 27, to everyone within its territory and under its jurisdiction, whether the person – or group of persons – are citizens of the country or not. Persons who are not (yet) citizens of the country in which they reside can form part of or belong to a minority in that country. This does not mean that migrants as such constitute a minority, but individual migrants can be part of a particular ethnic, religious or linguistic minority. Persons belonging to such minorities shall not be denied the right, in community with the other members of their group, to enjoy their own culture, to profess and practise their own religion, or to use their own language, whether they are citizens or not.

It is important to note, however, that the Committee placed a heavy emphasis on the limited content of the rights in Article 27: 'Given the nature and scope of the rights envisaged under that article .... Those rights simply are that individuals belonging to those minorities should not be denied the right to ...'. The point here is that the Committee focussed only on the passive or negative obligations contained in Article 27, not on the possible positive measures required, which

3 HRC General Comment No. 23 (fiftieth Session, 1994), Report of the Human Rights Committee, Vol. I, GAOR, forty-ninth Session, Supplement No. 40 (A149/40), 107-10.

have been elaborated more extensively in the UNDeclMin and in the Framework Convention for the Protection of National Minorities (FCNM).

It may also be asked whether 'national' minorities, the term used in the Framework Convention, are different from those listed in Article 27. Does this include only those who are 'nationals' of the country concerned? There is clearly no consensus on that; one of the reasons that no definition of 'national minorities' was agreed on was precisely that some wanted it to be limited to citizens, while others did not. In the implementation of the Framework Convention, some use citizenship as a restrictive criterion while others do not. Some interpret the term to include only those who form part of an 'ethnic nation', while others use a very different understanding. Usages therefore differ significantly, and no conclusions can be drawn merely on the basis of the term itself.

The main thesis in the following is that as a starting point, minority rights are applicable to all minorities, new or old, but when it comes to the requirement to take positive measures, the rights of the old minorities are stronger than the rights of new ones. The distinction between old and new should not, however, be confused with the citizenship issues. As pointed out in section V., there are many and different reasons why some groups of persons do not have citizenship. They can still be old minorities with a justified claim on positive measures.

IV. Testing the Appropriateness of the Distinction by Category of Minority Rights

In the following, I shall use the UNDeclMin as a basis. The same analysis could be pursued in relation to the Framework Convention. I start with comments on the rights set out in the Declaration Articles 2 and 3, and then examine the state obligations contained in Articles 4, 5, 6 and 1.

A. The Scope of Minority Rights in the Declaration

> Article 2(1): Persons belonging to national or ethnic, religious and linguistic minorities (hereinafter referred to as persons belonging to minorities) have the right to enjoy their own culture, to profess and practise their own religion, and to use their own language, in private and in public, freely and without interference or any form of discrimination.

Comment: This text is practically identical with Article 27 CCPR. There is generally no justification for distinction in this regard between old and new minorities.

> Article 2(2): Persons belonging to minorities have the right to participate effectively in cultural, religious, social, economic and public life.

Comment: The relevant distinction is not whether the minority is new or old but whether the person is a citizen or not. Those members of new minorities, who are citizens of the country, must be fully entitled to participate in the cultural, religious, economic and public life. Those among them who have not become citizens, must also as a general rule be entitled to participate, except where there are particular and justified restrictions applicable to non-citizens. This raises the broader question of the relationship between citizenship and human rights in general (see section V.).

> Article 2(3): Persons belonging to minorities have the right to participate effectively in decisions on the national and, where appropriate, regional level concerning the minority to which they belong or the regions in which they live, in a manner not incompatible with national legislation.

Comment: Again, the relevant distinction is not whether the minority is old or new, but whether the person concerned is citizen or not. Political rights can under human rights law be restricted to citizens, and in national practice it is the general rule that participation at the national level is restricted to citizens. There is a growing practice, however, at least in Western Europe, that lawful residents who have lived in the country for a certain period (often set to three years) are entitled to participate at the local and regional level, with voting rights, the right to election, and the right to hold public office at that level. Strictly speaking, however, states are not obliged to extend such rights to non-citizens, and this must be one of the reasons that the last sentence of Article 2(3) says that the participation must be 'in a manner not incompatible with national legislation'. There are also other considerations underlying that restriction, which will not be addressed here.

> Article 2(4): Persons belonging to minorities have the right to establish and maintain their own associations.

Comment: This is an application of the general right to establish and be member of associations (Article 22 CCPR and comparable regional provisions). As a general rule, new minorities are no less entitled to do so than old minorities. Any restriction would have to be based on the permissible limitations to the freedom of association, which in Article 22(2) CCPR are formulated in this way:

> No restrictions may be placed on the exercise of this right other than those which are prescribed by law and which are necessary in a democratic society in the interests of national security or public safety, public order *(ordre public),* the protection of public health or morals or the protection of the rights and freedoms of others.

None of these grounds could justify a general rule to prohibit new minorities from establishing and maintaining associations. It might be that in particular cases, the concern with national security could more easily justify restrictions on certain new minorities, but it would have to be explained in each case why that was needed.

> Article 2(5): Persons belonging to minorities have the right to establish and maintain, without any discrimination, free and peaceful contacts with other members of their group and with persons belonging to other minorities, as well as contacts across frontiers with citizens of other States to whom they are related by national or ethnic, religious or linguistic ties.

Comment: That they have a right to maintain contacts with other members of their group inside the country follows already from general human rights such as freedom of movement and freedom of association. This cannot in general terms be restricted to old minorities. On the basis of national security or public order, there may be some particular reasons applicable to special networks, but this has to be argued concretely and cannot be based on a general limitation of new minorities.

> Article 3(1): Persons belonging to minorities may exercise their rights, including those set forth in the present Declaration, individually as well as in community with other members of their group, without any discrimination.

Comment: The main purpose of Article 3(1) is not to regulate the application of the Minority Declaration to different kinds of minorities, but it has a bearing on that issue as well. What is at stake here is not the distinction between old and new minorities, but between new and old individuals in their exercise of minority and other rights. The general rule, reinforced by Article 3(1), is that no discrimination can take place in the enjoyment of their rights. This has to be interpreted, however, in light of other human rights provisions. In spite of the general rule in Article 3(1), distinctions can in some limited cases be made between those persons belonging to minorities who are citizens and those of the same minority who are not. As explained above, the main area where that distinction can be made is in regard to effective political participation, since under international human rights law political rights can be limited to citizens. A more complicated question arises where the state is obliged to take positive measures, such as ensuring teaching in the minority language in areas traditionally inhabited by a minority. Should also new immigrants enjoy those extended rights in line with the previously existing members of the same minority? In general, it seems that the answer should be in the positive, but a closer assessment of each case would appear necessary.

B. The Scope of State Obligations or Commitments

> Article 4(1): States shall take measures where required to ensure that persons belonging to minorities may exercise fully and effectively all their human rights and fundamental freedoms without any discrimination and in full equality before the law.

Comment: States are generally obliged to ensure human rights to everyone within their territory and subject to their jurisdiction. This obviously applies also to persons belonging to new minorities. Some restrictions can be made in regard to non-citizens (see section V.) but not to other members of 'new minorities'.

> Article 4(2): States shall take measures to create favourable conditions to enable persons belonging to minorities to express their characteristics and to develop their culture, language, religion, traditions and customs, except where specific practices are in violation of national law and contrary to international standards.

Comment: This is where distinctions start to become more acceptable. It follows already from Article 2(1) UNDeclMin and from Article 27 CCPR that states shall not prevent members of new minorities from expressing their characteristics and developing their culture. It is a different matter to argue that states shall take positive measures to ensure that different groups of immigrants shall be able to maintain their culture. If we take the case of the United Kingdom, in which there are many and numerous new minorities, the policy started with a general denial of a duty to support the new multiculturalism, but over time it changed into a greater acceptance or even positive attitude towards active support.[4] There is probably not yet, however, an international consensus on the duty to do so – on the contrary, the dominant attitude seems still to be an expectation that new arrivals will assimilate and that any effort to maintain their cultural identity will have to be done by themselves.

> Article 4(3): States should take appropriate measures so that, wherever possible, persons belonging to minorities may have adequate opportunities to learn their mother tongue or to have instruction in their mother tongue.

Comment: Probably the same goes here as in the previous case. States cannot and should not deny members of new minorities, through their own efforts – including running their own private schools, or in other ways – to ensure that their children learn their own language. There is probably no consensus, however, that the state is obliged to take positive measures for that purpose.

> Article 4(4): States should, where appropriate, take measures in the field of education, in order to encourage knowledge of the history, traditions, language and culture of the minorities existing within their territory. Persons belonging to minorities should have adequate opportunities to gain knowledge of the society as a whole.

Comment: The last part is certainly applicable to new as well as old minorities. In regard to the first part, the obligation is undoubtedly stronger with regard to old

4 John Rex, 'The Political Sociology of a Multicultural Society', in Daniele Joly, *Scapegoats and Social Actors* (London, 1998), 137-54, gives an interesting account of the changes in British policy in this regard.

than to new minorities. It would nevertheless be desirable that the children in the country as a whole have some acquaintance with the history, traditions and culture also of new minorities. It can hardly be required that they will have to learn or even achieve a rudimentary knowledge of the language of those new minorities.

> Article 4(5): States should consider appropriate measures so that persons belonging to minorities may participate fully in the economic progress and development in their country.

Comment: Much depends on the interpretation of this provision. States should ensure that there is no discrimination between members of majorities and minorities in the economic life of the country. There may be some acceptable limitations for non-citizens (see below) but not for members of new minorities as such. If, however, Article 4(5) is interpreted to mean that states shall ensure that the participation of minorities in the economic progress shall take into account the particular culture, tradition and way of organizing their economic activity, then this can hardly be stretched to include new minorities.

> Article 5(1): National policies and programmes shall be planned and implemented with due regard for the legitimate interests of persons belonging to minorities.
> Article 5(2): Programmes of cooperation and assistance among States should be planned and implemented with due regard for the legitimate interests of persons belonging to minorities.

Comment: This is an area where the concerns of the old minorities are much stronger than the ones of new minorities. The difficulty would be more or less the same as under Article 4(5): States should generally ensure that the legitimate interests of all residents are taken into account in national policies, but the obligation to take into account the particular way of life of minorities probably extend only to old minorities.

> Article 6: States should cooperate on questions relating to persons belonging to minorities, inter alia, exchanging information and experiences, in order to promote mutual understanding and confidence.

Comment: The primary concern underlying this provision is the relationship between kin-state and home-state where ethnic groups are divided by borders and where the kin-state is concerned with the fate of their ethnic kin in the neighbouring state. This is generally not the situation for new minorities, but it may apply in some particular cases, depending on how the notion of new minorities is defined. There are, however, good reasons to argue that even in relation to new minorities generally, there should be a degree of cooperation between the new home state and the state from which the minority originates. The arguments in favour are weaker than in relation to old minorities, but it can still be important in order to promote understanding and confidence.

> Article 1: States shall protect the existence and the national or ethnic, cultural, religious and linguistic identity of minorities within their respective territories and shall encourage conditions for the promotion of that identity.

Comment: States must clearly be obliged to protect the existence of all minorities against harassment and persecution by other members of society. This must apply to new as well as old minorities. States are also clearly obliged to respect the national or ethnic, cultural, religious and linguistic identities of new as well as old minorities, and to afford a reasonable degree of protection when that identity is attacked by other members of society. It is more uncertain whether states can be required to encourage conditions for the promotion of the ethnic, religious or linguistic identities of non-citizens, but it cannot be entirely neglected. Recent international instruments using the term 'identity' as part of the trend towards the protection and promotion of cultural diversity include Articles 29 and 30 of the International Convention on the Rights of the Child (CRC), which is applicable also to non-citizens, and Article 31 of the International Convention on the Protection of the Rights of All Migrant Workers and Members of Their Families,[5] which mainly applies to non-citizens. It sets less stringent requirements, however, on the state with regard to the protection of persons who have recently arrived to a country which they knew was not their own. The question is therefore not one of citizen versus non-citizen, but whether the group concerned has existed for a long time and sought to preserve its identity, or whether it consists of persons who have only recently arrived and who may also be numerically few, since immigrants under normal conditions come from many different countries and with different ethnic backgrounds. It cannot reasonably be expected that the state shall actively promote the identity of each of these smaller groups of new arrivals.

V. The Relevance of Citizenship for the Enjoyment of Human Rights, including Minority Rights

If faithfully implemented, human rights law reduces significantly the difference between the rights of citizens and non-citizens. In general terms, states are obliged to ensure the enjoyment of human rights to everyone within their territory and subject to their jurisdiction. The UDHR states that the rights contained within it shall be enjoyed by everyone, without discrimination; thus also by non-citizens. Article 2(1) CCPR reads as follows:

5 Adopted by the UN GA resolution no. 45/158 on 18 December 1990, entered into force on 1 July 2003. It has very few ratifications, almost none by the main host countries of migrant workers.

> Each State Party to the present Covenant undertakes to respect and to ensure to all individuals within its territory and subject to its jurisdiction the rights recognized in the present Covenant, without distinction of any kind, such as race, colour, sex, language, religion, political or other opinion, national or social origin, property, birth or other status.

The state shall ensure the rights contained in the CCPR to all individuals (not only citizens) within the territory of the state, and there shall be no distinction made in the enjoyment of these rights. There are, as we shall see, some important exceptions. But the main rule should be clear: Citizens and non-citizens should enjoy most of the civil rights contained in that CCPR without distinctions.[6]

The European Convention on Human Rights and Fundamental Freedoms has the same scope: Its Article 1 states that the state parties shall secure to everyone within their jurisdiction the rights and freedoms defined in the Convention. The CRC is even more explicit in its Article 2(1):

> States parties shall respect and ensure the rights set forth in the present Convention to each child within their jurisdiction without discrimination of any kind, irrespective of the child's or his or her parent's or legal guardian's race, colour, sex, language, religion, political or other opinion, national, ethnic or social origin, property, disability, birth or other status.

The International Covenant on Economic, Social and Cultural Rights (CESCR), Article 2(2) requires the state parties to guarantee that the rights contained in the CESCR will be exercised without discrimination on grounds listed there, such as national or social origin. Article 2(3), however, contains an exception: *Developing* countries can determine to what extent they would guarantee the economic rights contained in the Covenant to non-nationals. Antithetically, industrialized countries can make no such distinction. Other factors, such as legal residence, work permit and other elements may be relevant, but not citizenship as such.

While the UDHR had established that human rights were to be enjoyed by everyone, at least two of its articles contain restricting language – Article 21 on political rights and Article 13 on the right to freedom of movement.

The UDHR in Article 21(1), and the CCPR in Article 25 deal with the right to take part in the government of one's country, directly or through freely chosen representatives. Equally important is the right of everyone to equal access to public service in one's own country (UDHR, Article 21(2); CCPR, Article 25(c)).

The enjoyment of human rights is precarious when the person does not have the citizenship of his or her country of residence. Political rights are among the most precious of all human rights since their enjoyment makes it possible to influence the laws and policies of the country and therefore also to be able to protect one's own interests and value. It is particularly serious when many individuals

6 See on this point also HRC, General Comment No. 15, The Position of Aliens under the Covenant, dated 11 April 1986, UN Doc. HRI/Gen/Rev.1 (1994) at 18.

belonging to ethnic, religious or linguistic minorities or the weaker social groups are denied citizenship, since this will make it difficult to ensure reasonable protection for them. This can seriously weaken the functioning of democracy, one of its main functions being to ensure peaceful settlement of conflicts through effective participation by all groups.

The UDHR in Article 13 and the CCPR in Article 12 deal with freedom of movement. Everyone, citizen or not, is entitled to freedom of movement and residence within the borders of the state and to leave any country including his own, but the right to enter a country is limited to 'his own country'. This would at first sight limit the right of entry as a human right to citizens only, but it cannot be understood in such a rigid way. The Human Rights Committee, which is the official body supervising the implementation of the CCPR, has noted that in some circumstances, a non-citizen may enjoy protection under Article 12 of the CCPR. In this connection, considerations of non-discrimination, prohibition of inhuman treatment, and respect for family ties will have to be taken into account.

VI. Citizenship Controversies and their Relationship with Old Versus New Minorities

It is often assumed that persons without citizenship are relatively new arrivals and form the bulk of the so-called new minorities. The reality is more complex. Questions arise regarding persons who live in a territory which has come under new sovereignty and thus need a new citizenship as well as for those who have moved from their country of citizenship to another country to settle there.

A. Rights of Citizenship in Cases of State Succession

Four situations of state succession (when a territory is the subject of change of sovereignty) can be identified: (i) unification of states (ii) transfer of part of the territory to another state, (iii) dissolution of a state and the emergence of several newly independent states, and (iv) separation of part of the territory to become an independent state. The problems of citizenship arise for the residents of the territory who had already been citizens of the previous state.

The situations in category (i) do not give rise to doubt: The former citizenship is replaced by citizenship of the unified country. In the other situations, evidence from practice has been that nationality (citizenship) follows the territory. Residents should have an automatic option of citizenship of the state where their territory of residence is included, but may sometimes have the option to retain their former citizenship.

In situations of category (iii), the total dissolution of a state and the emergence of several newly independent states, the situation is different. Since the country no longer exists, the former citizenship no longer exists and can therefore not be retained. Citizenship has to be determined anew for all. As a general rule of thumb, residents will have to be given the citizenship of the new state in which they live and cannot normally demand to become a citizen of one of the other states emerging out of the dissolution.[7] Such other states are, of course, free to offer their citizenship but are not obliged to do so, unless special reasons therefore exist.

As a consequence of Article 7(2) of the CRC, at least one point can be made with great certitude: A child born on a state's territory has to be given the citizenship of that country if it otherwise would be stateless. Thus, in so far as otherwise stateless children are concerned, the principle of *jus soli* has now become universal law. To date, 191 states have ratified the Convention; the United States, which is the main state which has not ratified it, applies in any case the *jus soli* principle.

The best guidance in advanced legal opinion on these matters is to be found in the European Convention on Nationality (hereinafter 'the Nationality Convention'),[8] Articles 18 and 19. Preferably, the matter should be settled by treaty between the states concerned, but the principles to be followed in making such decisions shall according to Article 18 take into account human rights, including the principle that everyone has a right to a nationality and that statelessness shall be avoided. The burden of avoiding statelessness by extending its citizenship will fall mainly on the country of residence, and as mentioned above this will at least be so with regard to children born on that territory.

In sum, the evolution of human-rights-inspired international law at present gives reason to conclude as follows: In cases of state succession, citizens of the former state living habitually (as distinct from temporarily) on the territory under new sovereignty are entitled to obtain the citizenship of the state which has obtained sovereignty over the territory. Such persons shall always have the option to accept the offer of citizenship of the other country concerned, but are not obliged to take it, and the other country is not generally obliged to offer it. Both states are obliged to ensure that statelessness does not ensue, and the burden of proof will fall on the state of domicile to show that it has legitimate cause to deny citizenship to any person habitually resident there.

Is there a right to obtain citizenship of the state of residence in cases of state restoration? State restoration occurs when a previously independent state has been incorporated into a larger entity for some time but subsequently has regained its independence. The prime examples from recent time are the three Baltic states which were incorporated into the Soviet Union in 1940 and regained their independence in 1991.

Claims that situations of state restoration do not have to follow the rules applying to state succession are based on the assertion that restored states are entitled to reinstate the legislation on nationality as it stood before their incorporation and such states can thereby determine the allocation of nationality at restored

7 Summarizing the practice observed in previous times, Ian Brownlie concludes that 'the evidence is overwhelmingly in support of the view that the population follows the change of sovereignty in matters of nationality'. See Ian Brownlie, *Principles of Public International Law* (Oxford, 4th ed., 1990), 661-2.

8 Dated 6 November 1997, entered into force on 1 March 2000, ETS No. 166.

independence based on the previously existing law.[9] Such claims can only have validity when the incorporation of previously independent states has resulted from illegal threat or use of force, which arguably happened to the Baltic states in 1940.

During long periods of incorporation, migrations within that larger entity may have taken place at a large scale. Where the settlement has lasted for two or more generations before restoration takes place, allocation of citizenship cannot in the aftermath of restoration be handled in the same way as it would at the end of a regular military occupation. And yet it is not obvious that the descendants of those who arrived during the period of incorporation have an automatic right to citizenship in the restored country, even if they had citizenship of the larger state entity before the restoration of independence.

Due to their established domicile, however, they cannot be treated as aliens. If they do not immediately acquire citizenship, they would at least have the right to remain in the restored state and enjoy equality of treatment with nationals of the restored state in regard to social and economic rights, including access to work, with one exception: Until they obtain citizenship they can be excluded from such public service which involves the exercise of sovereign power. On this point see also the Nationality Convention, Article 20.

B. New Arrivals: Human Rights Requirements in Favour of Non-discriminatory Naturalization

Do migrants in the strict sense of the word, i.e. persons or their children who arrive in a country which they know is not their own, have a right to citizenship in their country of arrival? Many states practice the principle of *jus soli,* which means that children born on the territory as a general rule obtain citizenship of that country even if their parents were not citizens. Others restrict themselves to *jus sanguinis,* meaning that only children born of parents who already are citizens automatically *(ex lege)* obtain citizenship.

As a consequence of the evolution of human rights law, even those who otherwise apply the *jus sanguinis* principle have to apply the principle of *jus soli* to children born on their territory who would otherwise be stateless. Most immigrants, however, have another pre-existing citizenship in their country of departure, and their children can therefore not demand citizenship on the basis of statelessness. For persons who do not become citizens *ex lege,* states can bestow citizenship through naturalization. Is the host country obliged, at any stage, to naturalize those who have become permanent residents in the country? The Nationality Convention, Article 6 (acquisition of nationality) provides in its section 3 that states shall in their internal law provide for the possibility of naturalization of persons lawfully and habitually resident on its territory, and in such legislation the

9 A detailed discussion of the citizen issue in restored states is found in Ineta Ziemele, 'State Continuity and Nationality in the Baltic States and Russian Federation. International and Constitutional Issues', unpublished Ph.D. manuscript, Cambridge University, 1998.

time of residence required before an application can be lodged should not exceed ten years.

Controversial, and of great significance for minorities, is the question of whether the state can make distinctions between different sets of applicants for naturalization. This has traditionally been a jealously-guarded domestic prerogative, and international law remains weak on this point, but it is slowly changing under the impact of human rights. Distinctions on the grounds of ethnicity or culture could be held to be a violation of the International Covenant on the Elimination of All Forms of Racial Discrimination, particularly its Article 5(d)(iii), whereby state parties have undertaken to guarantee the right of nationality to everyone, without distinction as to race, colour or national or ethnic origin. The implication seems to be that preference cannot be given to particular ethnic groups among those who seek naturalization. In practice, however, several countries continue to give such preference. International law is unfortunately still rather vague on this issue.

Article 5 of the Nationality Convention provides that the rules of a state party shall not contain distinctions or include any practices which amount to discrimination on the grounds of sex, religion, race, colour or national or ethnic origin. Furthermore, states shall be guided by the same principle of non-discrimination between their nationals (citizens), whether they are nationals by birth or have acquired nationality subsequently.

VII. Concluding Theses on New Minorities: Their Rights and Protection

A frequent weakness in debates over definition is an underlying assumption that all groups which fall inside a possible definition should have the same rights, and that those who fall outside should not. This is not a fruitful approach. There is a great variety of minorities, living under highly different circumstances, with very different needs, and the justification for their protection varies greatly. Rather than striving to have one common definition of 'minorities' one should focus on which rights should be held by which type of minority under particular circumstances. Considerations of reasonability and proportionality have to be taken into account. This is not to say that there should not be some general standards on minority rights, but these should be conceived as broad frameworks within which any specific situations could be addressed in ways which correspond to the needs of the context and situation. International law does not in general terms make a distinction between old and new minorities, and this is so for very good reasons.

International standards of minority protection cover a broad set of rights and obligations, ranging from the universal principle of non-discrimination, through reinforcement of fundamental freedoms when applied in a minority context, to various forms of positive measures of lesser or greater burden in terms of resource allocation and in other ways. Members of all minorities, whether new or old, are entitled to the basic freedom from discrimination and the other fundamental freedoms. However, those parts of positive measures which constitute significant burdens on the state can more reasonably be reserved for old or traditional minorities.

The distinction between old and new minorities should not be based on criteria of citizenship, since the status as non-citizens is not always a result of recent arrival. But lack of citizenship can have serious consequences for members of minorities. In particular, it can seriously undermine their possibilities of effective participation in the political life of the country. For that and other reasons, it is also necessary to underline that states are no longer entirely free to determine their criteria of citizenship. International human rights law has already set important requirements to state legislation in this area, particularly in the context of state succession and state restoration.

*William A. Schabas**

'Ethnic Cleansing' and Genocide: Similarities and Distinctions

1. Introduction

On 18 April 2004, the Appeals Chamber of the International Criminal Tribunal for the former Yugoslavia (ICTY) concluded that the crime of genocide had been committed on the territory of the former Yugoslavia.[1] The determination brings to a conclusion much uncertainty in the case law of the International Tribunal. It finally provides an answer to the question: 'Was *genocide* committed in the former Yugoslavia? Until recently, there has been little disagreement about using the term 'ethnic cleansing' to describe the campaigns of brutal persecution of ethnic groups during the wars. Finally, it will be said, these practices have been called by their real name, genocide. The ruling is full of implications for two other protracted affairs, the ongoing and seemingly endless trial of Slobodan Milosevic before the ICTY[2] and the stalled and still-pending case filed by Bosnia and Herzegovina against the Federal Republic of Yugoslavia in 1993.[3]

* Professor of Human Rights Law, National University of Ireland, Galway and Director, Irish Centre for Human Rights.

1 *Prosecutor v. Krstic* (Case no. IT-98-33-A), Judgment, 18 April 2004, paras. 5-38.

2 See Michael Scharf and William Schabas, *Slobodan Milosevic on Trial: A Companion*, (New York and London, 2002).

3 See: Peter H.F. Bekker and Paul C. Szasz, "Casenote: Application of the Convention on the Prevention and Punishment of the Crime of Genocide", 91(1) *AJIL* (1997), 121; Laurence Boisson de Chazournes, "Les ordonnances en indication de mesures conservatoires dans l'affaire relative à l'application de la Convention pour la prévention et la répression du crime de génocide", 39 *Annuaire français du droit international* (1993), 514; Ben Gaffikin, "The International Court of Justice and the Crisis in the Balkans: Application of the Convention on the Prevention and Punishment of the Crime of Genocide (*Bosnia and Herzegovina v. Yugoslavia*, 32 *I.L.M.* 1599 (1993)", 17 *Sydney L. Rev.* (1995), 458; Thomas D. Grant, "Territorial Status, Recognition, and Statehood: Some Aspects of the Genocide Case (*Bosnia and Herzegovina v. Yugoslavia*)", 33 *Stanford J Int'l L.* (1997), 305; Christine Gray, "Application of the Convention on the Prevention and Punishment of the Crime of Genocide (*Bosnia and Herzegovina*

Minority Governance in and beyond Europe, ISBN 978-90-04-27648-2. pp. 39-60.

In the early years of the Tribunal's activities, the Prosecutor was extremely cautious in presenting indictments for genocide, provided for in Article 4 of the Statute of the International Criminal Tribunal for the former Yugoslavia,[4] opting for the broader and more general qualification of atrocities under the rubric 'crimes against humanity' found in Article 5. In 1999, Milosevic and four of his colleagues were indicted for crimes against humanity, but not genocide, with respect to the 'ethnic cleansing' of Kosovo.[5] A more recent reflection of the Prosecutor's ambivalent attitude towards genocide charges was her agreement to withdraw such a charge against Bosnian Serb leader Biljana Plavsic in return for a guilty plea to crimes against humanity.[6]

Initially, even the judges seemed disturbed by the Prosecutor's prudence, and criticized the reluctance to characterize 'ethnic cleansing' as the crime of genocide. In one case, the Tribunal took the rather unprecedented step of suggesting an indictment be reconsidered, writing:

> It emerged on the basis of the record that the policy of discrimination implemented at Blasenica, of which Dragan Nikolic's acts formed a part, was specifically aimed at 'cleansing' the region of its Muslim Population. In this instance, the policy of' ethnic cleansing' took the form of discriminatory acts of extreme seriousness which tend to show its genocidal character. For instance, the Chamber notes the statements by some witnesses which point, among other crimes, to mass murders being committed in the region .... The Chamber considers that the Tribunal may possibly have jurisdiction in this case under Article 4 of the Statute.[7]

However in the first genocide cases to go to trial, involving concentration camps in northwest Bosnia and violent campaigns of harassment directed against minorities, the judges of the trial chambers were unsatisfied with the evidence of a cam-

---

v. Yugoslavia (Serbia and Montenegro))", 43 *Int'l Comp. L. Q.* (1994), 704; William L. Hurlock, "The International Court of Justice: Effectively Providing a Long Overdue Remedy for Engaging State-Sponsored Genocide (Bosnia-Herzegovina v. Yugoslavia)", 12 *Am. U. J. Int'l L. & Poly* (1997), 299; Rafaëlle Maison, "Les ordonnances de la Cour international de justice dans l'affaire relative it l'application de la Convention pour la prevention et la repression du crime de genocide', 3 *EJIL* (1994), 381; Sandrine Maljean-Dubois, "I'affaire relative it l'application de la Convention pour la prevention et la répression du crime de génocide (*Bosnie-Herzégovine c. Yougoslavie*), Arrêt du 11 Juillet 1996, exceptions preliminaries", 42 *Annuaire français du droit international* (1996), 357.

4 UN Doc. S/RES/827 (1993), Annex, Art. 4.

5 *Prosecutor* v. *Milosevic et al.* (Case no. IT-99-37-1), Indictment, 22 May 1999.

6 *Prosecutor* v. *Plavsic* (Case no. IT-00-39&40/1), Plea Agreement, 30 September 2002, para. 9.

7 *Prosecutor* v. *Nikolic* (Case No. IT-94-2-R61), Review of Indictment Pursuant to Rule 61, 20 October 1995, para. 34.

paign to physically exterminate Bosnian Muslims as a group, and dismissed the charges of genocide.[8] Such activities might have been 'ethnic cleansing' but they were not, apparently, genocide. Only in *Krstic* did a Trial Chamber, in August 2001, find that a campaign of 'ethnic cleansing' had evolved, during what were the final weeks of the war in mid-July 1995, into full-blown genocide. It registered a conviction under Article 4 of the Statute against Bosnian Serb General Radovan Krstic for his involvement in the Srebrenica massacre.[9]

'Ethnic cleansing' has been part of the nomenclature of the Yugoslav wars since their beginning, and several commentators have been content to equate it with genocide.[10] The Commission on Human Rights' Special Rapporteur on extrajudicial, summary and arbitrary executions has said that 'ethnic cleansing' is no more than a euphemism for genocide.[11] The 1993 World Conference on Human Rights adopted a resolution on Bosnia and Herzegovina which said: "the practice of ethnic cleansing resulting from Serbian aggression against the Muslim and Croat population in the Republic of Bosnia and Herzegovina constitutes genocide in violation of the Convention on the Prevention and Punishment of the Crime of Genocide."[12]

In this respect, there can be no doubt about the influence of a carelessly drafted General Assembly resolution. In December 1992, as war raged in Bosnia and Herzegovina, the General Assembly evoked "the abhorrent policy of 'ethnic cleansing', which is a form of genocide."[13] This reference was reaffirmed in several subsequent resolutions.[14] During the debates on the December 1992 resolu-

8 *Prosecutor v. Jelisic* (Case no. IT-95-10-T), Judgment, 14 December 1999; *Prosecutor v. Sikirica et al.* (Case no. IT-95-8-I), Judgment on Defence Motions to Acquit, 3 September 2001; *Prosecutor v. Stakic* (Case o. IT-97-24-T), Judgment, 31 July 2003.

9 *Prosecutor v. Krstic* (Case no. IT-98-33-T), Judgment, 2 August 2001.

10 Drazen Petrovic, "Ethnic Cleansing – An Attempt at Methodology", 5 *EJIL* (1994), 342; Catherine A. Mackinnon, "Rape, Genocide and Women's Human Rights", 17 *Harvard Womens L. J.* (1994), 5, at 8; Lori Lyman Bruun, "Beyond the 1948 Convention – Emerging Principles of Genocide in Customary International Law," 17 *Maryland J. Int'l L. & Trade* (1993), 193, at 200. Also: John Webb, "Genocide Treaty – Ethnic Cleansing – Substantive and Procedural Hurdles in the Application of the Genocide Convention to Alleged Crimes in the Former Yugoslavia", 23 *Georgia J. Int'l Comp. L.* (1993), 377, at 402-3.

11 "Extrajudicial, summary or arbitrary executions, Note by the Secretary-General", UN Doc. A/51/457, para. 69.

12 UN Doc. A/CONF.157/24 (Part 1), 47-8.

13 "The Situation in Bosnia and Herzegovina", UN Doc. A/RES/47/121. UN Doc. A/47/PV.91, 99 (102 in favour, with 57 abstentions, on a recorded vote). The abstentions concerned a provision in the resolution calling for an arms embargo to be lifted, and had nothing to do with the reference to genocide.

14 "Situation of Human Rights in the Territory of the Former Yugoslavia: Violations of Human Rights in the Republic of Bosnia and Herzegovina, the Republic of Croatia and the Federal Republic of Yugoslavia (Serbia and Montenegro)", UN Doc. A/RES/48/153; "Rape and Abuse of Women in the Areas of Armed Conflict in

tion, a number of delegates described ethnic cleansing as "genocide"[15] or, more frequently, "genocidal",[16] as well as a "crime against humanity"[17] and a form of "apartheid".[18] The General Assembly debates are, however, stunningly laconic with respect to the assertion that ethnic cleansing is a form of genocide. This is especially striking when one considers that it was the General Assembly that drafted the 1948 Genocide Convention. Then, it formally and expressly rejected the equation between 'ethnic cleansing' and genocide. And significantly, another resolution adopted by consensus at the same session of the General Assembly in December 1992, entitled "'Ethnic Cleansing' and Racial Hatred", approached the question from the standpoint of racial discrimination and the protection of minorities and did not even refer to genocide or to the 1948 Convention.[19] Accordingly, the glib formulation by the General Assembly can hardly stand for any reliable legal authority. In some cases, General Assembly resolutions may be deemed to amount to declarations or codifications of customary international law, but these circumstances of adoption argue against any such conclusion with respect to the resolution on genocide and 'ethnic cleansing'.

'Ethnic cleansing' is probably better described as a popular or journalistic expression,with no recognized legal meaning in a technical sense. On the other hand, genocide is a precise legal term, first defined in a United Nations General Assembly resolution[20] and then developed in the 1948 Convention for the Prevention and Punishment of the Crime of Genocide:

> ... genocide means any of the following acts committed with intent to destroy, in whole or in part, a national, ethnical, racial or religious group, as such:
> (a) Killing members of the group;
> (b) Causing serious bodily or mental harm to members of the group;

---

the Former Yugoslavia", UN Doc. A/RES/48/143; "Rape and Abuse of Women in the Areas of Armed Conflict in the Former Yugoslavia", UN Doc. A/RES/49/205; "Rape and Abuse of Women in the Areas of Armed Conflict in the Former Yugoslavia", UN Doc. A/RES/50/192; "Rape and Abuse of Women in the Areas of Armed Conflict in the Former Yugoslavia", UN Doc. A/RES/51/115.

15 UN Doc. A/47/PV.86, 31 (Jaya, Brunei Darussalam); UN Doc. A/47/PV87, 14-5 (Khoshroo, Iran); UN Doc. A/47IPV.87, 24-5 (Elaraby, Egypt); UN Doc. A/47/PV.87, 46 (Huq, Bangladesh); UN Doc. A/47/PV.88, 22 (Shkurti, Albania).

16 UN Doc. N47/PV.86, 21 (Nobilo, Croatia); UN Doc. A/47/PV.86, 48 (Pirzada, Pakistan); UN Doc. N47/PV.87, 2 (Al-Ni'mah, Qatar); UN Doc. A/47/PV88, 65 (Ansay, Organization of the Islamic Conference).

17 UN Doc. A/47/PV86, 46 (Cisse, Senegal); UN Doc. A/47/PV.88, 65 (Ansay, Organization of the Islamic Conference).

18 UN Doc. A/47/PV88, 12 (Arria, Venezuela).

19 UN Doc. A/RES/47/80. See also: "Third Decade to Combat Racism and Racial Discrimination", GA Res. 48/91.

20 GA Res. 96(1).

(c) Deliberately inflicting on the group conditions of life calculated to bring about its physical destruction in whole or in part;
(d) Imposing measures intended to prevent births within the group;
(e) Forcibly transferring children of the group to another group.[21]

The 1948 definition has been reproduced essentially unchanged in subsequent international instruments, despite frequent efforts at amendment.[22] In national legislation, the crime of genocide is usually defined with reference to the 1948 Convention, although some legal systems have broadened its scope. Acknowledging that the traditional definition may evolve in the future, in the year 2000, Canada's parliament enacted a statute defining genocide with reference to the definition in the 1948 Convention, but allowing for an expansion of the concept to the extent this is reflected in customary international law.[23]

II. Defining 'Ethnic Cleansing'

The expression 'ethnic cleansing' may have first been used immediately following the Second World War by Poles and Czechs intending to 'purify' their countries of Germans and Ukrainians. But if this is the case, the language is certainly the direct descendant of expressions used by the Nazis in their racial 'hygiene' programmes. The latter had a term, *Säuberung* (cleansing), and their goal was to make German territory *judenrein*, that is, free of Jews.[24] The term 'ethnic cleansing' resurfaced in 1981 in Yugoslav media accounts of the establishment of 'ethnically clean territories' in Kosovo.[25] It entered the international vocabulary in 1992 when it was used to describe policies being pursued by the various participants in the Yugoslav wars aimed at creating ethnically homogeneous territories.[26] It was even employed by the parties to the conflict to describe the activities of their adversaries.[27]

---

21 Convention for the Prevention and Punishment of the Crime of Genocide, concluded on 9 December 1948, entered into force on 12 January 1951, 78 UNTS 277, Art. 2.

22 See: William A. Schabas, *Genocide in International Law*, (Cambridge, 2000).

23 *Crimes Against Humanity and War Crimes Act*, S.C. 2000, c. 24, ss. 4(3), 6(3).

24 Mark Kramer, "Introduction", in Mark Kramer, (ed.), *Redrawing Nations: Ethnic Cleansing in East Central Europe*, (Boulder, 2001), 1.

25 Petrovic, "Ethnic Cleansing -An Attempt ...", at 343.

26 See: Norman Cigar, *Genocide In Bosnia: The Policy of Ethnic Cleansing*, (College Station: Texas, 1995); Nathan Lerner, "Ethnic Cleansing", 24 *Israel YBHR* (1994), 103; Webb, "Genocide Treaty Ethnic Cleansing ..."; Damir Mirkovic, "Ethnic Cleansing and Genocide: Reflections on Ethnic Cleansing in the Former Yugoslavia", 548 *Annals Am. Acad. Pol. & Soc. Science* (1996), 191; Andrew Bell-Fialkoff, "A Brief History of Ethnic Cleansing", *Foreign Affairs*, Summer 1993, 110-21.

27 For example, *Prosecutor* v. *Blaskic* (Case no. IT-95-14-T), Judgment, 3 March 2000, para. 469; *Application of the Convention on the Prevention and Punishment of the Crime*

There have been a number of attempts to define 'ethnic cleansing'. According to the Security Council's Commission of Experts on violations of humanitarian law during the Yugoslav wars, "[t]he expression 'ethnic cleansing' is relatively new. Considered in the context of the conflicts in the former Yugoslavia, 'ethnic cleansing' means rendering an area ethnically homogeneous by using force or intimidation to remove persons of given groups from the area."[28] The Commission considered techniques of ethnic cleansing to include murder, torture, arbitrary arrest and detention, extrajudicial executions, sexual assault, confinement of civilian populations in ghetto areas, forcible removal, displacement and deportation of civilian populations, deliberate military attacks or threats of attacks on civilians and civilian areas, and wanton destruction of property.[29]

The Special Rapporteur of the Commission on Human Rights, Tadeusz Mazowiecki, said that "'[e]thnic cleansing' may be equated with a systematic purge of the civilian population with a view to forcing it to abandon the territories in which it lives."[30] The Commission itself, in the resolution adopted during its first special session in August 1992, said that "ethnic cleansing ... at a minimum entails deportations and forcible mass removal or expulsion of persons from their homes in flagrant violation of their human rights, and which is aimed at the dislocation or destruction of national, ethnic, racial or religious groups."[31] *Ad hoc* Judge Elihu Lauterpacht of the International Court of Justice defined ethnic cleansing as "the forced migration of civilians."[32] In a speech to the Security Council, Sir David Hannay of the United Kingdom said it was "the forcible removal of civilian populations."[33] Ambassador Colin Keating of New Zealand, in the General Assembly, said the term ethnic cleansing "covered a multitude of gross violations of human rights such as systematic expulsion, forcible relocation, destruction of dwellings, degrading treatment of human beings, rape and killings."[34] A member

of Genocide (*Bosnia and Herzegovina* v. *Yugoslavia (Serbia and Montenegro)*), Further requests for the Indication of Provisional Measures, 13 September 1993, [1993] ICJ Reports 325, at 432, para. 70.

28 "Interim report of the Commission of Experts Established Pursuant to Security Council Resolution 780 (1992)", UN Doc. S/35374 (1993), para. 55. Also: M. Cherif Bassiouni and Peter Manikas, *The Law of the International Criminal Tribunal for the Former Yugoslavia*, (New York, 1995), 608.

29 UN Doc. S/25274 (1993), para. 56.

30 UN Doc. S/PV.3134, para. 39. In an early report, Mazowiecki defined ethnic cleansing as "the elimination by the ethnic group exerting control over a given territory of members of other ethnic groups": UN Doc. A/47/666, UN Doc. S/24809 (1992).

31 "The Situation of Human Rights in the Territory of the Former Yugoslavia", CHR Res. 1992/ SI-1/1, preamble.

32 *Application of the Convention on the Prevention and Punishment of the Crime of Genocide (Bosnia and Herzegovina* v. *Yugoslavia* ..., Separate Reasons of Judge *ad hoc* Lauterpacht, 431, para. 69.

33 UN Doc. S/PY.3106 (1992), 36.

34 UN Doc. A/C.3/48/SR.6, para. 29.

of the Committee for the Elimination of Racial Discrimination described ethnic cleansing as a form of "enforced segregation".[35] In a 1998 resolution, the Sub-Commission on Prevention of Discrimination and Protection of Minorities defined it as "forcible displacement of populations within a country or across borders."[36]

The Prosecutor of the International Criminal Tribunal for the former Yugoslavia has often used the term 'ethnic cleansing' in indictments.[37] In some, she has described "an ethnic cleansing campaign which resulted in an exodus of Bosnian Muslim civilians",[38] and in others 'ethnic cleansing' has been described as "permanent removal"[39] or "forcible removal".[40] On occasion, the Prosecutor has used the term in inverted commas, which may imply some recognition of legal uncertainty surrounding its meaning.[41]

The Tribunal's judges have expressed considerable curiosity and interest about the meaning of 'ethnic cleansing'. In an early proceeding, held in accordance with Rule 61 of the Tribunal's Rules of Procedure and Evidence, the Trial Chamber asked the Prosecutor to define 'ethnic cleansing':

> Well, ethnic cleansing is a practice which means that you act in such a way that in a given territory the members of a given ethnic group are eliminated. It means a practice that aims at such and such a territory be, as they meant, ethnically pure. So, in other words, that that territory would no longer contain only members of the ethnic group that took the initiative of cleansing the territory. So, in other words, the members of the other group are eliminated by different ways, by different methods. You have massacres. Everybody is not massacred, but I mean in terms of numbers, you have massacres in order to scare these populations. Sometimes these massacres are selective, but they aim at eliminating the elite of a given population, but they are massacres. I mean, that is the point. So whenever you have massacres, naturally the other people are driven away. They are afraid. They try to run away and you find yourself with a high

35 UN Doc. A/CERD/SR.1003.

36 "Forced Population Transfer", S-CHR Res. 1998/27.

37 *Prosecutor* v. *Pandurevic* (Case no. IT-98-33), Indictment, 27 October 1999, para. 1.

38 *Prosecutor* v. *Popovic* (Case no. IT-02-57-I), Indictment, 26 March 2002, para. 8; *Prosecutor* v. *Nikolic* (Case no. IT-02-56-I), Indictment, 26 March 2002, para. 8; *Prosecutor* v. *Beara* (Case no. IT-02-58-I), Indictment, 26 March 2002, para. 8; *Prosecutor* v. *Nikolic* (Case no. IT-02-63-I), Indictment, 6 September 2002, para. 8; *Prosecutor* v. *Blagojevic* (Case no. IT-02-60-PT), Indictment, 27 May 2002, para. 19; *Prosecutor* v. *Borovcanin* (Case no. IT-02-64-I), Indictment, 6 September 2002, para. 8.

39 *Prosecutor* v. *Kovacevic* (Case no. IT-97-24-1), Indictment, 28 January 1998, para. 4; *Prosecutor* v. *Kvocka et al.* (Case no. IT-98-30/1-T), Amended Indictment, 1 August 2000, para. 4; *Prosecutor* v. *Brdjanin* (Case no. IT-99-36-T), Fifth Amended Indictment, 7 October 2002, para. 6.

40 *Prosecutor* v. *Tadic* (Case no. IT-94-1-A), Judgment, 15 July 1999, para. 204.

41 *Prosecutor* v. *Stakic* (Case no. 97-24-T), Indictment, 31 August 2001, para. 17.

> number of a given people that have been massacred, persecuted and, of course, in the end these people simply want to leave. They also submitted to such pressures that they go away. They are driven away either on their own initiative or they are deported. But the basic point is for them to be out of that territory and some of them are sometimes locked up in camps. Some women are raped and, furthermore, often times what you have is the destruction of the monuments which marked the presence of a given population in a given territory, for instance, religious places, Catholic churches or mosques are destroyed.
> So basically, this is how ethnic cleaning is practised in the course of this war.[42]

In another hearing, also held in the early years of the Tribunal's operations, Judge Jorda, who was presiding, asked prosecution witness James Gow, of King's College, London, whether "the concept of ethnic cleansing is to be found somewhere, either officially or in documents or proclamations as organized plans?" Professor Gow answered:

> The term ethnic cleansing has been widely used. It does have some history, but it has come to prominence and has been used in a widespread way in connection with the war in Bosnia and Herzegovina and, particularly, with the Serbian campaign there. The term is often attributed to one of the Serbian paramilitary leaders, Vojislav Seselj, in the current context. It has also been used by one of the other Serbian paramilitary leaders, Zeljko Raznjatovic (Arkan), and there is some film evidence, I believe, in which Arkan is giving instructions to his troops to be careful in this particular cleansing operation. But to say that there is some official document in which a plan for ethnic cleansing appears, I think, would be to take -would be to make too strong a statement. I have seen no evidence of an official document in which the term 'ethnic cleansing' is used, but the term has been used and it has been used by some of the people involved in the activity that they have been carrying out.[43]

The judges actually used the expression themselves, in their famous first ruling, on jurisdiction in the *Tadic* case, but it was generally encased in inverted commas or preceded by the words 'so-called', indicating their unease with the term as a legal or scientific concept.[44] In its 1997 judgment on the merits in the *Tadic* case, the Trial Chamber conducted an historical review of the former Yugoslavia, noting that Serbs themselves had been victims of 'ethnic cleansing' at the hands

42 42 *Prosecutor* v. *Karadzic and Mladic* (Case nos. IT-95-18-R61, IT-95-5-R61), Transcript of hearing, 28 June 1996, 10.

43 *Prosecutor* v. *Nikolic* (Case No. IT-95-2-R61), Transcript, 9 October 1995.

44 *Prosecutor* v. *Tadic* (Case no. IT-94-1-AR72), Decision on the Defence Motion for Interlocutory Appeal on Jurisdiction, 2 October 1995, paras. 32, 45, 53, 54, 99, 107. Also *Prosecutor* v. *Tadic* (Case no. IT-94-1-AR72), Decision on the Defence Motion on Jurisdiction, 10 August 1995, para. 16.

of Bulgarian and Hungarian occupying troops during the Second World War.[45] Observing, then, that it was "no new concept", the Trial Chamber expressed the view that Serb forces had adopted the "practice of ethnic cleansing" in order to achieve "the redistribution of populations, by force if necessary, in the course of achieving a Greater Serbia."[46] But it stopped shy of using the word genocide.[47] A few months later, in its sentencing decision in the same case, the same Trial Chamber referred to the 'ethnic cleansing' of the town of Kozarac, in the Prijedor region:

> ... as a consequence of the attack, which included two days of artillery barrage and an assault by a mechanised brigade of troops, some 800 civilians were killed out of a population of around 4,000. When the town had been captured, the Bosnian Serb forces proceeded to round up and drive out of the area on foot

45 *Prosecutor* v. *Tadic* (Case no. IT-94-1-T), Opinion and Judgment, 7 May 1997, para. 62.

46 *Ibid.*, para. 84. Also paras. 178, 188, 312, 373, 460, 479.

47 *Ibid.*, para. 62: "Many of these hard-fought and bloody conflicts took place in Bosnia and Herzegovina and many of the outrages against civilians, especially though by no means exclusively by Ustasa forces against ethnic Serbs, also took place there, particularly in the border area between Croatia and Bosnia and Herzegovina, where the Partisans were especially active and which is the very area in which Prijedor lies. A minister of the wartime Croatian puppet government had promised to kill a third of the Serbs in its territory, deport a third and by force convert the remaining third to Catholicism. Another urged the cleansing of all of the greatly enlarged Croatia of 'Serbian dirt'. Wholesale massacres of Serbs ensued; in six months of 1941 the Ustasa may have killed well over a quarter of a million Serbs, although the exact number is a subject of much controversy. Bulgarian and Hungarian occupying forces in other parts of Yugoslavia also engaged in massacres of Serbs *and in ethnic cleansing*. However, other ethnic groups also suffered in Prijedor, the Partisans killing many prominent Muslims and Croats in 1942 and again, in nearby Kozarac, in 1945." (my italics) Also *ibid.*, para. 84: "The objective of Serbia, the JNA and Serb-dominated political parties, primarily the SDS, at this stage was to create a Serb-dominated western extension of Serbia, taking in Serb-dominated portions of Croatia and portions, too, of Bosnia and Herzegovina. This would then, together with Serbia, its two autonomous provinces and Montenegro, form a new and smaller Yugoslavia with a substantially Serb population. However, among obstacles in the way were the very large Muslim and Croat populations native to and living in Bosnia and Herzegovina. To deal with that problem *the practice of ethnic cleansing was adopted*. This was no new concept. As mentioned earlier, it was familiar to the Croat wartime regime and to many Serb writers who had long envisaged the redistribution of populations, by force if necessary, in the course of achieving a Greater Serbia. This concept was espoused by Slobodan Milosevic, with ethnic Serbs widely adopting it throughout the former Yugoslavia, including Serb political leaders in Bosnia and Herzegovina and in Croatia. In addition to the concept of a Greater Serbia, there was also a concept on the part of Croats of the creation of a Greater Croatia that would include all Croats living in the territory of the former Yugoslavia." (my italics)

> the entire non-Serb population. During the course of the ethnic cleansing of Kozarac, many more civilians were beaten, robbed and murdered by Bosnian Serb paramilitary and military forces. The terrified population were then taken to the camps of Omarska, Keraterm and Trnopolje, where their ordeal continued. Some civilians, after their forced removal from Kozarac, were sent to Prijedor military barracks before being sent to the camps.[48]

In other words, 'ethnic cleansing' is equivalent to deportation,[49] a grave breach of the Geneva Conventions as well as a crime against humanity, and therefore a crime within the jurisdiction of the Tribunal.[50] The Tribunal has also described 'ethnic cleansing' as "ethnic separation by force"[51] or "forcible transfer".[52] In one judgment, a Trial Chamber said it was

> ... satisfied upon the evidence before it that there was a widespread and systematic attack against the non-Serb civilian population of the municipality of Visegrad at the time relevant to the Indictment. The attack took many forms, starting with the Serb take-over of the town and the systematic and large-scale criminal campaign of murders, rapes and mistreatment of the non-Serb population of this municipality, particularly the Muslims, which eventually culminated in one of the most comprehensive and ruthless campaigns of *ethnic cleansing* in the Bosnian conflict. Within a few weeks, the municipality of Visegrad was almost completely cleansed of its non-Serb citizens, and the municipality was eventually integrated into what is now Republika Srpska.[53]

But in the same ruling, it also used the term in inverted commas, once again suggesting perhaps that it was not a precise legal term or that it was a euphemism.[54] In yet another judgment, a Trial Chamber spoke of"what is colloquially

48 *Prosecutor* v. *Tadic* (Case no. IT-94-1-T), Sentencing Judgment, 14 July 1997, para. 38; also para. 56.

49 *Prosecutor* v. *Vasiljevic* (Case no. IT-98-32-T), Judgment, 29 November 2002, para. 191.

50 *Statute of the International Criminal Tribunal for the former Yugoslavia* ..., Art. 2, 5.

51 *Prosecutor* v. *Plavsic* (Case no. IT-00-39&40/1), Sentencing Judgment, 27 February 2003, para. 18.

52 *Prosecutor* v. *Krstic* (Case no. IT-98-33-T) ..., 622.

53 *Prosecutor* v . *Vasiljevic* (Case no. IT-98-32-T), Judgment, 29 November 2002, para. 58 (reference omitted, emphasis added).

54 *Ibid.*, para. 118. Also: *Prosecutor* v. *Nikolic* (Case no. IT-02-60/1-S), Sentencing Judgment, 2 December 2003, para. 59; *Prosecutor* v. *Kordic & Cerkez* (Case no. IT-95-14/2-T), Judgment, 26 February 2001, para. 851; *Prosecutor* v. *Krnojelac* (Case no. IT-97-25-A), Separate Opinion of Judge Schomburg, 17 September 2003, para. 14; *Prosecutor* v. *Delalic et al.* (Case no. IT-96-21T), Judgment, 16 November 1998, paras. 107, 213; *Prosecutor* v. *Kupreskic* (Case no. IT-95-16-T), Judgment, 14 January 2000, paras. 2, 38, 338.

referred to as 'ethnic cleansing'."[55] Another Trial Chamber of the Tribunal noted, in *Sikirica*, the relative paucity of genocide indictments, and the fact that virtually all of the prosecutions involved 'ethnic cleansing'. The Trial Chamber seemed to consider that 'ethnic cleansing' was better described within the framework of the crime against humanity of persecution.[56] In *Kupreskic*, a Trial Chamber stated that 'ethnic cleansing' was a form of crime against humanity, describing it as "a notion which, although it is not a term of art, is particularly germane to the work of this Tribunal."[57]

III. But Is 'Ethnic Cleansing' Genocide?

The crime of genocide is aimed at the intentional destruction of an ethnic group. 'Ethnic cleansing' would seem to be targeted at something different, the expulsion of a group with a view to encouraging or at least tolerating its survival elsewhere. Yet ethnic cleansing may well have the effect of rendering the continued existence of a group impossible, thereby effecting its destruction. In other words, forcible deportation may achieve the same result as extermination camps. But there is strong evidence that at least in the early years of the development of the concept of a crime of genocide, the forced expulsion, transfer or deportation that we now describe as 'ethnic cleansing' was not meant to be included within the definition.

The term 'ethnic cleansing' was unknown at the time the Genocide Convention was drafted. But the notion of 'rendering an area ethnically homogeneous by using force or intimidation to remove persons of given groups from the area' has a long history in international relations. In the 1940s, it was a recognized practice, and only in the late twentieth century has 'ethnic cleansing' come to be understood as a serious human rights violation.[58] For example, in post-Second World War Europe, the Allies forcibly removed ethnic German populations from areas in Western Poland. As many as fifteen million Germans were expelled and resettled pursuant to Article XIII of the 1945 Potsdam Protocol.[59] Indeed, during drafting of the Convention, the United States expressed concern that the proposed definition of the crime "might be extended to embrace forced transfers of minority groups such as have already been carried out by members of the United Nations."[60]

55 *Prosecutor* v. *Krstic* (Case no. IT-98-33-T) ... , para. 612.

56 *Prosecutor* v. *Sikirica et al.* ..., para. 90.

57 *Prosecutor* v. *Kupreskic* ..., para. 606.

58 Jennifer Jackson Preece, "Ethnic Cleansing as an Instrument of Nation-State Creation: Changing State Practices and Evolving Legal Norms", 20 *Human Rights Q.* (1998), 817.

59 A. De Zayas, "International Law and Mass Population Transfers", 16 Harv. Int'f L.] (1975),207; A. De Zayas, *Nemesis at Potsdam; The Expulsion of the Germans from the East*, (Lincoln, Nebraska, 1989); Freiherr Von Braun, "Germany's Eastern Border and Mass Expulsions", 58 *AJIL* (1964), 747.

60 "Comments by Governments on the Draft Convention prepared by the Secretariat, Communications from Non-Governmental Organizations", UN Doc. E/623. The

And while the Convention was being drafted, Palestinians were 'cleansed' from areas in the new state of Israel.[61]

Another contemporary indication of the attitude towards 'ethnic cleansing' appears in the debates of the 1952 session of the prestigious *Institut de Droit International*. Rapporteur Giorgio Balladore Pallieri listed twenty 'population transfer' treaties between 1913 and 1945, admitting that "il n'y a jamais de transfert vraiment volontaire des populations".[62] Pallieri concluded, with the logic of an ethnic cleanser, that there was nothing in international law to oppose the legitimacy of population transfers and that they were even, in certain circumstances, desirable. They were the consequences of the legitimate desire of all modern states to have loyal citizens, he said.[63] Pallieri's analysis was well received by most of the members of the Institute, including Max Huber, Jean Spiropoulos and Fernand de Visscher. Georges Scelle stood alone, deeming the whole idea repulsive and incompatible with the emerging law of human rights.

There is no doubt the drafters of the Genocide Convention quite deliberately resisted attempts to encompass the phenomenon of ethnic cleansing within the punishable acts of genocide. According to the comments accompanying the early Secretariat draft, the proposed definition excluded "certain acts which may result in the total or partial destruction of a group of human beings ... , namely ... mass displacements of population."[64] An accompanying commentary prepared by the Secretariat continued: "[m]ass displacement of populations from one region to another also does not constitute genocide. It would, however, become genocide

United States cited specifically paragraph 3(b), "destroying the specific characteristics of the group by: (b) Forced and systematic exile of individuals representing the culture of a group ...". The fears of the United States were not totally misplaced. One academic writer has said that "the expulsion of Germans and of persons of German descent living in the former eastern provinces of Germany and in eastern and southeastern European countries frequently took place under conditions that are classifiable as genocide": Hans-Heinrich Jescheck, "Genocide", in Rudolph Bernhardt, (ed.), *Encyclopedia of Public International Law*, Vol. II, (Amsterdam, 1995), 541-4, at 541. During United States Senate consideration of the Genocide Convention in 1950, James Finucane of the National Council for the Prevention of War testified about the United States's "genocidal intent, or genocidal carelessness, at Potsdam": United States of America, *Hearings Before a Subcommittee of the Committee on Foreign Relations, United States Senate, January 23, 24, 25, and February 9, 1950*, (Washington, 1950), 312.

61 Mark Tessler, *A History of the Israeli-Palestinian Conflict*, (Bloomington and Indianapolis, 1994), 291-307; Baruch Kimmerling and Joel S. Migdal, *Palestinians: the Making of a People*, (New York, 1993),146-56; Benny Morris, *1948 and After: Israel and the Palestinians*, (Oxford, 1990), 22; John Quigley, "Displaced Palestinians and a Right of Return", 39 *Harvard Int'l L. J.* (1998), 171.

62 Giorgia Balladore Pallieri, "Les transferts internationaux de populations", [1952] II *Annuaire de I'Institut de droit international*, 138-99, at 142-3.

63 *Ibid.*, 149.

64 UN Doc. E/447, 23.

if the occupation were attended by such circumstances as to lead to the death of the whole or part of the displaced population (if, for example, people were driven from their homes and forced to travel long distances in a country where they were exposed to starvation, thirst, heat, cold and epidemics)."[65] The unspoken reference here is to the mass displacement of Armenians within the Ottoman Empire in 1915, where the exposure to starvation, thirst, heat, cold and epidemics resulted in the death of hundreds of thousands.

In the Sixth Committee of the General Assembly, in 1948, Syria actually proposed an amendment to the definition of genocide corresponding closely to the contemporary notion of 'ethnic cleansing'. The Syrian amendment read: "[i]mposing measures intended to oblige members of a group to abandon their homes in order to escape the threat of subsequent ill-treatment."[66] The Syrian representative said "[t]he problem of refugees and displaced persons to which his delegations proposal referred had arisen at the end of the Second World War and remained extremely acute."[67] Yugoslavia supported the amendment, citing Nazi displacement of Slav populations from a part of Yugoslavia in order to establish a German majority. "That action was tantamount to the deliberate destruction of a group", said the Yugoslav delegate. "Genocide could be committed by forcing members of a group to abandon their homes", he added.[68]

But the United States argued that the Syrian proposal "deviated too much from the original concept of genocide."[69] For the United Kingdom, "the problem raised by the Syrian amendment was a serious one but did not fall within the definition of genocide."[70] The Soviets said that "[m]easures compelling members of a group to abandon their homes, in the case of acts committed under the Hitler regime, were rather a consequence of genocide."[71] The Syrian amendment was resoundingly defeated, by twenty-nine votes to five, with eight abstentions.[72]

The first consideration of the term 'ethnic cleansing' from a legal standpoint appears to be in the report of the Commission of Experts which was appointed by the Security Council in October 1992 to examine violations of international humanitarian law in the former Yugoslavia. The Commission stated that "'[e]thnic cleansing' is contrary to international law."[73] It suggested that in some cases 'ethnic cleansing' could be considered a breach of the Genocide Convention:

65 *Ibid.*, 24.

66 UN Doc. A/C.6/234.

67 UN Doc. A/C.6/SR.82 (Tarazi, Syria).

68 *Ibid.*, (Bartos, Yugoslavia).

69 *Ibid.*, (Maktos, United States of America).

70 *Ibid.*, (Fitzmaurice, United Kingdom).

71 *Ibid.*, (Morozov, Soviet Union).

72 UN Doc. A/C.6/SR.82.

73 "Interim report of the Commission of Experts Established Pursuant to Security Council Resolution 780 (1992)", UN Doc. S/35374 (1993), para. 55.

> Based on the many reports describing the policy and practices conducted in the former Yugoslavia, 'ethnic cleansing' has been carried out by means of murder, torture, arbitrary arrest and detention, extrajudicial executions, rape and sexual assault, confinement of civilian population in ghetto areas, forcible removal, displacement and deportation of civilian population, deliberate military attacks or threats of attacks on civilians and civilian areas, and wanton destruction of property. Those practices constitute crimes against humanity and can be assimilated to specific war crimes. Furthermore, such acts could also fall within the meaning of the Genocide Convention.[74]

Whether ethnic cleansing corresponds to genocide was also addressed before the International Court of Justice, in Bosnia's 1993 application against Yugoslavia. Bosnia had named Professor Elihu Lauterpacht of Cambridge University as its ad hoc judge, in accordance with Article 31(3) of the Statute of the International Court of Justice. In the Court's 13 September 1993 ruling on provisional measures, Judge Lauterpacht appended a separate opinion in which he asked "Has Genocide Been Committed?" He noted that

> the forced migration of civilians, more commonly known as 'ethnic cleansing', is, in truth, part of a deliberate campaign by the Serbs to eliminate Muslim control of, and presence in, substantial parts of Bosnia-Herzegovina ... Such being the case, it is difficult to regard the Serbian acts as other than acts of genocide in that they clearly fall within categories (a), (b) and (c) of the definition of genocide quoted above, they are clearly directed against an ethnical or religious group as such, and they are intended to destroy that group, if not in whole certainly in part, to the extent necessary to ensure that that group no longer occupies the parts of Bosnia-Herzegovina coveted by the Serbs. The Respondent stands behind the Bosnian Serbs and it must, therefore, be seen as an accomplice to, if not an actual participant in, this genocide behaviour. Should there be any disposition to regard 'ethnic cleansing' as no more than an aspect of a particularly vicious territorial conflict between Serbs and Muslims ... it must be recalled that the Respondent has itself also characterized 'ethnic cleansing or comparable conduct' as genocide ... Since the evidence presently before the Court of such 'genocide against the Serb ethnic group' is of a limited kind, and in terms of expulsion by Bosnian Muslims of Bosnian Serbs from the areas in which they were living does not approach the same order of magnitude as the expulsion of Bosnian Muslims by the Serbs, it would appear a fortiori that the Respondent also regards the 'ethnic cleansing' as carried out in this conflict as a breach of Article 11 of the Genocide Convention.[75]

74 *Ibid.*, para. 56.

75 *Application of the Convention on the Prevention and Punishment of the Crime of Genocide (Bosnia and Herzegovina v. Yugoslavia* ..., Separate Reasons of Judge *ad hoc* Lauterpacht, 431-2, paras. 68-70.

Judge Lauterpacht declared he was prepared to order, pursuant to the Genocide Convention, "a prohibition of' ethnic cleansing' or conduct contributing thereto such as attacks and firing upon, sniping at and killing of non-combatants, and bombardment and blockade of areas of civilian occupation and other conduct having as its effect the terrorization of civilians in such a manner as to lead them to abandon their homes."[76] These individual views were not, however, echoed in the majority decision.

IV. New Interpretations and a Cautious Approach

During discussion of the 'Elements of Crimes' of the Rome Statute of the International Criminal Court, in 1999-2000, the 'Arab Group' criticized a United States draft for failing to deal with the practice of ethnic cleansing as a means of genocide within the context of Article 6(b)(iii) of the Statute, which corresponds to Article II(c) of the Convention. Accordingly, "[t]his confirms the difficulty of enumerating all the so-called elements of crimes. It is more than likely that future events in the world will reveal other forms of genocide that have not been mentioned in this or similar proposals."[77] Article II(c) lists, as one of the ways of committing the crime of genocide, "deliberately inflicting on the group conditions of life calculated to bring about its physical destruction in whole or in part."

The problem with Article II(c), in terms of its relevance to the concept of 'ethnic cleansing', is the reference to physical destruction. It would seem that 'ethnic cleansing' does not necessarily aim at the physical destruction of the group, but rather its expulsion and transfer to another territory. *Physical* destruction may be a consequence of the transfer. Moreover, the perpetrators may be relatively indifferent to the consequences of the forcible transfer upon the future of the group. But in practice it will probably be difficult to prove that physical destruction was their intent or, to use the words of Article II(c), their *calculation*.

There is some precedent on this point. Until 1941, Nazi anti-semitic policies were directed towards convincing Jews in Germany to leave the country. Jews were required, of course, to pay a price for their freedom. Moreover, large numbers who attempted to leave were unable to find refuge because other 'civilized' states refused to admit them.[78] The Nazi policy, at the time, was one that we would today call 'ethnic cleansing'. Jews were incited to leave by various forms of persecution, including discriminatory laws and periodic outbursts of violence such as the *Kristalnacht* of 9-10 November 1938. After the war against the Soviet Union was

76 *Ibid.*, 447, para. 123(A)(ii).

77 "Proposal by Algeria, Bahrain, Comoros, Djibouti, Egypt, Jordan, Iraq, Kuwait, Lebanon, Libyan Arab Jamahiriya, Morocco, Oman, Palestine, Qatar, Saudi Arabia, the Sudan, the Syrian Arab Republic, Tunisia, United Arab Emirates and Yemen, Comments on the proposal submitted by the United States of America concerning terminology and the crime of genocide", UN Doc. PCNICC/1999/WGEC/DP.4, 3.

78 United States Holocaust Memorial Museum, *Historical Atlas of the Holocaust*, (New York, 1996), 25-7.

underway, the Nazi policy became destruction of the Jews of Europe, in whole or in part. No longer was emigration permitted, even if asylum was possible. At this point, the Nazi policy became genocidal. The District Court of Jerusalem, in the *Eichmann* case, noted this evolution in Nazi policy, commenting that "[t]he implementation of the 'Final Solution', in the sense of total extermination, is to a certain extent connected with the cessation of emigration of Jews from territories under German influence."[79] Until mid-1941, when the 'final solution' emerged, the Israeli court said "a doubt remains in our minds whether there was here that specific intention to exterminate", as required by the definition of genocide. The Court said it would deal with such inhuman acts as being crimes against humanity rather than genocide. Eichmann was acquitted of genocide for acts prior to August 1941.[80]

Recently, the German courts have proposed a new interpretation of the crime of genocide that enables it to encompass the concept of 'ethnic cleansing'. According to the Federal Constitutional Court, in a December 2000 ruling:

> the statutory definition of genocide defends a supra-individual object of legal protection, i.e. the *social* existence of the group [...] the intent to destroy the group [...] extends beyond physical and biological extermination [...] The text of the law does not therefore compel the interpretation that the culprit's intent must be to exterminate physically at least a substantial number of the members of the group.[81]

The German interpretation extends the scope of genocide by allowing it to encompass attacks on the existence of an ethnic group that fall short of physical extermination or destruction.

The drafting history of the Genocide Convention does not support such an interpretation. During preparation of the Convention, delegates unequivocally decided to *exclude* cultural genocide from its ambit.[82] In this respect, reference has already been made to the unsuccessful Syrian proposal. But one does not even need to refer to the *travaux preparatoires* of the Convention in order to see this, as it transpires from a literal reading of the text itself. First, there is the reference in Article II(c) to "physical destruction". Second, there is the exception to the general principle, by which the Convention applies only to physical destruction, that appears in Article II(e). Article II(e) is the final act of genocide in the list, and it addresses "forcibly transferring children of the group to another group". It was

---

79 *A.G. Israel* v. *Eichmann*, (1968) 36 ILR 5 (District Court, Jerusalem), para. 80.

80 *Ibid.*, para. 244(1-3); also, paras. 186-7.

81 Federal Constitutional Court, 2 BvR 1290/99, 12 December 2000, para. (III)(4)(a)(aa). Cited in *Prosecutor* v. *Krstic* (Case no. IT-98-33-T) ... , para. 1287.

82 UN Doc. AlC.6/SR.83 (twenty-five in favour, sixteen against with four abstentions). See also: *Yearbook of the International Law Commission 1991*, vol. II(2), 102. The debates are discussed in considerable detail in Schabas, *Genocide in International Law* ..., 179-89.

added to the Convention late in the drafting, on a proposal from Greece, which argued that despite the decision to exclude cultural genocide, there was one act of cultural genocide on which there was no disagreement, and that was forced transfer of children.[83] It seems straightforward enough that if the Convention specifically contemplates forcible transfer of *children*, it probably does not address the broader phenomenon of forcible transfer of populations as a whole.

Nevertheless, human rights treaties – and the Genocide Convention is not only the first[84] but it has been described as the quintessential human rights treaty[85] – should not be locked into rigid interpretations based either upon their *travaux preparatoires* or literal construction. As the Human Rights Committee indicated in a recent ruling, a human rights treaty "should be interpreted as a living instrument and the rights protected under it should be applied in context and in the light of present-day conditions."[86] Arguably, this is what the German Constitutional Court was doing in its December 2000 decision.

The judges of the International Criminal Tribunal for the former Yugoslavia have tread somewhat prudently here, however. In the *Krstic* judgment, after referring to the German case law, the Trial Chamber said that "despite recent developments", the prohibition of retroactive criminal law (*nullum crimen sine lege*) mandated a more conservative interpretation: "[C]ustomary international law limits the definition of genocide to those acts seeking the physical or biological destruction of all or part of the group."[87] More generally, several of the judges have warned against excessively broad interpretations of the crime of genocide, especially given that virtually anything that is not caught within the genocide net will in any event fall within the rubric of crimes against humanity.[88] In *Stakic*, a Trial Chamber said:

> It does not suffice to deport a group or a part of a group. A clear distinction must be drawn between physical destruction and mere dissolution of a group. The expulsion of a group or part of a group does not in itself suffice for genocide. As Kreß has stated, "[t]his is true even if the expulsion can be characterised as a tendency to the dissolution of the group, taking the form of its fragmentation or assimilation. This is because the dissolution of the group is not to be equated with physical destruction". In this context the Chamber recalls that a proposal

83 UN Doc. A/C.6/SR.82 (Vallindas, Greece).

84 It was adopted on 9 December 1948, just hours before the General Assembly voted on the Universal Declaration of Human Rights.

85 "Report of the International Law Commission on the work of its forty-ninth session 12 May-18 July 1997", UN Doc. A/52/10, para. 76. Also: *Prosecutor* v. *Kayishema and Ruzindana* (Case no. ICTR-95-1-T), Judgment, 21 May 1999, para. 88.

86 *Judge* v. *Canada* (Case no. 829/1998), Views, 13 August 2003, UN Doc. CCPRlC/78/D/829/1998, para. 10.3.

87 Prosecutor v. Krstic (Case no. IT-98-33-T) ..., para. 580.

88 See, for example, *Prosecutor* v. *Jelisic* (Case No. IT-95-10-A), Partial Dissenting Opinion of Judge Wald, 5 July 2001, para. 1.

> by Syria in the Sixth Committee to include "[i]mposing measures intended to oblige members of a group to abandon their homes in order to escape the threat of subsequent ill-treatment" as a separate sub-paragraph of Article II of the Convention against Genocide was rejected by twenty-nine votes to five, with eight abstentions.[89]

But while the judges of the ICTY may have rejected a broad and dynamic interpretation of the text of the provision, in their application of the law to the facts of the conflict in the former Yugoslavia they have shown a readiness to encompass within the definition of genocide acts of persecution that amount to 'forcible transfer' but that appear to fall short of physical destruction. Srebrenica is, of course, the paradigm, and it seems to lie on the fuzzy line that distinguishes 'ethnic cleansing' from genocide. There can be no question that the Bosnian Serb forces intended to forcibly transfer the Muslim population of Srebrenica, thereby creating an ethnically pure Serb territory in what was a highly strategic location. Many of the acts aimed at forcible transfer were comparable in brutality and horror to those perpetrated in many parts of the territory of the former Yugoslavia or, for that matter, in Kosovo in 1999. Both the Prosecutor and the judges have accepted that as a general rule, such acts of 'ethnic cleansing' fall short of the crime of genocide.

Srebrenica was different because the forcible expulsion of the Muslim population was also accompanied by the mass execution of 7,000 to 8,000 individuals. The victims were all male, and have been described as being of, military age' because it would seem that the young boys and the old men were spared, by and large. Indeed, the women, the children and the elderly men of the community were put on buses and moved from Srebrenica prior to the massacre of the menfolk. And this is where the ambiguity arises. Although the execution of the men looks unquestionably like an act of genocide, and one reminiscent of such World War II-era massacres as Babi Yar, the forcible transfer of the women, children and elderly men makes the overall crime look somewhat different. If the intent were truly to destroy the Muslim population of Srebrenica in a physical sense, why would the women and children, who are the guarantee of the *survival* of the community, be spared?

Faced with this ambiguity, both applicable decisions of the ICTY, that of the Trial Chamber and of the Appeals Chamber, have made findings of genocide. Acknowledging the factual uncertainties, they have devised a theory by which genocide was not part of the 'master plan' of ethnic cleansing for the Srebrenica enclave. Rather, they have treated genocide as something that was improvised very much at the last minute, as if it were a perverse strain of the disease of 'ethnic cleansing' that emerged somewhat spontaneously. The Trial Chamber had found that a plan to ethnically cleanse the Srebrenica enclave of Muslims "escalated" into a genocidal plan designed to "guarantee that the Bosnian Muslim popula-

89 *Prosecutor* v. *Stakic* ... , para. 519.

tion would be permanently eradicated."[90] Confirming this conclusion, the Appeals Chamber noted:

> The Trial Chamber has made findings that, as of 13 July, the plan to ethnically cleanse the area of Srebrenica escalated to a far more insidious level that included killing all of the military-aged Bosnian Muslim men of Srebrenica. A transfer of the men after screening for war criminals – the purported reason for their separation from the women, children and elderly at Potocari – to Bosnian Muslim held territory or to prisons to await a prisoner exchange was at some point considered an inadequate mode for assuring the ethnic cleansing of Srebrenica. Killing the men, in addition to forcibly transferring the women, children and elderly, became the object of the newly elevated joint criminal enterprise of General Mladic and VRS Main Staff personnel. The Trial Chamber concluded that this campaign to kill all the military aged men was conducted to guarantee that the Bosnian Muslim population would be permanently eradicated from Srebrenica and therefore constituted genocide.[91]

One of the problems with this approach was a lingering doubt about the individual accused. The judges were clearly not convinced that General Krstic had the intent to destroy the Muslims of Srebrenica. Krstic was an ethnic cleanser, not a *génocidaire*: "His own particular intent was directed to a forcible displacement."[92] Yet according to the Appeals Chamber, there were others, of course, at senior levels of the Serb forces, "to whom the forcible displacement was a means of advancing the genocidal plan."[93]

In this respect, the Tribunal is perhaps suggesting that the ambiguities of the treatment of the Muslims of Srebrenica may have been because of ambiguities within the Serb military staff itself The supreme commander, General Mladic, may have sought the physical destruction of the Muslims, and this explains the summary executions. General Krstic, on the other hand, intended to effect the forcible transfer, so he organized the buses for the women, children and the elderly. But if Mladic really planned to annihilate the Muslim community in Srebrenica, why did he allow the women, children and the elderly to escape? On this point, the reasoning of the Tribunal is unconvincing. The Appeals Chamber wrote:

> The fact that the forcible transfer does not constitute in and of itself a genocidal act does not preclude a Trial Chamber from relying on it as evidence of the intentions of members of the VRS Main Staff. The genocidal intent may be inferred, among other facts, from evidence of "other culpable acts systematically directed against the same group" ... In this case, the factual circumstances,

---

90 *Prosecutor* v. *Krstic* (Case no. IT-98-33-T) ..., para. 619.

91 *Ibid.*

92 *Prosecutor* v. *Krstic* (Case no. IT-98-33-A) ..., para. 133.

93 *Ibid.*

> as found by the Trial Chamber, permit the inference that the killing of the Bosnian Muslim men was done with genocidal intent. As already explained, the scale of the killing, combined with the VRS Main Staff's awareness of the detrimental consequences it would have for the Bosnian Muslim community of Srebrenica and with the other actions the Main Staff took to ensure that community's physical demise, is a sufficient factual basis for the finding of specific intent...[94]

The Appeals Chamber noted that the victims of the summary executions were not only men of military age. Some of them were "severely handicapped and, for that reason, unlikely to have been combatants."[95] Moreover, "the term 'men of military age' was itself a misnomer, for the group killed by the VRS included boys and elderly men normally considered to be outside that range. Although the younger and older men could still be capable of bearing arms, the Trial Chamber was entitled to conclude that they did not present a serious military threat, and to draw a further inference that the VRS decision to kill them did not stem solely from the intent to eliminate them as a threat ..."[96] Accordingly, for the Appeals Chamber, the summary execution of the men could not be accounted for on purely military grounds. It was aimed at something more: The theory of the Appeals Chamber is that the purpose of the executions was to compromise the survival of the community as a whole:

> The Trial Chamber was also entitled to consider the long-term impact that the elimination of seven to eight thousand men from Srebrenica would have on the survival of that community. In examining these consequences, the Trial Chamber properly focused on the likelihood of the community's physical survival. As the Trial Chamber found, the massacred men amounted to about one fifth of the overall Srebrenica community. The Trial Chamber found that, given the patriarchal character of the Bosnian Muslim society in Srebrenica, the destruction of such a sizeable number of men would "inevitably result in the physical disappearance of the Bosnian Muslim population at Srebrenica". Evidence introduced at trial supported this finding, by showing that, with the majority of the men killed officially listed as missing, their spouses are unable to remarry and, consequently, to have new children. The physical destruction of the men therefore had severe procreative implications for the Srebrenica Muslim community, potentially consigning the community to extinction.[97]

Yet it is uncontested that the Serbs intended to eliminate the Muslim community in Srebrenica. Even Krstic, who it has been acknowledged was a 'mere ethnic

---

94 *Ibid.*, paras. 33, 35.

95 *Ibid.*, para. 26.

96 *Ibid.*, para. 27 (references omitted).

97 *Ibid.* (references omitted).

cleanser', shared this objective. Speculation about the intent of those responsible for the summary execution of the men is therefore not particularly helpful here, because the permanent destruction of the Srebrenica Muslim community could also have been effected by putting the men on buses too.

And this explains the adoption, by the Tribunal, of its theory about 'procreative implications'. The killing of the men, according to the Appeals Chamber, would ensure the physical destruction of the Srebrenica Muslims because the women would no longer have children, and the group would then disappear. It must be said that there is no evidence whatsoever to suggest that this idea even crossed the minds of General Mladic and his co-conspirators. We have no *Mein Kampf* and no Wannsee Conference to imply a calculation whereby a summary execution of men would bring about the physical destruction of a group because of 'procreative implications'. Nor is there any manifestation of a similar approach elsewhere during the wars in the former Yugoslavia, so it cannot be suggested that this was a *modus operandi* of the Serb ethnic cleansers. And does the Tribunal's theory even make sense? Although there is no legal requirement that criminals carry out their crimes in a logical way, the Tribunal's inference that Mladic et al. intended the physical destruction of a group as a consequence of the 'procreative implications' of the killing of adult men has some unreasonable dimensions. If the young children are not killed, surely they will soon become adults and have children themselves. In Rwanda – a situation where the issue of genocide is beyond debate – Hutu women who were pregnant from Tutsi fathers were themselves massacred because of the concern that they would bear Tutsi children. Will not the offspring of the surviving children of Srebrenica's Muslims return to haunt the Serb ethnic cleansers, like the third generation Armenians do to the Turks who persecuted their grandparents? If Mladic really intended the physical destruction of the Muslims, didn't this even occur to him?

This is not to suggest that individual participants in the Srebrenica massacre may not have harboured genocidal ambitions. The Tribunal has already accepted the questionable proposition that an individual, acting alone, may commit genocide, in the absence of some overall plan or policy of a state or organized group.[98] But in *Krstic*, the Appeals Chamber spoke to the question of whether genocide was committed by the Serb forces, acting collectively. The fact that some of the Serb leaders may have intended genocide doesn't prove this is what happened any more than the fact others did not intend it – the case of General Krstic – proves the opposite. Even if Krstic knew of the genocidal intent of the others with whom he was involved, and this is the conclusion of the Tribunal, he still cannot be convicted of genocide unless the crime itself actually took place.

These uncertainties in the *Krstic* ruling of the Appeals Chamber probably reflect divisions among the judges themselves. The judgment is a compromise, the apparent result of concessions aimed at reaching a consensus. For some of the

98 *Prosecutor* v. *Jelisic* (Case No. IT-95-1O-A), Judgment, 5 July 2001, para. 48. Also: *Prosecutor* v. *Kunarac et al.* (Case no. IT-96-23 & IT-96-23/1-A), Judgment, 12 June 2002, para. 98.

judges, it must have been unthinkable that the most terrible massacre committed in Europe since the Holocaust would not be labelled genocide. The consequence has been to muddy the distinction between 'ethnic cleansing' and genocide. Srebrenica stands as a unique event in the Yugoslav wars. Perhaps it is best to see it as the exception that proves the rule. The Tribunal's theory by which a genocidal plan for the Muslims of Srebrenica emerged literally in the final hours of an ethnic cleansing campaign that had been underway for some three years supports the inference that, by and large, the Bosnian Serbs, and with them the leaders of the Federal Republic of Yugoslavia, did not intend to commit genocide. To this extent, the conclusions in *Krstic* may actually assist Milosevic before the ICTY and Serbia before the International Court of Justice in the pending cases.

*Andrea Krizsán**

Ombudsmen and Similar Institutions for Protection against Racial and Ethnic Discrimination

I. Introduction

Article 13 of the 2000 EU Race Directive[1] defines the requirement for member states to designate bodies for the promotion of equal treatment for all without discrimination on grounds of racial or ethnic origin. The tasks the Directive attributes to such bodies include assisting victims in pursuing their complaints, conducting independent surveys on discrimination, publishing reports and making recommendations on issues relating to discrimination. The message conveyed by the Directive is that, in order to put the equal treatment principle in place, it is not enough to issue new legislation and leave it to regular judicial procedure for implementation, but that additional efforts are necessary. Bodies combating discrimination and promoting diversity are one major pillar of such additional efforts.

One type of institution that clearly fits the Directive's description of such bodies, which has been in place in some countries of Europe from before the document's inception and has been working towards the above aims, is the ombudsman institution and, specifically, the ombudsman institution that specializes in minority or discrimination issues.

Throughout the past few decades, starting perhaps with the creation of the Commission for Racial Equality (CRE) in the UK in 1976, a variety of bodies combating racial discrimination and promoting equal treatment have been established. Some of them in the form of commissions with regulatory functions and complaint procedures, others as centres against racism, and others, since the mid-1990s, as specialized ombudsman institutions.[2] Despite the undeniable differences

* Research Fellow, Center for Policy Studies, Central European University, Budapest, Hungary.

1 Council Directive 2000/43/EC of 29 June 2000 implementing the principle of equal treatment between persons irrespective of racial or ethnic origin.

2 See a report on bodies combating discrimination that existed before the Race Directive's requirements went into force. European Commission Directorate-General for Employment and Social Affairs, *Promoting Diversity: 21 Bodies Promoting Diversity*

Minority Governance in and beyond Europe, ISBN 978-90-04-27648-2. pp. 61–84.

between the different models, mainly determined by the different institutional and political cultures of the respective countries, from the years of experience of working with discrimination their grounding principles seem to have converged and a set of common principles has evolved from the activity of these institutions. These institutions can be seen as more than just examples of good practice: the careful scrutiny of cases allows us to identify the characteristic features of this recently emerged institutional solution: specialized bodies combating discrimination. Ombudsman institutions working in this field fit this group of institutions and, as this paper will argue, many aspects of the ombudsman model can be seen as cornerstones of this institutional model. The type of specialized ombudsman we talk about here is a hybrid between classical ombudsman institutions and regulatory agencies. This paper will attempt to look primarily at the ombudsman type institutions but will reflect on the common sets of working principles that ground the work of most of these bodies.

The aim of this paper is twofold. First, it will attempt to show how several features required by bodies working towards the implementation of equal treatment can be related to or even derived from classical ombudsman institutions. It will show how the ombudsman institution, a centuries-old but flexibly adopted institution, can be seen as having informed the idea for the bodies proposed by the Directive. Secondly, the paper will attempt to substantiate the necessity for having specialized agencies beyond courts for dealing with racial and ethnic discrimination. It will do so by analyzing some of the specific features of specialized ombudsman institutions and also of other specialized agencies that informed the conception of the Directive, such as the CRE in the UK.

II. The Ombudsman Institution in General

The ombudsman institution originates in Sweden where it has operated since the beginning of the nineteenth century.[3] It was established with the purpose

and Combating Discrimination in the European Union (Office for Official Publications of the European Communities, Luxemburg, 2002), at <http://europa.eu.int/comm/employment_social/publications/2003/ke4702705_en.html>. For an earlier review of the same bodies, see also European Commission Against Racism and Intolerance, "Examples of Good Practices: Specialised Bodies to Combat Racism, Xenophobia, Antisemitism and Intolerance at National Level", CRI (2004) 06, at <http://www.coe.int/T/E/human_rights/Ecri/1ECRI/3-General_themes/2-Examples_of_good_practices/1-Specialised_Bodies/ECRI04-6%20good%20practices%20specialised%20bodies%20final.pdf>.

3 For a history of the ombudsman institution see Gerald E. Caiden, Niall MacDermot and Alec Sandler, "The Institution of Ombudsman", in Gerald E. Caiden (ed.), *International Handbook of the Ombudsman*, (Greenwood Press, Westport Connecticut, 1983); Walter Gellhorn, *Ombudsmen and Others: Citizens Protectors in Nine Countries* (Harvard University Press, Cambridge, Massachusetts, 1966); Donald C. Rowat, *The Ombudsman: Citizen's Defender* (George Allen and Unwin, London, 1967); Donald C. Rowat, *The Ombudsman Plan* (University Press of America, London, 1985); Frank

of investigating the complaints of private citizens against public authorities. The ombudsman was meant to be the representative of citizens against the state and the misuse of its powers. The ombudsman is an independent person appointed by the legislative power who has the power to investigate all public authorities upon individual complaints or upon his/her own initiative and to make recommendations, however, without having wide enforcement powers. Its means of enforcement are persuasion, conciliation and, if these do not work, publicity. The institution is a watchdog over justice and equity in the ways in which the state deals with its citizens.

The second part of the twentieth century saw the spread of the institution all over Europe and the world. The definition of the ombudsman institution today is much looser and much more inclusive than it was 50 years ago. The adaptation of the original model to different political and legal systems widened several – until then unquestionable – elements of the definition. Today, the institution of the ombudsman reflects a set of principles with regard to appointment, scope and means of the institution. Along these principles, there are large variations among the ombudsmen of different countries. The first section will discuss these principles and show the possibilities for variation along them, with special emphasis on some of the particular elements that are relevant from the point of view of ombudsman institutions that work to combat discrimination.

A. The Aim of the Institution

The aim of the ombudsman institution is, as put by Caiden, MacDermot and Sandler, the protection of the dignity of man and the reduction of distance between rulers and ruled. As they write:

> The existence of an independent ombudsman office denotes a clear indication by the rulers that they recognize obligations and duties to the ruled, that the ruled should be treated justly, promptly and courteously, that they should be granted their due according to the law, and that public business should be conducted honestly and efficaciously.[4]

The ombudsman is an institution for the achievement of justice and equity. It can criticize illegal behaviour, but a breach of law is not necessary: unreasonable or unjust behaviour is sufficient grounding for the action of the ombudsman. Even if a decision is procedurally correct it can still be considered unreasonable, unjust or inhumane by the ombudsman if it is bad in its effects. The ombudsman will consider the quality of the decision.[5] Thus, he/she not only provides for proce-

---

Stacey, *Ombudsmen Compared* (Clarendon Press, Oxford, 1978); Bengt Wieslander, *The Parliamentary Ombudsman in Sweden* (The Bank of Sweden Tercentenary Foundation and Gidlunds Bokforlag, Stockholm, 1994).

4 Caiden, MacDermot and Sandler, "The Institution of Ombudsman ...", 4.

5 Stacey, *Ombudsmen Compared* ....

dural justice but also for substantive justice. As such, the institution is a remedy for human rights violations, a remedy that works as a complement to courts and tribunals. In many cases, court procedures tend to be too slow, too costly, too formal and sometimes unnecessarily adversarial. The ombudsman institution fares better than courts with respect to these features as well. Finally, the ombudsman complements the work of the courts not only in the field of individual complaints but also through its strategic powers, using formal investigations as a means to revealing structural or institutional problems, or injustice about which for some reason no complaints were raised.

B. Independence

One of the main features of the ombudsman institution is its independence from those investigated. However, this principle can be interpreted in different ways. The classical ombudsman model achieves its independence through its being appointed by the legislative power. In this interpretation, the ombudsman works as the eyes the parliament keeps on the executive power.

A more extreme case is one that aims to achieve certain independence also from the legislative, by appointing the ombudsman for a longer period than the parliamentary cycle.[6] In the 1980s, however, despite the strong opposition of some experts on the institution,[7] the principle of independence was widened to include also what we call today executive ombudsmen. Executive ombudsmen are not appointed by the parliament but by some part of the executive. Executive ombudsmen are usually responsible for the protection of special categories of rights or have the task of supervising compliance with an act concerning some right (e.g. consumer protection, freedom from ethnic discrimination, equality between sexes). Thus, the specialized ombudsmen are most often appointed by the relevant ministry or state department. The emphasis in the work of executive ombudsmen is on executive practice: on enforcement and implementation of laws, and on specialized know-how for dealing with a special field of human rights. An important part of the work of executive ombudsmen is policy-oriented strategic work. However, they also deal with individual complaints. In their case, the importance of the principle of independence is reduced: independence for executive ombudsmen means independence from the organization or institution investigated, rather than independence from state administration in general.

C. The Scope of Investigations

Another principle grounding the ombudsman institution concerns the scope of its investigations. The classical model of the ombudsman was created to inves-

6 Hungary is such a case. The ombudsman is appointed for six years based on the recommendation of the president. Thus, not every parliament has its own ombudsman. Act LIX. of 1993 on the Parliamentary Commissioner for Civil Rights, Section 4.

7 Caiden, MacDermot and Sandler, "The Institution of Ombudsman ...", 12.

tigate only public authorities. With the spread of the institution, however, this has widened too. A possibility for widening is moving from the original scope of investigation – public authorities – to investigation directed at the public sector in general, which includes bodies or organizations providing different goods and services for the public such as healthcare, education, insurance or financial services, regardless of whether the provider is entirely or partially state-owned, or even a church, in cases where it provides a public service.[8] A more radical option for widening the scope of investigation of ombudsmen is the private sector ombudsman. It can be said that "the public sector has no monopoly over bad decision-making and bureaupathologies".[9] Though fear exists that widening the scope of action of the institution to include the private sector might result in the dilution of the concept, at the end of the day if the private sector ombudsman is seen to have "as many as possible of the characteristics of the classical ombudsman"[10] and, most importantly, is seen as independent from those being investigated, it can be considered an ombudsman. It seems that executive ombudsmen, as argued, being in most cases the specialized ones, tend to have a wider scope of action. Enforcement of a right, or an Act regulating one particular right, can rarely be effective if requested only by public authorities. However, in no case will private life fall within the scope of ombudsman action. The widening of the ombudsman's remit extends only to the publicly performed activity of privately owned or managed bodies (e.g. employment practices of private companies, data processing of private banks, service provision by private hospitals).

D. Powers and Instruments

What makes the ombudsman institution truly specific besides compliance with the above-described principles of independence and control over public life is its powers and instruments. The ombudsman has power to investigate individual complaints of aggrieved citizens and has strategic powers to conduct investigations on its own initiative. Easy access is one of the main features of the institution with respect to individual complaints. Complaints are investigated free of charge and, in most cases, there is no formal requirement for making the complaint, meaning that the ombudsman will sometimes help in formulating the complaint itself In general, it takes a much shorter time de facto for the ombudsman to resolve complaints than would be so in the case of court procedures. Also, the procedures conducted by the ombudsman are much less adversarial than court proceedings: firstly in the sense of focusing on investigation; and secondly in the sense that the aim of the institution is not to find and punish the wrongdoer but

8 The Danish Ombudsman Act says in Section 9: "The jurisdiction of the Ombudsman shall extend to the Established Church, except in matters which directly or indirectly involve the tenets or doctrines of the Church".

9 Caiden, MacDermot and Sandler, "The Institution of Ombudsman ...", 12.

10 Mary Seneviratne, Ombudsmen in the Public Sector (Open University Press, Buckingham, Philadelphia, 1994), 5-6.

to make him or her understand the incorrectness of the respective action and to persuade this person that the highlighted action resulted in treating the victim inhumanly and unfairly, and thus reinstatement is due. Meanwhile, persuasion also has the advantage of preventing the wrongdoer from repeatedly committing the same action. These features make the institution one that is easily accessible for people who are disadvantaged, who cannot afford to start proceedings before courts, who cannot formulate their complaints or who just want to avoid for different reasons prolonged and costly adversarial procedures.[11]

Ombudsmen can start formal investigations, as mentioned, on their own initiative and can investigate individual cases, but can also be more general in the scope of their action and look at institutional problems or general failures in the workings of some field of the public sector. The ombudsman generally has access to all information, files and documents concerning the investigated case. Upon finding some injustice, the means the ombudsman can use are again characteristic. Conciliation, persuasion and mediation are the means available to the ombudsman. Its approach is not supposed to be adversarial and the institution has no effective power to enforce its opinion. However, recommendations can be made and, upon non-compliance, publicity can be used. The means available to ombudsmen for fighting against violations of rights show that the institution is to have an educational role even in the case of solving individual complaints. The aim is not necessarily only to settle the particular issue at stake but to make the 'respondent' learn from the mistake, to understand the inhumanity, unjustness or irrationality of the provision or criterion applied, or of the practice used. The recommendations of the ombudsman will thus aim on the one hand at the resolution of grievances and on the other hand, at a change of practices.

Many ombudsmen recognize the educational role as one of their most important functions.[12] Education occurs through individual persuasion but also through what Baroness B. Serota[13] calls indirect impact: through annual reports presented to parliament or the appointing state department, through codes of practice and standards of good practice in the different fields that are provided for the employees of relevant bodies, offices or for any other concerned party. She argues that "the aim of indirect impact should be not just to improve practices in particular areas but to establish benchmarks to which authorities can relate their practices".[14] The annual reports presented to the appointing body will have the aim, on the one hand, of making public the activity and the findings of the ombudsman and, on the other hand, of making recommendations concerning legislation, policy and practices based on the individual complaints received by the ombudsman and the formal investigations conducted on own initiative. Thus, the institution pro-

11 Caiden, MacDermot and Sandler, "The Institution of Ombudsman ...", 4.

12 Larry B. Hill, "The Self-Perception of Ombudsmen: A Comparative Survey", in Caiden (ed.), *International Handbook* ..., 43-59.

13 Baroness B. Serota, "The Evolution of the Role of the Ombudsman. Comparisons and Perspectives", in Caiden (ed.), *International Handbook* ..., 38-39.

14 *Ibid.*, 39.

vides some kind of feedback on how existing laws, policies and practices operate and where amendment or new legislation or policy is needed. Even though the ombudsman will not always have the power to make suggestions on the substance of change, it can yet signal its necessity and show the nature of the problem.

This concise and descriptive discussion of the general ombudsman concept is not meant to do justice to the incredible richness and complexity of the ombudsman institution and its evolution. It is only meant to highlight some of the grounding features of the institution and some crucial points of flexibility connected to the concepts that are fundamental to specialized ombudsman institutions working to combat discrimination and, more widely, to specialized bodies combating discrimination. The next section will reflect on how each of these specific features gains relevance for the purposes of our argument here.

III. Specialized Ombudsman Institutions Combating Discrimination

Let us now examine what the main features of the specific ombudsman institutions working on combating discrimination are and, more widely, of the specialized bodies working in this field. Special emphasis will be given to two issues: first, how the above-described elements of the ombudsman idea inform the working of these institutions; and second, why such bodies are necessary for an adequate assurance of equal treatment without discrimination on grounds of race or ethnicity. Explanations will be grounded in a complex understanding of the nature of the phenomenon of racial discrimination and in a thorough understanding of some of the foundational ideas behind establishing such specialized bodies in relation to the phenomenon of discrimination.

The specific need for specialized bodies to combat discrimination[15] was first raised in 1997 at the European level by the European Commission against Racism and Intolerance (ECRI) of the Council of Europe. The ECRI spoke about the need to establish specialized bodies to combat racism, xenophobia, antisemitism and intolerance at a national level. ECRI's General Policy Recommendation No. 2 on the necessity of establishing such specialized bodies,[16] directed at member states of the Council of Europe, states that these institutions may take the form of, among others, national commissions for racial equality, ombudsmen against ethnic discrimination, Centres/Offices for combating racism and promoting equal opportunities or even bodies with the wider objective to promote and enforce human rights in general. The minority ombudsman or the ombudsman against ethnic discrimination is one form that fits the ECRI Recommendation, a form chosen by Sweden, Hungary and Finland.

15 The Paris Principles in 1991 set out the principles for national institutions for the promotion and protection of human rights in general.

16 ECRI General Policy Recommendation No. 2 of 1997 on specialised bodies to combat racism, xenophobia, antisemitism and intolerance at national level, Council of Europe, CRI (97)36.

What are the crucial common features of these institutions, how do they relate to the ombudsman model and how do they serve the purposes of combating discrimination?

A. The Aim of the Institution

The objective of the specialized ombudsman institution is generally to work towards the promotion of ethnic justice and equality, a formula used by the Swedish Ombudsman against Ethnic Discrimination.[17] Meanwhile, the ECRI Recommendation states that specialized bodies should have the responsibility to "work towards the elimination of the various forms of discrimination" and "to promote equality of opportunity and good relations between persons belonging to all different groups in society".[18] MacEwen argues that since racism and discrimination are pervasive in society and "include the way we look, behave, talk, react, socialize and mediate, conciliate and even judge",[19] enforcement agencies need to be established by the state. Through these agencies the state goes above the formal structures to dismantle not only social processes and personal mind-sets sustaining discrimination, but also to address the disadvantage (both economic and cultural) of a racially determined social underclass,[20] that is to perceive and deal with racial discrimination within the framework of an anti-discrimination project[21] not just an anti-discrimination law. Thus, the aim of specialized enforcement agencies is to promote substantive equality of opportunity instead of just formal equal treatment.

The creation of an ombudsman combating discrimination has an even more important symbolic meaning than the existence of a general ombudsman. Having a specialized ombudsman for this field denotes the recognition by the state of its obligations towards a disadvantaged part of its population, namely citizens belonging to national, ethnic or racial minorities. It indicates, as in the case of the general ombudsman, that rulers "recognize obligations and duties to the ruled [meaning here those belonging to minorities]",[22] but it also indicates that this group of citizens has to be treated with special concern – their just and equitable treatment deserving special consideration. This consideration is especially justifiable since members of national, ethnic or racial minorities are generally more

17 Peter Nobel, "Experience and Practice of the Ombudsman", Proceedings of the 2nd Round Table of European Ombudsman, 27-28 June 1988, Strasbourg, at <http://www.coe.int/T/E/Human_rights/cddh/4._Other_activities/O5._Round_Tables/Proceedings%202nd%20Round%20table%20E.asp#P2347 _229705>.

18 ECRI General Policy Recommendation No. 2 of 1997. Principle 3(a).

19 Martin MacEwen (ed.), *Anti-Discrimination Law Enforcement: A Comparative Perspective* (Ashgate, Aldershot, 1997), 2.

20 *Ibid.*

21 Andrew Koppelman, *Antidiscrimination Law and Social Equality* (Yale University Press, New Haven, London, 1996).

22 Caiden, MacDermot and Sandler, "The Institution of Ombudsman ...", 4.

vulnerable to the abuse, unreasonable or irrational behaviour of rulers; their difference makes them more vulnerable to violations of their human dignity. Their relationship with the 'rulers' is in most cases even more unequal than in the case of the other categories of the 'ruled'. In most cases, members of minorities are more dependent on the state than majority members: the state in their case will not only have to provide its regular service, but will also have to provide for the protection of the minority from the eventual abuses of the majority. As the Hungarian Minority Parliamentary Commissioner formulated,[23] the minority ombudsman will not only be a mediator in the conflict between 'rulers' and this special category of 'ruled', but will also mediate between the two groups of 'ruled': the majority and the minority. The importance of the specialized ombudsman institution has to be regarded within this symbolic context.

B. Independence

As noted above, the specialized ombudsman may be either a parliamentary or governmental (executive) ombudsman. The Swedish Ombudsman against Ethnic Discrimination is a body dependent on the executive just as the CRE is. The justification for this lies with the importance of their strategic enforcement powers, the regulatory and policy-shaping functions they play, and their promotional powers on the particular field of rights. Obviously, the specialized ombudsman stands as closely to the general ombudsman model as it stands to what MacEwen calls specialized enforcement agencies.[24]

It is an ombudsman in all its powers, means and instruments, and it is a specialized enforcement agency in not being restricted only to the review of state actors and public administration, and in having jurisdiction only over issues connected to one special field of rights. In the case of the executive model of the ombudsman, the relevant state department recognizes the role this institution can play, not only in handling individual complaints, but also in summarizing issues coming up in complaints or in investigations undertaken on its own initiative, in making recommendations concerning development of policies and legislation in the field, and also in the promotional work needed for efficient enforcement of the respective category of rights. The advantage of the executive ombudsman is being within the executive and thus having the necessary leverage, yet being outside it as well and, as such, dealing with the rights issues in a technocratic, expert way, thus separating them from the political realm. The independence of the institution still remains a crucial feature of these specialized ombudsman institutions, as well as of specialized bodies combating discrimination. However, this independence is operationalized through other means, not through the checks and balances between the legislative and the executive powers, as used by parliamentary ombudsman institutions.

23 Interview conducted with Jeno Kaltenbach in April 1999.

24 According to MacEwen, specialized enforcement agencies belong to the larger category of nondepartmental public bodies. MacEwen, *Anti-Discrimination Law ...*, 5.

In the case of the parliamentary model of ombudsman, as used in Hungary or Finland, the emphasis is put on independence from the executive. In these cases too, being completely independent from the administration will not prevent the executive from consulting the ombudsman in important questions pertaining to policies concerning minority issues, yet, if dissatisfied with the work of the ombudsman (e.g. too severe criticism of administration), the executive will have no power to influence or eventually dismiss the ombudsman.

Independence is an important component of the ECRI Recommendation. The document shows how independence can be secured differently than through the classical ombudsman solution. The Recommendation conceptualizes independence through three elements. The first element concerns funding: the specialized bodies "should be provided with sufficient funds to carry out their functions and responsibilities effectively, and the funding should be subject annually to approval by the parliament". The second element that is considered to be important from the point of view of independence is the ability to function without interference from the state and the guarantees necessary for independence in appointing staff, managing resources and expressing views publicly. The third element concerns the appointment and dismissal of members or incumbents: guarantees shall be provided for preventing arbitrary dismissal, non-renewal and appropriate guarantees for fair appointment. However, independence, as perceived along these three terms, can be realized with carefully designed legislation by executive ombudsmen or, eventually, by enforcement agencies just as well as it can be by the classical model of independent parliamentary ombudsmen.[25] MacEwen argues that, even if enforcement agencies are acting on behalf of the central government, they are not part of the central government. Incumbents are most probably selected on the basis of their specialized expertise in the field, experience and skills shown in their previous work, and this tends to decrease problems with both accountability and with political bias.

No matter how it is conceptualized in the individual cases, the independence criterion is one of the foundational criteria for specialized bodies just as it is for ombudsman institutions. The ombudsman institution proved flexible enough to accommodate new forms of independence even in its country of origin.[26] The focus seems to have shifted away from accountability to the parliament to the requirement of firm legal basis, clear mandate, budgetary guarantees and guarantees to prevent unfair dismissal. The importance of the criteria remain, however, unquestionable: in a Europe where the state is the largest employer and service provider and, therefore, most probably also the largest discriminator, independence from state intervention is a must for a body combating discrimination

25 ECRI General Policy Recommendations No. 2 of 1997. Principle 5, Sections 1-4.

26 The parliamentary vs. executive ombudsman debate was resolved in Sweden by focusing rather on a firm legal basis for the institution and a legally defined mandate. See European Commission, Promoting Diversity: 21 *Bodies* ..., 3.

C. Scope of Action

Despite the restrictive scope of action of the classical ombudsman model, consistent action to combat discrimination seems to require that the scope of action of the specialized ombudsman institution extends beyond public administration to public life in general; that is, to include private employers and private service providers as well. This can be justified by the aim of fighting discrimination and the special vulnerability of members of minorities; recognizing the fact that they will face very similar problems and types of discrimination coming from privately owned actors in public life. Even though the state is in most cases the largest employer and the largest service provider and covering the arbitrary and unjust activity of public administration will mean covering a large proportion of the violations of rights of minorities members, it will still exclude a large number of very similar violations committed by non-state actors. Once the aim of the ombudsman is the advancement of racial equality, or the fight against racial discrimination, it is very difficult to justify why this implies only investigation of abuses committed by state actors. The Hungarian Minority Ombudsman's activity illustrates this case well. The Ombudsman, who has a mandate restricted to the public sector, has repeatedly tried to extend his actions indirectly to private employers and private service providers, in order to overcome the inconsistencies deriving from his limited mandate.[27] There is also an efficiency argument in favour of extending the scope of action for minority ombudsmen to private actors. Investigation, proof of and evidence for discrimination cases requires special skills and know-how.[28] However, this know-how is similar for all cases of discrimination, regardless of whether it has been committed by a local government as employer or a privately-owned company as employer. Centralizing this expertise in dealing at a non-judicial level with racial discrimination cases will further the efficient handling of these problems. The minority ombudsman seems to be one type of ombudsman institution for which the extension of the scope of action beyond public administration is justified by the nature of the specialization: combating discrimination on the grounds of race and ethnicity.

D. Functions of the Institution

The sets of functions that are attributed to specialized ombudsmen combating discrimination are truly specific. Functions attributed to other specialized bodies working in this field are also consistent with these. The Swedish Ombudsman against Ethnic Discrimination has three sets of duties: to strive to ensure that ethnic discrimination does not occur in working life or other areas of society; to

27 Andrea Krizsán, "The Hungarian Minority Parliamentary Commissioner and the Anti-discrimination Principle", PhD thesis, Department of Political Science, Central European University, Budapest (2001), 290-291.

28 Commission for Racial Equality, *Second Review of the Race Relations Act 1976* (CRE, London, 1992), 48-49.

assist anyone subjected to ethnic discrimination and safeguard their rights; and to initiate measures against ethnic discrimination and to promote good relationships between different ethnic groups.[29] The Finnish Minority Ombudsman makes policy proposals and provides legal advice and juridical assistance to victims.[30] The Hungarian Minority Ombudsman investigates individual complaints and initiates ex officio investigation of discrimination cases, reviews relevant legislation and policy, and comments on legislation and policy with relevance to the field that is in preparation, and raises awareness of issues related to minorities.[31]Similarly, the CRE has three sets of functions defining its work: to work towards the elimination of discrimination; to promote equality of opportunity and good relations between persons of different racial groups; and, finally, to keep under review the Race Relations Act and to recommend amendments when necessary.[32]

As mentioned at the very beginning of the paper, the EU Race Directive also projects three main sets of tasks for bodies combating discrimination: assisting victims; conducting independent surveys on discrimination; and publishing reports and making recommendations on issues relating to discrimination. Similarly, the functions and responsibilities enumerated in the ECRI Recommendation[33] can be grouped in three major clusters: policy-making and legislative functions; enforcement functions; and, finally, promotional and educational functions. The first group, the policy-making and legislative functions, include tasks such as the monitoring of the content and efficiency of the relevant existing legislation and governmental policies and making recommendations concerning their amendment or modification, as well as counselling the legislative and executive branches of government concerning improvement of legislation and policies in the field or concerning the making of new laws and policies. The second group of functions, enforcement functions, is aimed at the enforcement of the rights of individual victims and at the strategic enforcement of the rights of relevant minority groups. The Recommendation includes here functions such as providing assistance and legal aid to victims, if provided for by the national legislation, support for or eventually bringing cases before the judiciary, hearing cases and seeking extra judicial settlements through conciliation, all of these supported by the powers to obtain evidence and all relevant information and documents from the concerned parties. Finally, promotional powers are understood by the ECRI document to include providing information and advice to relevant bodies and institutions, counselling

29 Act Against Ethnic Discrimination 1994, Sections 2-4. The new Act on the Ombudsman against Ethnic Discrimination 1999 adds to the above the task of preventing discrimination and supervising the workings of the Act on Measures against Discrimination on the Labour Market 1999.

30 European Commission, *Promoting Diversity: 21 Bodies* ..., 22.

31 Krizsán, "Ombudsman and Similar Institutions ...".

32 Race Relations Act 1976, Section 43(1).

33 There are 13 functions mentioned altogether. ECRI General Policy Recommendation No. 2 of 1997, Chapter C: Functions and responsibilities of specialised bodies, Principle 3.

actors in specific relevant areas on standards of anti-discriminatory practice, promoting and participating in the training of different key groups within society in tolerance, anti-racism and anti-discriminatory practices, promoting awareness of discrimination issues in society, including preparation and distribution of information and other materials and, finally, supporting and cooperating with organizations that have objectives similar to that of the specialized body.

MacEwen, based on his examination of eight different anti-discrimination law enforcement agencies, identifies four groups of functions such agencies have to undertake. The first set consists of promotional functions, including issuance of guidance and codes of practice, education and training, networking, and research in the area. The second and the third set are enforcement powers, which he divides into two groups: investigation of individual complaints; and strategic investigations, pattern and practice cases and formal or ex officio investigations. The fourth group of functions he writes about include advising the government on law and practice, assessing the efficiency of existing law and policies, as well as previewing legislation and policies in the field and commentary connected to them.[34]

It is obvious from the clusters of functions attributed to minority ombudsman institutions that the aim of these institutions extends beyond simple individual enforcement of the right not to be discriminated against to a very wide understanding of enforcement, an understanding according to which in order to have a relatively full enforcement of this right more is needed than enforcement in individual cases of violation. The functions suggest that promotion of awareness within society concerning the problem of racism and its moral unacceptability, and of recognition and tolerance towards national, ethnic or racial differences, is part of the enforcement process and, moreover, that re-educating the public and changing prejudices and prejudiced mind-sets is also part of it. They also suggest that often discrimination penetrates the structures of society and its systemic form cannot be addressed by enforcement only on the individual level, but only through careful assessment, with the help of system-wide remedies. Finally, the function to assess and evaluate relevant legislation and policy, to suggest amendments and new policy and legislation, shows that it is not enough to address the issue of racial discrimination in the different fields where it may occur, but that permanent coordination and supervision and evaluation of the efficiency of the overall anti-discrimination policy is needed, and that the special focus and expertise of the specialized ombudsman institution allows for doing this appropriately.

E. Specialized Ombudsman Institutions for Combating Discrimination

Having seen some of the cornerstone ideas defining the specialized ombudsman institution combating discrimination, the question is: how can these features be used for the special needs of combating discrimination on grounds of race or ethnicity?

34 MacEwen, *Anti-Discrimination Law* ..., 19.

In the field of assisting individual complainants, the institution first of all has procedural advantages. The means available to the minority ombudsman institution, the ability to make complaints free of charge, the absence of formal requirements in pursuing a complaint, the fact that the ombudsman will assist the complainant in formulating the complaint if necessary and, finally, the fast and non-adversarial procedure, are all advantageous for victims of discrimination. These procedures will be advantageous for those who have a lower level of education and perhaps cannot formulate their complaint, who cannot afford to pay the costs of a judicial procedure or who lack the self-confidence to raise their voice.[35] All of these factors – poverty, lower level of education, lower self-confidence – fall in most cases with a disproportionate impact on members of ethnic minorities. Thus, the access of groups such as the Roma in Hungary to the ombudsman will allow them to make complaints with respect to discrimination with far greater ease.

The methods of investigation used by the specialized ombudsman – the specific methods of solving cases – such as persuasion, conciliation and the threat of publicity can, in many cases, provide an alternative to the protracted and costly adversarial procedures and to the mostly individualized remedies provided by the court procedure.

Violations in this field are often committed out of ignorance; many times racism plays a role only unconsciously. Not many institutions, organizations or bodies want to see themselves being described as racist in the media. This is again a reason why the proceedings of minority – ombudsman – type institutions present a real alternative to the sanction-oriented judicial procedure. Persuasion will also further the education of 'respondents', convincing them of the abusive character of their procedure and sometimes showing them possible alternative good practices. Indeed, it has been shown in connection to the work of the CRE that institutions and employers are more willing "to accept advice and introduce widespread change when confronted privately with evidence of inequality, than they were after a more public and accusatory investigation".[36] Conciliation can often bring an easy remedy to the violation of the human dignity of the victims. Sometimes apologies and recognition of fault is what victims are looking for and the ombudsman is able to persuade the 'respondent' to provide it. The emphasis of the ombudsman's procedure is more on compensating the victim, defining the problem and preventing its future occurrence than on blaming the wrongdoer.

This is not to say, of course, that the ombudsman proceedings shall replace court procedures. Complainants may be motivated by different goals when they pursue their complaints: some of them see their cases as part of a political struggle, others want public acknowledgment of their ill treatment and others want their

35 Laurence Lustgarten, *Legal Control of Racial Discrimination* (Macmillan Press, London, 1980), 191.

36 Mary Coussey, "The Effectiveness of Strategic Enforcement of the Race Relations Act 1976", in Bob Hepple and Erika Sczyczak, *Discrimination and the Limits of the Law* (Mansell Publishing Limited, London, 1992), 44.

financial loss to be compensated.[37] The specialized ombudsman cannot be an adequate instrument for all cases. Especially in cases of intentional direct discrimination (where a person intentionally treats another less favourably on racial grounds), the importance of "the threat of sanction, the deterrent effect that shapes behavior by making compliance more attractive than the financial costs or physical and psychological punishment that follows upon non-compliance"[38] as used by courts and tribunals cannot be disregarded. However, the elimination of racial discrimination and achievement of equal opportunities regardless of race or ethnicity is what Lustgarten calls a more programmatic end, which requires changes in the actions of people in a systematic way, requires changing the mentality of people. As Koppelman wrote, it necessitates an anti-discrimination project, a project of social reconstruction.[39] The anti-discrimination project has to proceed on three levels. The first is the level of racial meanings: that is, of racially biased beliefs and values shared by the members of society. The second level is the level of racially significant practices, meaning the discriminatory practices that are constructed by the beliefs and values attacked on the first level. The third level is called, by Koppelman "racially tainted distribution": that is, the distribution of wealth and power that emerges from racially significant practices, which are addressed under the second level. Thus, the issue to be addressed becomes much wider than a procedural approach would suggest. The antidiscrimination project implies judicial work with adequate negative sanctions having a preventive effect, but it also implies shaping action in a specific direction, i.e. among others using directive remedies. In most cases, courts cannot provide such remedies.[40] The ombudsman institution is allowed to provide such remedies either directly, in individual cases, or indirectly through its strategic powers. The direct remedies provided by the ombudsman may not be enforceable[41] and are certainly disregarded in some cases but, in other cases where there is good intention, the expertise of the ombudsman is indeed appreciated and regarded as a help. The minority ombudsman may address the anti-discrimination project on all of its three levels: its powers of promotion, awareness raising and education of the public will attack the problem of racial discrimination on the level of racial meanings, of beliefs and values shared

37 Lustgarten, *Legal Control* ..., 201.

38 Lustgarten, *Legal Control* ..., 224.

39 Koppelman, *Antidiscrimination Law* ..., 92-99.

40 A successful exception is found in US jurisprudence and especially in the activity of the US Supreme Court. Despite its common law system, this was never adopted by British courts. Lustgarten argues that the CRE can make up for the failure of courts in providing directive remedies. Lustgarten, *Legal Control* ..., 236.

41 This is one of the major differences between specialized ombudsman institutions and some other specialized bodies combating discrimination. For example, two such specialized bodies even have the power to act as quasi-judicial bodies, which can issue formal rulings in cases of discrimination: the Dutch Equal Treatment Commission and the Office of the Director of Equality Investigations (ODEI) in Ireland. See European Commission, *Promoting Diversity: 21 Bodies* ..., 12.

by the members of the society. Its enforcement powers and its powers to review policy and legislation and to recommend policies and legislation will act on the other two levels. The second level, that of racially significant practices, will especially be addressed by the wide enforcement powers the institution has, partly by its enforcement powers relating to individual complaints and partly by its strategic powers. The third level, that of racially tainted distribution, will mostly be addressed by the powers of the institution to issue guidance for good practices, codes of good practice, to recommend policies both for actors in society such as employers, local authorities, healthcare institutions, insurance companies and for the state. The ombudsman may be the most appropriate institution to work out guidelines for different forms of affirmative action programmes or other programmes for improving substantive equality of opportunity.

Direct intentional discrimination cases are the least interesting ones for minority ombudsman institutions. Once proof of intent is available, or intent can be inferred, liability should be established and remedies made available for the victim. Direct discrimination cases, if brought, should always go before courts, which have the appropriate enforcement powers to handle them. The strategic powers and soft enforcement powers available to minority ombudsman institutions are mostly inappropriate and unnecessary for handling such cases. However, the support of the institution could eventually be useful in providing specialized help in gathering circumstantial evidence.

The role of minority ombudsmen in dealing with indirect discrimination cases is much more extensive than is the case with direct discrimination. Even though the institution's powers are not appropriate to compensate individual victims, its soft powers will certainly be very much appropriate for bringing about changes in systemically discriminatory practices. Also, the concentration of expertise in a specialized body like the minority ombudsman will be necessary to apply the sophisticated methods of proof, especially statistical evidence, required for showing discriminatory patterns and practices.

Indirect discrimination cases are a field that exemplifies well how the special prerogatives of the institution can be used to combat discrimination. As the EU Race Directive defines it, indirect discrimination shall be taken to occur where an apparently neutral provision, criterion or practice would put persons of a racial or ethnic origin at a particular disadvantage compared with other persons, unless that provision, criterion or practice is objectively justified by a legitimate aim and the means of achieving that aim are appropriate and necessary.[42] Analysis on the work of the CRE, a forerunner in Europe in the implementation of the concept of indirect discrimination, proves useful in understanding some of the advantages of the specialized ombudsman institution. Cases of indirect discrimination may occur without the intent to discriminate or to cause disadvantage to the members of a minority group and, as such, liability is problematic in such cases. In the absence of liability, judicial remedies can at best provide an injunction to cease the operation of the indirectly discriminatory practice or requirement: it is difficult,

42 EU Race Directive, Article 2(2)(b).

if not impossible, to argue for damages for the victims.[43] Given the difficulties one faces when trying to prove indirect discrimination,[44] and the lack of incentive for victims to bring the case (absence of damages), few indirect discrimination cases can be brought before courts and even fewer can be successful. However, the specialized ombudsman institution does "not require adherence to formal rules of evidence and procedure. [It] may form an opinion favourable to the complainant on the basis of less weighty evidence than would be needed to establish a prima facie case in legal proceedings".[45] Investigation of indirect discrimination rather falls within the strategic powers of the specialized ombudsman institution. It can be achieved by using the ombudsman's own data bank for proof, or collecting proof in its investigations or sometimes commissioning research from experts or research institutes working in the field. The specialized ombudsman institution's support and involvement seems indispensable in addressing cases of indirect discrimination, at least at the moment when courts in most European countries are rather inexperienced and sometimes too conservative to deal with the phenomenon.

There is a considerable variation between different specialized bodies, including specialized ombudsman, concerning their prerogatives with respect to individual complaints and with respect to their interference with judicial procedures. Some specialized bodies remain closer to the classical ombudsman model in that they do not have more power than to make recommendations and their recommendations have no binding force. At this end of the spectrum, the specialized institutions remain completely independent of the courts, they provide an alternative legal remedy – a soft one – besides the remedies provided by courts.[46] Another possibility is that when specialized bodies have the mandate to bring cases before the courts, or at least participate in preparing important discrimination cases for court proceedings, i.e. by providing legal aid for bringing cases, providing expert opinions for the procedures, or writing amicus curiae on the cases.[47] A mandate to bring cases before courts does not mean, however, that the specialized bodies will bring all their cases before the courts. Usually, the only cases considered for support and legal aid in court procedures are those that bring up some matter of principle, i.e. their appropriate presentation and success will result in the development of the legal approach towards racial discrimination. The other extreme of the spectrum is the already mentioned case when specialized bodies have quasi-

43 Lustgarten, *Legal Control* ..., 233.

44 Lustgarten, *Legal Control* ..., 211-213. See also Geoffrey Bindman, "Proof and Evidence of Discrimination", in Hepple and Sczyczak (eds.), *Discrimination and the Limits* ..., 50-66.

45 UK Home Office, "Racial Discrimination ...", Cmnd. 6234, White Paper presented to Parliament in September 1975 (HMSO, London, 1976), 9-10.

46 The Hungarian Minority Ombudsman falls into this category.

47 Most specialized bodies fall under this category (e.g. the Swedish Ombudsman against Ethnic Discrimination, UK Commission for Racial Equality).

judicial powers.[48] Choosing one model or the other depends on the institutional culture and the political sensitivities of the given country. What follows necessarily from the objectives and advantages of this type of institution, however, is its capacity to provide expertise not only in offering alternative, extrajudicial solutions for cases of racial discrimination but also in preparing and bringing discrimination cases successfully before courts. This is important, not only from the point of view of the particular discrimination cases at issue, but also from the point of view of the development of judicial practice and the education and increased sensitivity of the judiciary regarding these matters. The expert knowledge input of specialized ombudsman and specialized bodies in judicial procedures dealing with discrimination is one of the most important profits flowing from the establishment of such institutions for handling individual cases of discrimination, and more widely for the process of combating discrimination.

F. Strategic Powers

However, beyond the advantages such institutions offer in addressing individual complaints of discrimination, the role they play in combating racial discrimination by means of their strategic powers is even more important. As Lustgarten rightly shows, the strategic powers of "a public body with unusual powers" are justified by the weakness of individual remedies as far as racial discrimination is concerned. He argues, with reference to employment discrimination, that "individual enforcement can at best produce an erratic series of changes in the behavior of individual employers".[49] On the other hand, "complaints are random in their incidence and significance. Most victims do not complain. Many do not know that they have suffered discrimination. Others are reluctant to complain because they do not want to relive the humiliation, which they have suffered, or because they have no confidence in the effectiveness of the complaint procedure and the redress, which it is likely to provide for them. Some complaints are trivial, others misconceived. Although it is necessary for the law to provide effective remedies for the individual victims, it is also essential that the application of the law should not depend upon the making of individual complaint".[50] Besides the questionable efficiency of approaching racial discrimination through individual remedies and the questionable significance and number of complaints, there is also the difficulty of proving discrimination, the necessity in many cases to use statistical data, which is usually only available (if at all) to the discriminator. These three factors make the strategic powers of the specialized ombudsman crucial for an effective fight against discrimination.

48 For example, the Dutch Equal Treatment Commission and the ODEI of Ireland.

49 Lustgarten, *Legal Control ...*, 241.

50 See UK Home Office, "Racial Discrimination ...", 9, for an argument on the necessity of creating the Commission for Racial Equality in the UK. See also Hepple and Szyszczak (eds.), *Discrimination and the Limit ...*.

The strategic powers of the ombudsman allow the institution to intervene when and where it deems necessary in the public interest. The ombudsman has the power to initiate formal investigations into specific institutions, bodies or into some general aspect of public life (e.g. minority education, discriminatory practices used by employment agencies). His targets can be chosen, based on the expertise of his staff and eventually on the signals coming from individual complaints, so that they can have long-term importance, so that "they make [a greater] general impact on the incidence of discrimination than even a substantial number of successful individual complaints will make".[51] Applebey and Ellis argue that formal investigations are especially important in the following four situations:

(1) in cases of "victimless discrimination" – situations in which there has traditionally been discrimination and in which members of the victim groups do not even file complaints any more;
(2) cases when too many people are affected by the discrimination and, in the absence of class action, it would be very resource and time consuming to have all victims start procedures individually;
(3) "where practices are very complicated and require the ascertainment of facts which are beyond the capacity and resources of an individual";
(4) "where the individual who has been discriminated is in fact a member of a clearly defined group and the Commission [CRE] feels it essential to investigate further in the interests of the remaining members of the group".[52]

The ombudsman institution also takes part in policy shaping through its strategic powers. The reports of its formal investigations, as well as annual reports, are presented before parliament or the government department appointing the ombudsman with relevant recommendations and suggestions concerning laws and policies in the field of anti-discrimination policy.

The specialized ombudsman can also function as a kind of data bank concerning court and tribunal cases of discrimination, successful methods of proof, available data for evidence (for example, relevant statistical and demographic data), data concerning public interest law firms dealing with such cases and information concerning legal aid available for those who choose or have to choose litigation. The minority ombudsman will thus act as a mediator in many individual cases, will provide necessary information for going to court and eventually will transfer the complaint to the relevant body. It will also function as a centre for expertise in addressing complaints by members of minorities concerning the violation of their rights on grounds of race, national or ethnic origin.

51 Lustgarten, *Legal Control ...*, 242.

52 George Applebey and Evelyn Ellis, "Formal Investigations: the Commission for Racial Equality, and the Equal Opportunities Commission as Law Enforcement Agencies", 236 *Public Law* (1984), 273-275.

The minority ombudsman also conducts research into issues of racial discrimination or orders relevant policy-oriented research from specialized research institutes, researchers or experts working in the field. The institution and its experienced staff will probably have a quite good perspective in determining what kind of research is needed for the advancement of anti-discrimination policy and what research might further best the enforcement of the right not to be discriminated against.

The strategic powers of the ombudsman institution will also have a role in defining and coordinating the anti-discrimination policy of a particular country and in finding an appropriate solution to address the issue as widely and as comprehensively as possible. By summarizing the issues brought up by individual complaints and looking at the general trends as shown by individual complaints and general investigations undertaken on its own initiative, the ombudsman will have the most refined image of the workings of the existing anti-discrimination policy of the country. Given the relatively recent developments of the right not to be discriminated against and the ambiguities about it even at the international level, the ombudsman will play an active part in finding an adequate solution for the implementation of this right at the national level. The power the institution has, to refer beyond national law to international documents, will give the specialized ombudsman an even better understanding of the potential for improvements in protection against racial discrimination at the national level. Channeling this expert information back into the policy-making process has great potential for continuously improving the policy-making process and policies in the field.

G. Promotional Powers

Underlying the entire idea of the ombudsman institution in general and the ombudsman institution that specializes in combating discrimination, in particular, is the task of educating the public. This task informs the way the ombudsman will try to solve individual complaints, but is also part of the strategic powers of the institution. The specialized ombudsman also has a role to play in initiating public debates concerning recognition of minorities and tolerance, can initiate campaigns to teach the public about the rights of minorities, but also educates by making public the results of its investigations, by eventually publicizing good practice and by criticizing abuse. Regular media appearances either connected to investigated cases or connected to relevant issues on the public agenda are used by both the Swedish Ombudsman against Ethnic Discrimination and the Hungarian Minority Ombudsman.

Codes of practice showing good practice in important fields where discrimination can occur may be provided by the ombudsman to the relevant actors in the field. Good practice codes will, on the one hand, help actors to avoid racial discrimination and, on the other hand, may also provide guidance on how to improve equality of opportunity for the members of a disadvantaged minority, how to design appropriate and acceptable affirmative action programmes, and how to monitor policies.

H. Balancing between the Different Functions of the Institution

The specialized ombudsman institution, as presented here, is a rather pro-activist institution. It seems to be a hybrid between the general ombudsman institution, as it originated in Sweden, and a specialized regulatory agency. The argument is that an institution having the flexibility, powers and independence characteristic of the ombudsman institution and the expertise and specialization of specialized enforcement agencies plays a pivotal role in combating discrimination. A valid concern that comes up upon analyzing the extensive list of tasks such specialized agencies might have is that the extensive strategic powers and promotional powers as described here will conflict with the individual complaint-solving task of the institution and none of them will in fact be efficient enough. This strategically important point remains to be addressed by each institution. If all individual complaints are considered and dealt with in detail, much less capacity will remain for the use of strategic and promotional powers. The ombudsman must therefore strike a balance between the three groups of functions in a way in which the legislative intent standing behind the institution will best be reflected. The case of the CRE provides one solution: the equilibrium is reached by not considering all individual complaints but only those which raise a question ofprinciple, those of a complexity that it is unreasonable to expect the complainant to deal with unaided or other cases chosen for any other special consideration.[53] This shows that in the case of the CRE, at least partly, individual complaints are also perceived as aiding the strategic powers. However, in order to choose this strategy there has to be available alternative remedy: courts and tribunals have to be accessible to the refused individual victims; they also have to be willing to adequately consider such cases and there must exist an adequate law regulating race relations with adequate sanctions, procedures of proof and evidence on the basis of which courts can make their decisions. In the absence of these conditions, the ombudsman will have to work as a proxy for the courts, meaning that the institution will have an immense individual caseload, leaving much less free capacity for exercising strategic and promotional powers. The Hungarian Minority Ombudsman institution's work, for example, throughout its first eight years of activity served as a proxy for judicial work on discrimination cases in the absence of an appropriate legal framework regulating discrimination. In these circumstances, the Ombudsman has chosen to concentrate most of its capacities on addressing individual complaints and working towards the improvement of the legal and policy context, and consequently has allocated far fewer resources to promotional functions.[54]

53 Lustgarten, *Legal Control* ..., 191.

54 Krizsán, "Ombudsman and Similar Institutions ...", 302-303.

IV. Why Do We Need Specialized Institutions for Combating Discrimination?

A very important challenge that has to be addressed if writing about specialized bodies combating discrimination casts doubts on the grounding premises of the institution. This argument is: in a well-functioning constitutional democratic legal system, regular courts and tribunals and general administrative remedies will be sufficient to cope with the problem of racial discrimination; there is no need for a soft institution such as the specialized ombudsman, because it cannot add anything to the way the judiciary and the executive are addressing the problem.[55]

The question is: why should a state establish specialized ombudsman institutions or other specialized bodies in order to efficiently and comprehensively combat discrimination on grounds of ethnicity or race? Why not just leave it to the already existing and functioning institutions of the state? One short and pragmatic answer to this question is that all states with comprehensive progressive anti-discrimination legislation and policy use the specialized agency model.[56] It seems that there are currently no viable alternatives to this model. Even in the legal context provided by countries such as the US, the UK, Sweden or the Netherlands, a specialized body for dealing with the enforcement of anti-discrimination law and policy is deemed necessary. Moreover, the Race Directive, along with the Council of Europe's ECRI Recommendation, provides for it.

There is a substantive answer to this question as well. As argued in the previous chapter, racial discrimination means more than the sum of individual discriminatory acts, it is a structural phenomenon that has its roots and effects in the personal mind-sets of people, in racially determined acts and decisions and in the racially tainted distribution of resources within society. If racial discrimination is perceived as such, the random decisions of courts and tribunals only address a few superficial manifestations of what racial discrimination is, leaving aside most of the structural, of the systemic problem. As MacEwen formulates: anti-discrimination law in itself has only a marginally ameliorative impact given the persistent and pervasive nature of racial discrimination; this is why anti-discrimination law has to be accompanied by other policies and strategies that have a more holistic approach to discrimination.[57] Specialized bodies combating discrimination, among them ombudsmen, are part of such a holistic approach. The specialized ombudsman, due to its extensive powers, will promote a structural approach to the issue of racial discrimination and will address the problem at all three levels

55 This argument has been formulated by some of the experts working in the office of the Hungarian Minority Commissioner, among others. Behind the argument stood the presumption that the Hungarian legal system is not a mature one yet. Thus, the minority ombudsman institution temporarily has a role to play, but as soon as the deficiencies of the legal system are solved (a matter of years) the institution will basically cease to be functional.

56 MacEwen, *Anti-Discrimination Law* ..., 234.

57 *Ibid.*, 10.

where it occurs. Class action is considered to be a legal instrument that makes up for some of these problems because it makes court procedures cheaper, it provides moral support for the complainant through creating a class and it sheds light on the size and importance of the racial discrimination issues. However, the introduction of class action seems to require major changes in European legal systems and, given its repercussions for other fields of litigation and the several procedural difficulties that go with it, its introduction has been treated very cautiously.[58] Meanwhile, the specialized ombudsman institution, especially if provided with the tools to give legal support or assistance in court cases or to eventually bring cases before court, takes on some of the major advantages of class action: it makes up for the financial difficulties some litigants may have in suing, provides supportive solidarity and encourages complainants to come forward, and remedies to some extent the inequality of bargaining power between the complainant and the respondent. Through its investigations of systemic discrimination, the specialized ombudsman also points to the extent and importance of the problem of racial discrimination. Pannick argues, referring to specialized bodies combating discrimination in the UK, that "legal actions by the CRE or the EOC could achieve much of what the class action is designed to achieve, particularly if the CRE and the EOC were empowered to commence litigation without receiving a complaint from a victim and if the court were to be empowered to grant damages to a defined class of victims in addition to declaratory and injunctive relief".[59]

It is also important to mention that, unlike courts, on the one side, or government departments, on the other side, specialized agencies have access both to individual complaints, which often show the fallacies of laws and policies in place, as well as have the means to make recommendations regarding legislation and policy towards government departments and the legislative power. Thus, they are in an exceptional position to see the practical workings of the relevant existing laws and policies and also to intervene in the policy-making process by recommending necessary amendments, thus channelling information between the enforcement of legislation and the legislative power.

Another important advantage of the specialized ombudsman model is its specialization – the fact that it concentrates on a single issue area. Dealing permanently with the same type of problem – that of discrimination – will result, on the one hand, in specialized knowledge of the area and, on the other hand, in special sensibility towards a very complex problem. Neither of these is available to courts or other bodies providing administrative remedies because they only meet discrimination cases once in a while and thus do not have the opportunity to develop special sensitivity or know-how towards any particular issue, as it is only one of several others to be dealt with in everyday cases. This specialization is also economic from the point of view of efficient adjudication: it is more economic to develop specialization in one agency that will help in preparing cases or

58 For advantages and disadvantages of class action see David Pannick, "Class action and discrimination law", 10(1) *New Community* (1982), 16-26.

59 *Ibid.*, 24.

(if allowed under national legislation) eventually bring them before courts than to have a person who specializes in such issues at every body adjudicating such cases. Specialized bodies are cheap, informal, accessible and provide specialized expertise. This makes them suitable for participating in one way or another in the adjudication of discrimination cases.

Another important advantage of these institutions is that they try to solve cases not by the adversarial approach of courts or tribunals but in a more conciliatory manner, aiming for the persuasion of the parties concerning the wrongness of discrimination and thus the prevention of reoccurrence, rather than blaming the wrongdoer.

Finally, as mentioned in the examination of the general ombudsman model, the specialized ombudsman promotes a concept of justice and equity, which can be more extensive than the one codified in the laws. Sometimes the ombudsman might find abuse of constitutional or human rights also when the act is not prohibited as unlawful by statutory law. The specialized ombudsman thus has the opportunity to give a relatively wide interpretation to rights, sometimes using relevant international standards or good practices from other countries as reference points.

Thus, to summarize, the ombudsman institutions that specialize in combating racial or ethnic discrimination complement the activity of courts and other bodies providing legal remedy first with their unique strategic enforcement powers, second by providing alternative methods for solving individual complaints and third by promoting a wider understanding of constitutional rights than is provided for by statutory law. These reasons together justify the establishment of such institutions for the better enforcement of the right not to be discriminated against on grounds of ethnicity or race.

The new specialized institutions established under the Race Directive or earlier but with the same purpose in mind have clearly learnt a lot from the ombudsman model. Their independence, their emphasis on solving complaints by extrajudicial means, their aim of compensating for the inequality of bargaining power between victims and perpetrators, their capacity to uncover abuses even if there is no complaint, their focus on educating the public or the role they play in developing and improving the understanding of concepts of rights are all derived from the centuries-old idea of the ombudsman institution. The philosophy of ombudsman institutions, even if it has relatively little to say about specialization and expert work in the field of one particular human right, still provides the rationale for how these institutions are to function.

*David Smallbone**

Ethnic Minority Entrepreneurship, Diversity and Competitiveness

I. Introduction

A. *Entrepreneurship as an Agent of Change*

It is increasingly recognized that entrepreneurship plays a central role in economic development and that entrepreneurs are key elements of change in market economies.[1] However, as well as contributing to the development of more competitive economies, fostering entrepreneurship has increasingly been seen by policy-makers as a means of combating social and economic exclusion, by encouraging enterprise in disadvantaged communities and localities. In this context, entrepreneurship appears to offer a mechanism for drawing marginalized ethnic minorities and immigrant communities into the mainstream of societies and economies, with potential benefits at both the macro and micro levels.

There is already a good deal of literature on ethnic minority entrepreneurship focusing on its contribution to social inclusion. By contrast, this particular paper examines the arguments and evidence to support the proposition that ethnic diversity, as such, is a potential source of competitiveness, through the involvement of members of ethnic minorities in entrepreneurship. The involvement of ethnic minorities in entrepreneurial activities has attracted growing interest in recent years for various reasons. One of them is that as well as contributing to reducing social exclusion and raising living standards in groups that are often among the more disadvantaged in society, it can be argued that, from an economic standpoint, the ability of European economies to be entrepreneurial depends on their ability to encourage and support entrepreneurship in all sections of society, including ethnic minorities. The argument needs to be viewed in the wider con-

* Professor of Entrepreneurship and Small Business, Small Business Research Centre, Kingston University.

1 Sander Wennekers and Roy Thurik, "Linking Entrepreneurship and Economic Growth", 13(1) *Small Business Economics* (1999), 27–55.

Minority Governance in and beyond Europe, ISBN 978-90-04-27648-2. pp. 85-104.

text of the growing evidence of the links between entrepreneurship and economic development at the national level.

In the UK, for example, the current strategic framework for government policy with respect to small businesses includes 'enterprise for all' as one of its seven priority themes, referring to "the encouragement of more enterprise in disadvantaged communities and disadvantaged groups".[2] Because of a tendency for ethnic minorities to concentrate in particular localities, the development of some local economies—and the standards of living within them—may be heavily influenced by the nature and extent of ethnic minority involvement in self-employment and business ownership. As a consequence, the UK government views the promotion of different forms of entrepreneurship as a mechanism for developing those communities and areas.

The rest of this paper is concerned with ethnic minority entrepreneurship in the UK. In the UK context, ethnic minority communities are a result of a long history of immigration, which includes migrants from former colonial territories, as well as, more recently, asylum seekers and migrants from other member states of the EU. In established ethnic minority communities, members include second- and third-generation migrants, who have been born and educated in the UK. Following a discussion of some of the distinctive characteristics of and challenges facing ethnic minority entrepreneurs and a summary of ethnic minority involvement in entrepreneurship in the UK, the proposition that ethnic diversity may be a source of potential competitive advantage will be examined. The case of London is used to illustrate the argument, partly because it represents one of the most ethnically diverse cities in Europe and partly because the research on which this paper is based was commissioned by the London Development Agency (LDA).[3] If supported, the proposition is potentially powerful in political terms, since it suggests that an ethnically diverse society is potentially stronger economically than a less diverse one, with potential welfare gains for the population as a whole. As a consequence, policies designed to encourage and support ethnic minority business development may be justified by the potential economic benefits for the society, as well as promoting greater social inclusion for ethnic minorities.

B. *Challenges Facing Ethnic Minority Entrepreneurs*

Since most ethnic minority-owned businesses (EMBs) are small firms, they share many of the characteristics and challenges faced by small firms more generally. These include frequent problems in raising finance to start a business and/or expand (particularly in the early stages) and deficiencies in certain core management competencies, such as marketing and financial management skills. One

2 Small Business Service, "Business Plan 2004", at <http://www.sbs.gov.uk/SBS_Gov_files/researchandstats/SBS_busplan2004>, 10–23, at 10.

3 The author acknowledges the substantial contribution of Dr John Kitching and Rosemary Athayde from the Small Business Research Centre at Kingston University to the project on which this paper is based.

of the distinctive characteristics of small firms in comparison with their large firm counterparts is a more limited internal resource base (particularly in terms of finance and management) and many EMBs share with other small firms the constraints that stem from this. As a consequence, a case can be made for policy intervention designed to assist EMBs in overcoming such constraints, in order that they may fulfil their potential contribution to social inclusion and economic development. Some previous research has also drawn attention to the tendency of EMBs to focus, initially at least, on coethnic customers and markets, either because of the intrinsically ethnic nature of the product or service being offered for sale or because of a reliance on informal sales and 'marketing' methods based largely on word of mouth. Finally, the informality that is commonly found in the recruitment practices of small—and particularly very small—enterprises can be associated with a reliance on coethnic labour in small EMBs, which means that growth is likely to be associated with increased employment opportunities for members of ethnic minorities.

At the same time, it is important to recognize the diversity of ethnic minority business activity that exists within a single country, as well as internationally. In the UK, for example, there is a considerable diversity between ethnic minority groups, as well as between generations within the same ethnic group, which, in some cases, can affect the distinctiveness of this type of enterprise compared with other small firms. There is also a variety of experience between different countries, according to the social, economic and political contexts in which particular ethnic minorities are found. This diversity is reflected in the types of business activity chosen by members of different ethnic groups, the strategies they use to mobilize resources (such as the degree of reliance on social capital to raise finance), as well as their wider business behaviour.

Cultural factors can affect the value placed on entrepreneurship and the motives for starting a business, although it is important also to recognize the role of 'opportunity structures' presented by the social and economic context as a contributory factor in this regard, as well as cultural influences. For example, while culture may contribute to the members of some minority groups having a longstanding ambition to start their own businesses (e.g. Nigerians in the UK), translating this ambition into action may be influenced by the pattern of opportunities and difficulties they face in the labour market. Clearly, there are many interrelationships between ethnicity, culture and enterprise, which mean that EMBs are a heterogeneous group, yet share many of the underlying characteristics of the small business population more generally.

One aspect of the heterogeneity of ethnic minority involvement in entrepreneurship in an international context is the relationship with immigration, since in most cases ethnic minority populations have resulted from a process of in-migration at some stage. This is important because the timing, scale and circumstances in which immigration has taken place affects the skills and resources available for entrepreneurship, as well as the high propensity of some ethnic minority groups to seek to engage in entrepreneurial activity.

II. Ethnic Minority Entrepreneurship in the UK

A. The National Picture

According to the 2001 census, non-white ethnic minorities account for 8% of the UK population (9% in England).[4] Indians are the largest ethnic minority group, followed by Pakistanis, Mixed Ethnic groups, Black Caribbean, Black Africans, Bangladeshis and Chinese. The non-white population of the UK is heavily concentrated in the major urban areas, with approximately two thirds living in just five cities (London, Manchester, Birmingham, Bradford and Leicester). This reflects a wider international tendency for ethnic minority communities to cluster in large cities, particularly where the minority communities consist of migrant groups. Overall, ethnic minority communities in the UK are younger and growing more rapidly than white communities, which means that the proportion of the total population comprising ethnic minorities is predicted to rise.

Turning to the involvement of ethnic minorities in business ownership, it is estimated that, in 2004, there were a total of 4.3 million small and medium-sized businesses (SMEs) in the UK, accounting for more than half of total employment in private sector businesses.[5] More than 0.25 million of these businesses were owned by members of an ethnic minority group and may be characterized as ethnic minority businesses (EMBs), contributing an estimated £15 billion to the UK economy annually. EMBs in the UK are also increasing as a proportion of the total business stock, reflecting a growing share of the total number of new business start-ups in the country annually during the 2000-05 period.[6]

B. London: an Ethnically Diverse City

London is the most ethnically diverse city in the UK and one of the most ethnically diverse cities in the world.[7] For centuries, London has been (and remains) the first destination for most migrants, defined as those born abroad, into the UK.[8] Ethnic minority groups constitute 29% of the London population and today

4 Office of National Statistics, "2001 Census", 2006, at <http://www.statistics.gov.uk/CCI/nugget.asp?ID=455&Pos=4&ColRank=2&Rank=1000>.

5 Stella Mascarenhas-Keyes, "Ethnic Minority Small and Medium Enterprise in England: Diversity and Challenges, 2006", Paper presented at the 51st Conference of the International Council for Small Business, Melbourne, 18–21 June, 1–38, at 2.

6 Barclays Bank, "Black and Minority Ethnic Business Owners: a Market Research Perspective", SME Research Team, Barclays Bank (1995), at <http://www.newsroom.barclays.co.uk/imagelibrary/detail.asp?MediaDetailsID=4379>.

7 Lisa Benton-Short, Marie Price and Samantha Friedman, "Globalization from Below: the Ranking of Global Immigrant Cities", 29(4) *International Journal of Urban and Regional Research* (2005), 945–959, at 947.

8 BBC, "Born Abroad: an Immigration Map of Britain", (2005), at <http://news.bbc.co.uk/1/shared/spl/hi/uk/05/born_abroad/html/overview.stm>.

London is home to nearly two million migrants. There are at least 50 non-indigenous communities based in London with populations of 10,000 or more. Table 1 gives a broad overview of ethnic minority categories[9] in London, showing that the two largest groups were Asian/Asian British and Black/Black British. Since ethnic minority communities are typically younger and also growing more rapidly than white communities, their share of London's population is growing, to an estimated 33% by 2011.[10]

Table 1: Ethnic Minorities in London

Ethnic Group	Total London	Percentage London
White	5,103,203	71.2
Mixed	226,111	3.2
Asian/Asian British	866,693	12.1
Black/ Black British	782,849	10.9
Chinese/Other ethnic group	193,235	2.7
Total	7,172,091	100.0

Source: *Mackintosh 2005.*

A distinctive characteristic of ethnic minorities in the UK, compared with some continental European countries, is the high proportion of second and third generation migrants, reflecting the longstanding nature of the UK as a destination for migrants, particularly for those from former colonial territories. Many of London's EMB groups are children or grandchildren of first generation migrants. For example, almost 60% of Black Caribbeans and almost 50% of Bangladeshi and Pakistani people in London were born in the UK. This is important because people born, reared and educated in the UK might be expected to have different motivations and resources with respect to entrepreneurial activities compared with newly-arrived migrants, as a result of having been brought up and educated in the host country environment.

Ethnic diversity is also reflected in the wide variety of languages spoken by minority groups. In the case of London, it is reported that more than 300 languages are spoken, with almost one in four schoolchildren speaking a language other than English at home, reflecting the migrant status of their families in many cases. In policy terms, the Regional Language Network in London is actively pro-

9 In the UK censuses of population in 1991 and 2001, respondents were asked to which of a number of specified ethnic groups they belonged. The main ethnic groups specified included: White, Mixed, Indian, Pakistani, Bangladeshi, Other Asian, Black Caribbean, Black African, Other Black, Chinese, Other Ethnic Groups. See for more detail <http://www.statistics.gov.uk/cci>.

10 London Development Agency, "Redefining London's BME Businesses, 2005", at <http://www.lda.gov.uk/upload/pdf/Main_Research.pdf>, 1–37, at 18.

moting foreign language support as a central element in the capital's preparation for the 2012 Olympic Games. In these terms, London's linguistic diversity (which is now viewed as a potential asset) is associated with its ethnic diversity, which in turn reflects its attraction to migrants over a long period of time. This includes the most recent period, when sources of in-migration have included new member states of the European Union.

As far as London's ethnic minority businesses are concerned, the most up-to-date source of data is the London Annual Business Survey 2004 (LABS 2004), which in 2004 was based on a telephone survey of 4,008 private sector businesses in the capital.[11] The sample data was weighted to reflect the broad sector, size and location characteristics of the business population in London, in order to enable grossed-up estimates of the responses to be produced with respect to a range of business characteristics and types of behaviour. Based on this survey, almost one in four businesses in London (22.6%) can be classified as EMBs. Collectively, it is estimated that they employed 504,700 people or 19% of total private sector employment in the capital. Asian owners comprised 10.7% of the total, while Black owners represented 4.6% (see Figure 2). The remaining businesses were made up of Mixed-race (4.3%) and Other (3.0%) ethnic groupings.

Figure 1: Ethnicity of London's Business Owners

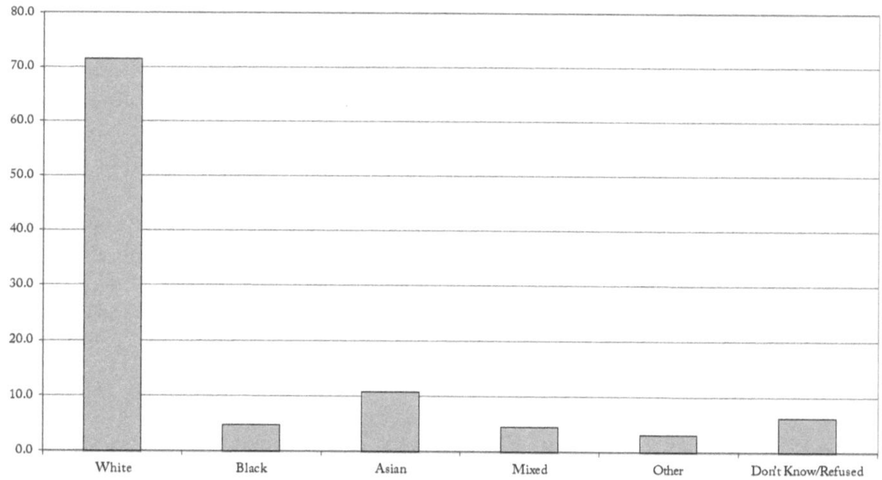

Source: London Annual Business Survey, 2004

11 London Development Agency/Business Link, "London Annual Business Survey 2004", Report of the London Development Agency (2005), 1–61, at <http://www.lda.gov.uk/server/show/ConWebDoc.1298>. The fieldwork for the 2004 survey was undertaken in September and October by BMG Research, and analysis and report writing were carried out by the Small Business Research Centre, Kingston University.

The largest ethnic minority business group is from South Asia (i.e. from India, Pakistan, Bangladesh, Sri Lanka, Afghanistan and Nepal). Black-owned businesses are the next largest groups (i.e. from Black Caribbean and Black African groups). The third largest group is from East Asia (i.e. from China, Japan, Vietnam, Korea, Indonesia and the Philippines). The smallest group is from West Asia (Turkey, Turkish Cypriot and Kurdish communities, and groups from the Middle East). There are around 10,000 Indian-owned businesses, accounting for an annual sales turnover of more than £20 billion; 4,000 Pakistani-owned businesses; 900 Bangladeshi-owned businesses; and approximately 16,000 Black Caribbean and Black African business owners, turning over around £10 billion.[12] In gender terms, the LABS report showed that black women had the highest level of business ownership (17.9%), compared with 12.1% of white women and 5.2% of Asian women.[13]

A consistently reported characteristic of EMBs is their tendency to be mainly small and microenterprises. The evidence from London confirms this, with Black- and Asian-owned business establishments employing 4.1 and 5.9 people, respectively, on average, which is significantly lower than the London average of 8.7 (all mean values). Mixed-race-owned businesses employed on average 15.6 people. EMBs have also traditionally tended to be disproportionately concentrated in low entry threshold sectors (such as catering and retailing), although there are also a number of new emerging fields of activity (such as information technology and creative industries), the latter often involving second or third generation migrants, who are typically better educated than their parents. The evidence for London shows that EMBs are more likely to be involved in the wholesale and retail trades, as well as real estate, renting and business service activities. Asian-owned businesses were most likely to be involved in the wholesale and retail trades (39.6%), whereas Black (35.7%) and Mixed-race (40.5%) owned businesses were most likely to be in real estate, renting and business service activities.

III. Ethnic Diversity and Competitiveness

A. An Overview

Diversity is currently topical in policy circles, driven by a combination of the social inclusion and competitiveness agendas and fuelled by the writings of Richard Florida[14] in the context of wider globalization debates. Diversity competitiveness linkages may be explored at the micro (individual enterprise) and/or the macro

---

12 *Ibid.*

13 London Development Agency, "London Annual Business Survey 2004", at <http://www.lda.gov.uk/upload/pdf/London_Annual_Business_Survey_2004.pdf>.

14 Richard Florida, *The Rise of the Creative Class*, revised edition (New York: Basic Books, 2004); and Id., *Cities and the Creative Class* (London and New York: Routledge, 2005).

(e.g. city/region)[15] levels. At its simplest, city/regional competitiveness can be defined in terms of the trading performance of the city's/region's enterprises. As a consequence, city/regional competitiveness can be enhanced by creating and sustaining the conditions that enable local enterprises to trade successfully. Cities/ regions may enable businesses to become successful by offering close proximity to resource suppliers and markets and through the availability of assets that are external to but benefit individual enterprises. Such assets include the public infrastructure (e.g. transport links, communications), a local skills base, knowledge and technology spillovers and high levels of trust between economic actors. Each of these assets can potentially enable businesses to achieve a higher level of performance than would otherwise be possible.

The rest of this section considers ways in which ethnic diversity (defined in terms of the proportion of the population composed of EMBs, their distribution between EMB groups, and the associated social and cultural differences) might be an asset that enhances competitiveness. From a policy perspective, there is interest in identifying the existence of such linkages as well as the ways in which policy intervention might contribute to enhancing the role of diversity in stimulating city/region competitiveness.

Ethnic diversity at the level of the city/region can, potentially, contribute to business competitiveness through a variety of causal mechanisms. A recent review of the international evidence base in this regard (in which the author was involved) led to the identification of seven potential diversity competitiveness links.[16]

1. Entrepreneurship and new venture creation, associated with the high propensity of some minority groups to be involved in entrepreneurial activity
2. Ethnic diversity as a source of creativity and innovation
3. Exploitation of diaspora-based linkages by ethnic minority businesses for business development purposes
4. Supplier diversity, where an ethnically diverse supply base can be a source of innovation in the purchasing organization and/or enable it to access ethnically diverse markets
5. Ethnic diversity and tourism, where ethnic minority events and activities contribute to a more attractive tourist 'offer'
6. Ethnic attraction, where an ethnically mixed population may enhance the attractiveness of a location for foreign direct investment from countries of origin, and

15 Here the term 'city/region' is used as a generic label to refer to sub-national territories, while recognizing that recent discussion distinguishes cities and regions in order to indicate their interrelations. See, for example, Office of the Deputy Prime Minister, "Cities, Regions and Competitiveness", Second Report of the Working Group of Government Departments, at <http://www.communities.gov.uk/pub/481/ CitiesregionsandcompetitivenessPDF758Kb_id1127481.pdf>.

16 London Development Agency, "The Competitive Advantage of Diversity: an Introduction to the Project and Mid-Term Research Findings", Report prepared by the Small Business Research Centre, Kingston University (2005).

7. Workforce diversity, on the basis that there is a business case, as well as one based on social equity, for employers recruiting, retaining and developing job seekers from minority ethnic groups.

Because this paper is focused on the links between ethnic diversity, entrepreneurship and competitiveness, only the first five themes listed above are considered; themes six and seven are more applicable in the case of large enterprises and less concerned with aspects of entrepreneurship.[17] In each case, hypotheses are put forward specifying the mechanisms through which ethnic diversity might generate specific competitiveness effects, which are then considered in relation to the available evidence.

B. *Ethnic Diversity and Entrepreneurship*

Increasing attention—for example, in the UK,[18] the Netherlands,[19] Germany,[20] Canada[21] and Australia[22]—is being paid to ethnic minority and immigrant business ownership and policy issues associated with it. Moreover, the tendency for some ethnic minority groups to be disproportionately involved in entrepreneurship is a consistent feature in the international literature. For example, in the UK, self-employment rates vary considerably between ethnic minority groups. According to the 2001 census of population, Chinese, Pakistani, Indian and White Irish groups have the highest rates of self-employment in London, at over 20% of those in work in each group. This contrasts with Black Caribbean, Black African and Other Black groups, which have among the lowest rates at 10–13%. In each minority ethnic group, male self-employment is considerably higher than female.

---

17 For a review of the evidence base with respect to the remaining themes and a more detailed review of those covered in this paper, see *ibid.*

18 Monder Ram and David Smallbone, "Policies to Support Ethnic Minority Enterprise: the English Experience", 15(2) *Entrepreneurship and Regional Development* (2003), 151–166.

19 Robert Kloosterman, Joanne van der Leun and Jan Rath, "Mixed Embeddedness: (In) Formal Economic Activities and Immigrant Businesses in the Netherlands", 23(2) *International Journal of Urban and Regional Research* (1999), 252–266.

20 Antoine Pecoud, "Entrepreneurship and Identity: Cosmopolitanism and Cultural Competencies among German-Turkish Business People in Berlin", 30(1) *Journal of Ethnic and Migration Studies* (2003), 3–20.

21 Robert B. Anderson and Robert J. Giberson, "Aboriginal Entrepreneurship and Economic Development in Canada: Thoughts on Current Theory and Practice", in Curt H. Stiles and Craig S. Galbraith (eds.), *Ethnic Entrepreneurship: Structure and Process* (Elsevier, Amsterdam, London, 2004), 141–170.

22 Jock Collins, "Cultural Diversity and Entrepreneurship: Policy Responses to Immigrant Entrepreneurs in Australia", 15(2) *Entrepreneurship & Regional Development* (2003), 137–149.

In this context, ethnic diversity can contribute to competitiveness if members of ethnic minority groups start businesses offering new goods and services, or enter established markets. By extending the range of products available in the marketplace, the former is an inherently more innovative process than the latter, with potentially more enduring effects on economic development. The demand for ethnic-based products can foster business opportunities for local inner-city providers of products such as food and drink.[23] Entry into established markets is a less innovative means by which ethnic diversity can contribute to city/region competitiveness, namely, through the cheaper provision of goods and services already available. One UK example was the move into low-order retailing in several inner cities by Asians during the 1970s and 1980s.[24] Market entry puts pressure on already existing firms to lower prices or improve efficiency in order to retain market share. Unless hitherto untapped demand exists or market growth can absorb an expansion in the business stock, it might lead though to effects on existing businesses.[25]

C. *Ethnic Diversity, Creativity and Competitive Advantage*

A major contributor to the diversity competitiveness debate is Richard Florida,[26] who argues that diversity, in its various forms, influences economic competitiveness indirectly by fostering creativity and innovation, which is the principal driving force of economic development. Creative people, he suggests, are attracted to tolerant places, where there are low barriers to entry. Tolerant places provide the habitat where all forms of creativity (artistic, cultural, technological and economic) can take root and flourish. Creative people move to such places because they provide opportunities to validate their identities as creative. Places with diverse mixes of creative people, it is argued, are more likely to generate new combinations of ideas and resources which, in turn, lead to greater innovation, firm formation, job generation and economic growth.

Florida has developed three quantitative indices of diversity to rank cities/ regions (the Gay Index, Bohemian Index and Melting Point Index), plus a fourth, composite, index. These diversity indices are then correlated with measures of human capital, high-technology industry and economic performance. Associations

23 Michael Porter, "The Competitive Advantage of the Inner City", 73(3) *Harvard Business Review* (1995), 55–71.

24 Trevor Jones, Giles Barrett and David McEvoy, "Market Potential as a Decisive Influence on the Performance of Ethnic Minority Business", in Jan Rath (ed.), *Immigrant Businesses* (Basingstoke: Macmillan, 2000), 37–53, at 41.

25 Monder Ram, Tareq Abbas, Balihar Sanghera and Geoffrey Hillin, "Currying Favour with the Locals: Balti Owners and Business Enclaves", 6(1) *International Journal of Entrepreneurial Behaviour & Research* (2000), 41–55.

26 See, for example, Florida (2004), *op.cit.* note 14; Id. (2005), *op.cit.* note 14; and Sam Youl Lee, Richard Florida and Zoltan Acs, "Creativity and Entrepreneurship: a Regional Analysis of New Firm Formation", 38(8) *Regional Studies* (2004), 879–891.

are strongest with the Composite Diversity Index, suggesting that all three influences contribute. Taken individually, the Gay Index is the strongest predictor of the performance indices, followed by the Bohemian Index and then the Melting Pot Index, although the latter appears to be more important in smaller cities. It is not suggested that gays, bohemians or immigrants cause economic growth directly but rather that their presence in a particular city/region is an indicator of a place that is open and conducive to new ideas.

Two criticisms can be made of Florida's work from the standpoint of ethnic diversity and competitiveness. First, his Melting Pot Index is a measure of *immigrants* rather than *ethnicity* and it should not be assumed that all immigrants into the US are from visible minorities. In fact, Florida suggests there is no correlation between the proportion of non-whites in a city/region and the concentration of high-tech industry.[27] Second, correlation alone does not provide a sound foundation for making causal inferences. Beyond proposing a vague notion of a 'creative ecosystem', Florida does not discuss the precise causal mechanisms through which ethnic diversity generates creativity and economic development effects.[28]

In empirical terms, there is some evidence of the role of ethnic diversity in stimulating creativity and innovation in relation to London's creative industries, referring specifically to London's Asian population's contribution to the music and performing arts and software and computing sub-sectors.[29] Music and the performing arts are good examples of activities where diversity can feed into creativity through fusion, by drawing on different cultural traditions and creating something new. In such cases, an individual's ethnicity and cultural experience has a major potential input into the creative process and may thus be regarded as a key element in the core business concept. Another example is the fashion business, where there is strong interest from young Asians in developing traditional designs into forms that are suitable for contemporary garments. A successful fusion can lead to products that have an appeal both in the mainstream as well as narrowly Asian markets. Young British Asians are in a good position to achieve that, since the fusion reflects their own experience. The link between diversity, creativity and innovation may also apply between individual firms within clusters of firms, as well as within firms. The principle of fusion in relation to ethnic and cultural diversity can also be a source of innovation in ethnic minority firms involved in the food processing sector.

The relatively high value-added nature of the business activities involved in London's creative industries, which are typically knowledge or skill based, contrast with the low value-added nature of many of the traditional areas of Asian business activity in the UK, in sectors such as clothing, catering and low-order

27 Florida (2004), *op.cit.* note 14 at 254.

28 Michael Storper and Anthony Venables, "Buzz: Face-to-Face Contact and the Urban Economy", 4 *Journal of Economic Geography* (2004), 351–370.

29 David Smallbone, Marcello Bertotti and Ignatius Ekanem, "Diversification in Ethnic Minority Business: the Case of Asians in London's Creative Industries", 12(1) *Journal of Small Business and Enterprise Development* (2005), 41–56, at 49.

retailing. In this context, it is perhaps not surprising that Asian businesses in the creative industries are typically owned and run by second or third generation migrants, many with graduate level education. The higher value-added characteristic is an important one for Asian entrepreneurship (in a UK context), in view of the recognition by policy-makers of the need to encourage the diversification of minority ethnic business activity out of low value-added, low entry threshold activities into higher value-added activity. The trend can potentially contribute to more competitive Asian business development, as well as to increased social inclusion, with potential welfare gains for the society as a whole.

D. *Exploiting Diaspora Networks*

Ethnic diversity at the city/region level may enhance business competitiveness by enabling or stimulating business owners to commercially exploit diaspora links, which may be viewed as a form of social capital. While accepting that commentators attach multiple meanings to the term 'diaspora',[30] the term is used in this paper to refer to the dispersion of ethnic and national groups across international borders. No assumptions are made regarding diaspora members' self-identities vis-à-vis their host societies or their orientations towards any putative homeland. Diaspora networks vary in terms of the number of actors they incorporate, their location, the benefits they can make available to individual members and the strength of relations between network actors, all of which can influence business competitiveness. Business owners may exploit diaspora networks in two main ways: firstly, to access resources that are unavailable or more expensive to acquire from other sources; and, secondly, to provide a market for goods and services. Cities and regions that are home to EMB groups possess a potential competitive asset if these diaspora-based linkages can be exploited commercially.

International studies show extensive use of ethnic-based networks to access sources of finance, labour, information and markets for goods and services.[31] Rath, for example, refers to networks as being instrumental in acquiring knowledge, distributing information, obtaining capital, recruiting labour and establishing strong

30 Roger Brubaker, "The 'Diaspora' Diaspora", 28(1) *Ethnic and Racial Studies* (2005), 1–19, at 1.

31 For example, James Rauch, "Business and Social Networks in International Trade", 39 *Journal of Economic Literature* (2001), 1177–1203; Jock Collins, "Chinese Entrepreneurs: The Chinese Diaspora in Australia", 8(1/2) *International Journal of Entrepreneurial Behaviour & Research* (2002), 113–133; David Smallbone, Rosemary Athayde and John Kitching, "Ethnic Diversity, Entrepreneurship and Competitive Advantage in a Global City", Paper presented to the 51st Conference of the International Council for Small Business Annual Conference, Melbourne, 18–21 June; Gordon Cheung, "Chinese Diaspora as a Virtual Nation: Interactive Roles between Economic and Social Capital", 52 *PS* (2004), 664–684.

relations with clients and suppliers.[32] Ethnic networks in Canada were considered essential to business success for the Asian, Chinese, Indian, Korean, Sri-Lankan, Vietnamese and Jewish communities; and in the US for Chinese, Asian, Iranian, Korean, Jewish and African-American communities (among others).

A number of UK studies have also found that EMB groups use diaspora-based networks to access valuable resources and to provide markets for products.[33] McEwan, Pollard and Henry stress the importance for the ethnic food and Bhangra music industries in Birmingham of import/export linkages with countries of origin, such as India and China.[34] Jones, Ram and Edwards highlight the importance of drawing on local and illegal coethnics as a source of labour in the West Midland's restaurant and clothing sectors; many businesses would simply not survive without undocumented immigrant labour.[35]

Some EMBs are able to generate business with companies based abroad because they have been exposed to a blend of knowledge and experience from their own culture and Western culture. For example, a small London-based EMB operating in design, was able to offer packaging services to foreign companies that wanted to invest in London and needed help in tuning their packaging to the tastes of English customers.[36] Sunrise Radio is another UK example of the competitive advantages of an Asian network. This media company has radio stations in seven cities in England and Scotland with high concentrations of Asian communities. Transnational elements of the company include five national radio stations in Sri Lanka, two in Mauritius and one in Dubai. Additionally, anecdotal evidence suggests that London's diversity contributes to attracting people looking for ethnic-based products in, for example, Chinese medicine.

Trust is an important component of ethnic networks, without which they would not function effectively.[37] Trust is a necessary condition for the sustain-

32 Jan Rath, "The Commodification of Cultural Resources in a Historic Inner City: Amsterdam Chinatown from an International Comparative Perspective", Paper presented at the Conference on The Future of the Historic Inner City of Amsterdam, September 2002, University of Amsterdam.

33 Nick Henry, Cheryl McEwan and Jane Pollard, "Globalization from Below: Birmingham – Postcolonial Workshop of the World?", 34(2) *Area* (2002), 117–127.

34 Cheryl McEwan, Jane Pollard and Nick Henry, "The 'Global' in the City Economy: Multicultural Economic Development in Birmingham", 29(4) International Journal of Urban and Regional Research (2005), 916–933.

35 Trevor Jones, Monder Ram and Paul Edwards, "Ethnic Minority Business and the Employment of Illegal Immigrants", 18(2) *Entrepreneurship & Regional Development* (2006), 133–150, at 140.

36 Smallbone, Bertotti and Ekanem, *op.cit.* note 29.

37 Collins, *op.cit.* note 31 at 122; David Smallbone, Fergus Lyon and Xiao Li, "Trust, Co-operation and Networking in an Immigrant Business Community: the Case of Chinese-owned Businesses in the UK", in Hans-Hermann Hohmann and Friederike Welter (eds.), *Trust and Entrepreneurship: A West-East Perspective* (Cheltenham and Northampton, MA: Edward Elgar, 2005); McEwan, Pollard and Henry, *op.cit.* note 34.

ability of networks, and the deterrence of opportunistic behaviour that could undermine them is enforced by the threat of expulsion from the network. At the same time, networks also need to be open to new members; otherwise, such "efficiency enhancing *domestic* networks" can actually impede international trade.[38] Encouraging business start-up in areas of high concentration can generate agglomeration benefits but can also harm the interests of *existing* business owners by increasing levels of competition.[39]

It is important to recognize the role of the broader social context, rather than focusing exclusively on ethnic resources and networks, as an influence on business competitiveness. The 'mixed embeddedness' thesis suggests that competitiveness depends not only on business owners' embeddedness in ethnic networks but also their capacity to draw on and exploit wider market and institutional contexts,[40] which can vary spatially. EMB groups often operate in product markets that do not require high financial outlays or high skill or qualification levels, as these are easier to enter. Because of this, coethnic markets are often very competitive and dependence on them is likely to constrain business performance and growth.[41] The concept of 'breakout' was introduced to describe the capacity of EMB-owned enterprises to reach customers beyond the ethnic group.[42] In order to achieve this, business owners may have to exploit their 'weak ties',[43] which are those with whom they do not have close relationships but possess key resources or can become important customers. This contrasts with a continued reliance on 'strong ties' (e.g. family members and others with whom the owner has close relations) to provide key resources.

E. *Supplier Diversity*

It can be argued that a diverse supply base can contribute to enhanced performance for the purchasing organization, whether this is a large corporate or a public sector organization. In this regard, the US experience provides useful evidence of the business case for supplier diversity. One argument is that small businesses can

---

38 Rauch, *op.cit.* note 31, emphasis in original.

39 Ram, Abbas, Sanghera and Hillin, *op.cit.* note 25.

40 Jan Rath and Robert Kloosterman, "Outsider's Business: a Critical Review of Research on Immigrant Entrepreneurship", 34(3) *International Migration Review* (1999), 657–681; Robert Kloosterman and Jan Rath, "Immigrant Entrepreneurs in Advanced Economies: Mixed Embeddedness Further Explored", 27(2) *JEMS* (2001), 189–202.

41 Giles Barrett, Trevor Jones, David McEvoy and Chris McGoldrick, "The Economic Embeddedness of Immigrant Enterprise in Britain", 8(1/2) *International Journal of Entrepreneurial Behaviour and Research* (2002), 11–31.

42 For a review, see Monder Ram and Trevor Jones, *Ethnic Minorities in Business, Report of the Small Business Research Trust* (Small Business Research Trust, London, 1998).

43 Mark Granovetter, "Strength of Weak Ties", 78(6) *American Sociological Review* (1973), 1360–1380.

offer a more customized and flexible solution than larger providers, either alone or in partnership. Diversity may also be viewed as a source of creativity and innovation, implying that supplier diversity may enhance the innovative and entrepreneurial propensities of the organization. Another factor is the potential public relations value for the organization in terms of being able to demonstrate diversity of suppliers to match the diversity of its customer base. There is also the potential reputation value for an organization from being known to support socially beneficial initiatives and actively promote equal opportunities.

Because of a tendency for many ethnic minority businesses to be focused on low value-added activity, an important policy priority is to help to diversify the ethnic business sector by helping EMBs to exploit new market opportunities. This can be achieved by assisting established EMBs to 'break out' of a reliance on coethnic markets into 'mainstream' markets, which in many cases will be a necessary step for these businesses to grow. More fundamentally, it can involve taking steps to open up completely new markets for EMBs, thereby offering an opportunity to diversify the ethnic business base. In this context, in the UK, there are a number of supplier diversity programmes that seek to increase the access of EMBs and other small firms to procurement contracts. thereby increasing the diversity of the supply base. Such initiatives offer a potential mechanism for facilitating the diversification of EMBs into higher value-added activity, with public sector procurement as a potentially valuable tool for achieving this.[44]

In the UK, there has been considerable interest recently in examining the US experience, where this type of initiative has a longer track record and public policies for ethnic minority businesses have included procurement preference initiatives for some years. Many states now have an office for minority businesses and a network of local branches, though not in all cases, because of political opposition to the principles of affirmative action. Affirmative action is based on 'set-aside' public procurement contracts whereby a minority business that is within 5% of the lowest bid will be awarded the contract. In the private sector also, there are numerous examples in the US of corporate supplier diversity programmes. Support for supplier diversity is said to be strongest in the US automobile industry, where Ford, Daimler-Chrysler and General Motors spent a total of $8.5 billion on diversity supplier contracts in 2001. Major corporations (i.e. Fortune 500 companies) are using their public websites to support supplier diversity initiatives. For instance in Cincinnati, Kroger, which operates supermarkets under the names Fred Meyer, Ralphs, Smith's, King Soopers, Dillon, Fry's and City Market, has a 'supplier diversity programme' that seeks to ensure that minority-owned and female-owned businesses are part of their mainstream supply base. Unfortunately, there has been little evaluation of such programmes, making it difficult to assess the impact they have had on ethnic-minority-owned businesses and the amount of 'deadweight' involved in such initiatives (in other words, how many ethnic

44 Monder Ram and David Smallbone, "Ethnic Minority Enterprise: Policy in Practice", Research Report RR001/01, Small Business Service, at <http://www.sbs.gov.uk/SBS_Gov_files/researchandstats/EMBreport.pdf>.

minority businesses would have become suppliers without being involved in a particular initiative).

It has been suggested that affirmative action supplier diversity policies in the US have contributed to the diversification of second generation minority-owned enterprises, as well as to local economic development in disadvantaged urban areas.[45] At the same time, the US model of prioritizing disadvantaged groups in awarding procurement contracts has, not surprisingly, led to allegations of favouritism and attempted misuse by those excluded from the programme and criticisms regarding the effects of bidding procedures on the quality of supplies. In fact, litigation against specific cases of minority business preferment and state-wide referendums resulted in the states of California and Washington banning preferment based on race or ethnicity, thus weakening its effectiveness as a policy tool to help minority businesses. Critics of 'preferential procurement' argue that it puts qualified non-EMBs at a disadvantage and that these schemes can be poorly administered. It is also argued that the difficulties EMBs face in accessing procurement contracts stem from their small size and lack of experience, due to the young age of many of these firms.

Supplier diversity programmes are relatively new to the UK and therefore tend to be in the very early stages of development.[46] In the UK, the key drivers for supplier diversity are economic development, equal opportunities and corporate social responsibility, although some private sector companies claim to base their initiatives on 'the business case'. Attempts have been made to assist in building the capacity of small EMBs to meet the requirements of procurement opportunities created. One example is 'Fit-to-Supply', which is an intermediary-led initiative, run by Business Link for London. The programme provides information to participating EMBs about supply opportunities, as well as training to help firms achieve the quality standards of purchasers.

F. *Ethnic Diversity and Tourism*

Ethnic diversity can also contribute to city/regional competitiveness (a so-called 'diversity dividend') by attracting visitors/tourists to ethnocultural events and to ethnic precincts providing a range of retail and food and drink outlets.[47] Urban tourism currently accounts for approximately 30% of European tourism and is expected to continue to grow. European examples include tropical carnivals in London's Notting Hill, Berlin and Rotterdam; the Bollywood film festival in The Hague; and the Turkish Klein Istanbul in Berlin. However, traditional countries

45 Thomas Boston, *Affirmative Action and Black Entrepreneurship* (London: Routledge, 1999).

46 Monder Ram and David Smallbone, "Supplier Diversity Initiatives and the Diversification of Ethnic Minority Businesses in the UK", 24(4) *Policy Studies* (2003), 187–204.

47 Jan Rath (ed.), *Tourism, Ethnic Diversity and the City* (London and New York: Routledge, 2006).

of settler immigration acknowledged the potential of cultural diversity a long time ago and were ahead of Europe in this regard. Examples include the Chinese Quarter in Melbourne since the 1970s and Chinatown in New York; Chinatown in Vancouver opened up to tourism in the 1930s.[48]

One attempt at an integrated policy initiative focused on ethnically based tourism is the Hague's 'City Mondial' project, which was part of a wider 'Big Cities Policy' in the Netherlands to address social needs in deprived city districts.[49] The aim was to offer an integrated approach combining physical, economic and social measures with locally based initiatives involving local residents and representative groups (e.g. housing associations and voluntary groups). Local governance was a key feature of the policy and social cohesion a key aim.

The Hague is the most segregated city in the Netherlands and is home to 8 of the 15 most deprived neighbourhoods, with more than 40% of the population being of non-Dutch origin. Although the second cultural city of the Netherlands (after Amsterdam) historically, the cultural potential of immigrants had not been recognized and exploited. The tourist sector was identified as an important component of regeneration strategy because it provides many jobs to lower-skilled residents. City Mondial was perceived as a major opportunity to enrich the cultural repertoire of The Hague and to encourage the economic activities of immigrants. More than 80% of the population in the district covered by City Mondial have an ethnic background and they now form one of the fastest growing groups of entrepreneurs in the city, mainly in the hospitality and retail sectors. Many new shops and restaurants have opened in recent years and the City Mondial Foundation has developed a range of activities. Strong local networks were one of the factors behind the success of the initiative. At the same time, many of the ethnically based activities are said to run in parallel, with little crossover or joint participation by different ethnic groups,[50] suggesting that there may be missed opportunities for creativity and innovation, compared with a situation where a higher degree of interaction occurs.

It has been suggested that in order to reap the 'diversity dividend' from ethnic tourism, certain conditions need to be in place.[51] To be successful, the ethnic tourist sector needs to be integrated into a larger existing tourist industry and be included in mainstream promotion. In addition, Zukin argues there is a 'critical infrastructure', comprised of knowledge workers that design cultural production, such as marketing bureaux, tourist boards and national and local government, which influences the popularity of particular ethnic activities.[52] These actors need to work together to promote ethnic cultural activities with a commit-

48 Rath, *op.cit.* note 32.

49 Van Kempen, "Big Cities Policy in the Netherlands", 91(2) Tijdschrift voor Economische en Sociale Geograffe (2000), 197–203.

50 *Ibid.*

51 Rath, *op.cit.* note 32.

52 Sharon Zukin, "Urban Lifestyles: Diversity and Standardization in Spaces of Consumption", 35(5–6) *Urban Studies* (1998), 825–883.

ted organization or individual taking the lead. There also needs to be a critical mass of consumers for the ethnic tourist sector to take off, as well as a critical mass of ethnic attractions to sustain tourist interest. The social and regulatory infrastructures must be capable of supporting the development of a regular precinct into a tourist attraction. Finally, small innovative EMB businesses need to be nurtured through business development programmes designed to support growth and facilitate quality upgrading.

However, there are also a number of potentially negative influences of such developments that need to be carefully managed. For example, in a study of 12 English cities, Hankinson found that local residents were not always involved in such initiatives because the perceived benefits were targeted at outside business interests rather than helping local communities.[53] The displacement of low-rent residents and small businesses is just one of the negative effects of tourism development in previously deprived areas highlighted by other researchers.[54]

IV. Conclusions and Wider Implications

Examination of the UK experience with respect to ethnic minority entrepreneurship demonstrates that self-employment and business ownership can provide a route for immigrant-based ethnic minorities to play an active role in a host society, as well as a means for individuals to earn a living and achieve a degree of self-fulfillment. The above average propensity of members of some ethnic minority groups to be involved in entrepreneurial activity must be viewed as positive overall, even if the social inclusion effects may sometimes be exaggerated.[55] While some of this involvement in entrepreneurship may initially have been driven by need, which in some cases may have included negative experiences in seeking employment in mainstream labour markets, it is misleading to characterize all ethnic minority entrepreneurship in Britain in such terms. What is also unquestionable is the significant and growing contribution that ethnic-minority-owned businesses are making to the UK economy, particularly from those that are members of well-established ethnic minority communities. Moreover, as generational change contributes to a shift towards greater involvement in higher value-added activities, the nature and extent of this contribution is likely to increase.

At the same time, increasing attention should be paid to the needs and aspirations of members of newly arrived migrant groups from Central and Eastern Europe and asylum seekers, about whom the evidence base is currently thin. Since creating and developing a business requires resources, as well as aspiration and commitment by individuals, the ability of members of minority and/or immigrant

53 Graham Hankinson, "Location Branding: a Study of the Branding Practices of 12 English Cities", 9(2) *Journal of Brand Management* (2001), 127–142, at 137.

54 Zukin, *op.cit.* note 52.

55 Robert Blackburn and Monder Ram, "Fix or Fixation? The Contribution and Limitations of Entrepreneurship and Small Firms to Combating Social Exclusion" 17(1) *Entrepreneurship and Regional Development* (2006), 73–85.

groups to successfully follow such a path is likely to be affected by the nature and extent of the resources they are able to mobilize. While the social capital that often exists within such communities is undoubtedly a potentially valuable asset in this regard, it is unlikely to be sufficient in itself if finance and human capital resources are limited.

The argument that ethnic (and other forms) of diversity can contribute to the competitiveness of an economy is an attractive one because it emphasizes the integrated nature of contemporary societies and the interdependence between their members. If the proposition can be supported with convincing evidence, there is a potentially powerful message to be disseminated within society, with implications for social inclusion. However, in this context, it must be recognized that, although a number of hypothesized links between ethnic diversity and competitiveness can be identified, the empirical evidence required to confirm, refine or reject these is currently rather scarce. While a number of the suggested causal connections seem plausible, without further systematic research it is difficult to argue whether such connections exist in practice, how strong such connections are and what conditions support or hinder their influence in practical terms. This conclusion is consistent with feedback received in regard to ongoing research being undertaken by Kingston University for the London Development Agency, from other academic researchers and government policy-makers from around the world. This includes informants in Australia, Canada and the US, who were approached as experts on ethnic minority business or representatives of agencies with an interest in the topic. Most of them reported an interest in the topic being investigated, yet few were able to provide, or point the research team towards, convincing evidence to support ethnic diversity competitiveness links. At the same time, the lack of previous evidence underlines the potential contribution of the case studies and empirical research being undertaken in London.

Recognizing the limitations of the existing empirical evidence, detailed examination of specific links suggests that the high propensity of some ethnic minority groups to engage in entrepreneurship is undoubtedly a potential asset for a city, provided more can be channelled into higher value-added activity. In addition, diaspora-based linkages are undoubtedly a potential asset of London's EMB population, as far as mobilizing resources and exploiting new markets is concerned. However, further research is required in order to clarify the circumstances in which such linkages are most likely to be positively exploited. In the creative industries, in particular, there is some evidence of diversity contributing to the development of innovation that is generating profitable business opportunities, as well as employment. The overall conclusion is that ethnic diversity may be a potential asset for city competitiveness but the evidence currently available requires strengthening before significant public policy resources are committed to seeking to enhance it.

While it may be argued that the position of London is unique with regards to the diversity of its ethnic minority population, the principles discussed in this paper are worth exploring and potentially transferable to other contexts. Perhaps the key point to note is that while diversity is a source of *potential* competitiveness, resources are needed to exploit it, which in some ethnic minority communities requires a strong supplementary or pump-priming role for public policy.

*Rainer Hofmann**

Political Participation of Minorities

I. Introduction[1]

At the outset, I should like to thank the organizers of this event for having entrusted me with the task to speak to you tonight on the issue of 'political participation of minorities'. It is a great personal pleasure to be here in this beautiful city of Bozen/ Bolzano, which I have known for more than 40 years, a city which—just like the entire region of South Tyrol—has made enormous progress during this period. This progress, which has been achieved in many fields, has been most considerably facilitated and enhanced by the fact that the political leaders of this region—and to pay tribute to only one of them I should like to mention Dr Silvius Magnago—have been quite successful in establishing a political system that, based upon the agreements known as the 'package', resulted in a system of power-sharing and integration of the three linguistic groups residing in the region. As we all know, South Tyrol is today—together with the Åland Islands and the Eastern cantons of Belgium—generally considered as a 'model' for a successful solution to a previously most problematic situation of frequently tense majority–minority relations. And I trust that you all agree with me when I say that one of the reasons for this success story is the fact that the South Tyrolean model is based on a concept of power-sharing that—notwithstanding some recent debates as to the need to adapt it to changing circumstances—provides for effective political participation of all the linguistic groups residing in the region.

This brings me to the topic of my lecture, namely the 'political participation of minorities'. I shall start by briefly addressing the question as to the reason *why* we need political participation of persons belonging to minorities. I shall then—equally briefly—address the issue of *who* should be able to participate in this process of political participation; this means obviously that I shall deal with

---

* Professor of Constitutional and International Law at the University of Frankfurt/ Main, Germany.

1 This is the annotated version of the first EURAC Annual Minority Rights Lecture held on 30 November 2006 in Bolzano/Bozen.

Minority Governance in and beyond Europe, ISBN 978-90-04-27648-2. pp. 105–118.

the definition of the term 'minority', in particular whether only persons belonging to 'traditional', or 'autochthonous' or 'old' minorities should be included or whether also persons belonging to immigrant or other groups whose members have recently settled in the region concerned should, as 'new' minorities, be entitled to—and, if so, to what extent—political participation. Finally—and this will constitute the main part of my lecture—I shall present the various modalities of political participation or, in other words, *how* the political participation of minorities can be successfully implemented.

Before I do so, I should like to conclude this introduction with two remarks of a more personal nature: first, I should like to ask for your understanding that I shall rely to a large extent on the pertinent practice established by the Advisory Committee under the Council of Europe Framework Convention on National Minorities (FCNM). I shall do so not only because I feel more familiar with this practice than, for example, with the practice established by the OSCE High Commissioner on National Minorities (HCNM), although I shall, of course, take into due account the Lund Recommendations on the Effective Participation of National Minorities in Public Life, adopted on 1 September 1999.[2] Second, I should like to stress how much this lecture owes to the extensive work done on this issue of political participation by two outstanding experts, namely Marc Weller,[3] Director of the Flensburg-based European Centre for Minority Issues, who unfortunately cannot be with us tonight, and Professor Joseph Marko, who is our host tonight.[4]

2 Lund Recommendations on the Effective Participation of National Minorities in Public Life, adopted 1 September 1999, at <http://www.osce.org/hcnm/documents/recommendations>. On the Lund Recommendations, see Krzysztof Drzewicki, "The Lund Recommendations on the Effective Participation of National Minorities in Public Life – Five Years After and More Years Ahead", 12(2-3) *International Journal on Minority and Group Rights* (2005), 123-131; Kristin Henrard, "'Participation', 'Representation' and 'Autonomy' in the Lund Recommendations and their Reflections in the Supervision of the FCNM and Several Human Rights Conventions", 12(2-3) *International Journal on Minority and Group Rights* (2005), 133-168; and Sally Holt, "The Lund Recommendations in the Activities of the HCNM", 12(2-3) *International Journal on Minority and Group Rights* (2005), 169-188.

3 See, for example, Marc Weller, "Article 15", in *id.* (ed.), *The Rights of National Minorities. A Commentary on the European Framework Convention for the Protection of National Minorities* (Oxford University Press, Oxford, 2005), 429-461; and *id.*, "DH-MIN Handbook on Minority Consultative Mechanisms", Council of Europe Document DH-MIN(2006)012, at <http://www.coe.int/T/E/human_rights/minorities/>.

4 See, for example, Joseph Marko, "Effective Participation of National Minorities. A Comment on Conceptual, Legal and Empirical Problems", Council of Europe Document DH-MIN(2006)014, at <http://www.coe.int/T/E/human_rights/minorities/>.

II. Why Is There a Need for Political Participation of Minorities?

The answer to this question results from the correct assessment that only those minorities whose members feel that the state in which they reside is also 'their' state, that it also 'belongs to them', will be prepared to fully integrate themselves into that state and its structures. This, in turn, will contribute considerably to stability and peaceful majority–minority relations. To achieve this end, effective participation is clearly a *conditio sine qua non*. It is, therefore, no surprise that the right to effective participation in cultural, economic and social life and in public affairs—and this lecture will be focused on the latter aspect, i.e., political participation—is generally accepted, as is reflected in paragraph 35 of the 1990 OSCE Copenhagen Final Document[5] and by its guarantee in Article 15, FCNM. It has also been the subject of the above-mentioned 1999 Lund Recommendations on the Effective Participation of National Minorities in Public Life, as further specified by the quite detailed 2001 Warsaw Guidelines to Assist National Minority Participation in the Electoral Process.[6] So, effective political participation of minorities serves a twofold aim: by adding to the stability of peaceful majority–minority relations, it also contributes considerably to the preservation and promotion of the distinct identity of minorities.

III. Who is Entitled to Participate in the Process of Political Participation?

As stated above, this question leads us to one of the most controversial issues relating to the situation of minorities under both domestic and international law, i.e., the question as to the conditions under which a group of persons constitutes a minority—or, more precisely, a national minority in the sense of international law, which includes ethnic, linguistic and religious minorities. For obvious reasons, I have to refrain from attempting to provide you with adequate information as to the relevant situation in the domestic legal orders of the 46 Council of Europe member states, but shall focus on the situation under international law.

However, this self-imposed limitation does not make things easier: most of you will know that, notwithstanding serious efforts, there is as yet no definition of the term 'national minority' that is accepted by all concerned, in particular by the states and the minorities themselves. There are, however, some basic elements that are common to all such definitions and that may be traced back to the

5 CSCE Copenhagen Document, adopted 29 June 1990, at <http://www.osce.org/documents/odihr/1990/06/13992_en.pdf>.

6 Warsaw Guidelines to Assist National Minority Participation in the Electoral Process, adopted 1 January 2001, at <http://www.osce.org/documents/hcnm/2001/01/240_en.pdf>. In this context, see also David Hine, "Electoral Systems, Party Law and the Protection of Minorities", Council of Europe Document DH-MIN(2006)013, at <http://www.coe.int/T/E/human_rights/minorities/>.

proposal made by Professor Francesco Capotorti in the late 1970s.[7] They usually include some objective elements and one subjective element. The basic element is, of course, constituted by the distinctive features (e.g., history, language, religion, ethnicity, lifestyle) of the relevant minority group as compared with the majority population of a given state. Additional objective elements are the numerical inferiority of minorities (a notion that does not exclude a group that constitutes a numerical majority in a given region of a state from being able to rely on the protection offered by international law to national minorities due to their numerically inferior situation from a country-wide perspective; the German-speaking population here in the region of South Tyrol is a prime example thereof) and their non-dominant position. The necessary subjective element could be called the common will of the members of a group to preserve their distinctive characteristics, which is generally implicit in cooperative efforts to protect and promote their ethnic, linguistic or religious identity and their refusal to be assimilated by the majority. While these elements seem to be recognized, in principle, by all parties concerned, the current discussion mainly relates to the following two issues: does a group need to have resided for a certain minimum period of time in the territory in which its members live or, in other words, do they need to have a certain historic link to that territory? And do only those persons belong to a minority who have the citizenship of the state in which they live?

Regrettably, no clear answer can be given: the situation under domestic law seems to be quite varied, as is also reflected in the pertinent statements made by states parties to the FCNM, either upon ratification or in their state reports. The Advisory Committee consistently held that some of the provisions of the FCNM—such as Article 11(3) with its explicit reference to areas traditionally inhabited by persons belonging to a national minority—would obviously be applicable only to 'old' minorities. In contrast thereto, it is clear that Article 6 of the FCNM applies to "all persons living on the territory" of a given state party and, thus, also to persons belonging to 'new' minorities.[8] Furthermore, I find it possible to argue that other provisions, such as Articles 3, 5, 7, 8 and—for that matter—also 15 of the FCNM could also, at least in certain circumstances, be applicable to persons belonging to 'new' minorities. Based on this analysis, the Advisory Committee opted for a flexible approach that makes it possible to consider the inclusion of persons belonging to such groups in the application of the FCNM on an article-by-article basis. As a result, the Advisory Committee expressed its opinion that the competent state authorities should "consider the issue in consul-

7 Francesco Capotorti, "Study on the Rights of Persons belonging to Ethnic, Religious and Linguistic Minorities", UN Doc. E/CN.4/Sub.2/384/Rev. 1 (1979).

8 See, for example, first opinion on Austria, para. 35; second opinion on Denmark, para. 76; first opinion on Germany, paras. 137-140; second opinion on Germany, paras. 66-87; first opinion on Italy, para. 40; second opinion on Italy, para.78; first opinion on Norway, para. 36; second opinion on Norway, paras. 72-92; and first opinion on Sweden, para. 37.

tation with those concerned". It made it clear, however, that it strongly favours an inclusive approach.[9]

The HCNM has also consistently favoured such an inclusive approach; on the other hand, it must be seen that he was mainly concerned with situations in which the 'new' minorities had not come into existence as a result of inter-state migration but rather as a consequence of prior intra-state movements: I am referring to the situation subsequent to the restoration of the sovereignty of the Baltic states, the dissolution of the Soviet Union or the break-up of Yugoslavia. And, indeed, there might be good reasons to differentiate between persons who have come to a specific area as citizens of the state of which the area concerned was then a part and—even more so—who have been born there, on the one hand, or persons who have moved to another country as migrant workers and might never have expected close links with the state in which they—and their children and grandchildren—came to reside, on the other hand.

In the end, I think it is indeed preferable to opt for such an inclusive approach, which would make it possible, albeit on a right-by-right (or article-by-article) basis, to extend the personal applicability of minority rights also to persons belonging to such 'new' minorities. This conclusion applies, in my opinion, also as regards the right to political participation. However, I find it essential to stress that this does not mean that 'old' and 'new' minorities would have the same scope of rights; so, in the context of the right to effective political participation, I find it quite possible—and, indeed, imperative—to accord more extensive rights to persons belonging to 'old' minorities than to persons belonging to 'new' minorities. I shall come back to this issue when I discuss the next point of my lecture—namely, the question as to *how* effective political participation of minorities can be implemented.

IV. How Can the Effective Political Participation of Minorities be Implemented?

In line with the conclusion of the above discussion as to the personal scope of the right to effective political participation, in the following section I shall first deal with the issue of how this right can be implemented as concerns (persons belonging to) 'old' minorities and then discuss this issue as regards (persons belonging to) 'new' minorities.

Before I shall do so, it is necessary to define the scope of the term 'political participation' as it will be used in this lecture. The starting point will be Article 15 of the FCNM, as it is the only 'hard law' provision applicable to most European states. Obviously, the above-mentioned Lund Principles and Warsaw Guidelines will be taken into account as appropriate.

9 See, for example, first opinion on Azerbaijan, para. 20; first opinion on Croatia, para. 17; second opinion on Croatia, paras. 27-30; second opinion on the Czech Republic, paras. 25-29; first opinion on Estonia, para. 17; second opinion on Estonia, paras. 25-27; and first opinion on Sweden, para. 16.

At the outset, it must be stressed that the actual text of Article 15 of the FCNM provides only limited guidance as to the scope of the term 'political participation'; the situation improves considerably, however, if the Explanatory Report to the Framework Convention and, in particular, the quite extensive pertinent practice of the Advisory Committee are taken into account. On the basis thereof, I shall structure the following part of my lecture as follows: I shall begin by briefly addressing the issue of 'effective political participation and state construction'. Since all European states that are Council of Europe member states must be democracies and respect the rule of law (*Rechtsstaaten*), the representation of minorities in elected legislative bodies is of utmost importance. Therefore, in the second section of this part of my lecture, I shall discuss 'effective political participation and electoral representation'. Finally, it is important to keep in mind that electoral representation *per se* might not result in—or guarantee—effective participation in all situations: this applies, in particular, with respect to numerically smaller minorities, which, even under benevolent legal conditions, might simply be too small to achieve sizable electoral representation; for them—but not only for them—alternative means are needed and they will be dealt with under the heading of 'effective political participation and consultative mechanisms'.

A. Effective Political Participation and State Construction

As you know, scholars in general and legal scholars in particular are often considered—rightly or wrongly—to seek to adapt realities to their structural approaches to problems or, in other words, to bend reality in such a way that it fits their own preconceptions. On the other hand, a certain amount of systematization might indeed contribute to clarify issues. So, in an 'ideal' world, minorities would either live in a territorially compact settlement or be dispersed throughout the whole territory of the state concerned. Obviously, such factual conditions do impact on how state construction will benefit the effective political participation of minorities.

From a comparative constitutional law point of view, Europe offers a very wide variety of state constructions: we find everything from very centralized states with no regional structures whatsoever (or where administrative districts still resemble the traditional French *département* as established under Napoleon) and limited local government powers, to centralized states with limited regional structures (sometimes construed as entities of territorial autonomy for certain minorities) and possibly far-reaching local government powers, to truly regional states (including states with asymmetrical power structures) with differing local government powers, to semi- and fully federal states with, again, differing local government powers.

Now, how can the different forms of state construction be used best in order to achieve effective political participation? At the outset, I must stress that Article 15 of the FCNM is silent on this issue—i.e., it does not favour any specific kind of state construction. This is also reflected in the pertinent practice of the Advisory Committee, which has, however, underlined in a number of opinions the importance of territorial autonomy for preserving and promoting the distinct identity of minorities;[10] it held, therefore, that territorial changes to the administrative structures of a country that might have detrimental effects on the situation of minorities must be avoided.[11]

Obviously, both the factual conditions of minority settlement and the traditions of state construction must be taken into account when assessing the potential of different models of state structures for improving the political participation of minorities. From a systematic point of view, there are, in principle, two options available, the appropriateness of which depends, to a large extent, on such factual conditions of minority settlement and such traditions of state construction: while Joseph Marko uses the terms "cultural autonomy" and "territorial autonomy",[12] Marc Weller differentiates between "functional layering of public authority" and "territorial layering of public authority".[13] Notwithstanding some—I would say minor—differences, they both refer to quite similar concepts as you will see right now.

1. Cultural Autonomy or Functional Layering of Public Authority

Generally speaking, the concepts of cultural autonomy or functional layering of public authority may be usefully applied in situations where a minority does not constitute the majority or a sizable minority of the population in a given region of a state but finds itself dispersed throughout the whole territory of a state.[14] In such a situation, some states (e.g., Hungary) have opted for the introduction of a system endowing institutions established under public law with the power to regulate—or at least to have a most significant say in the regulation of—'cultural affairs', including, in particular, the running of public education institutions, such as *Kindergärten* and schools, or the management of their own cultural institutions or media, such as publicly funded radio and TV broadcasting programmes. The important aspect here is the fact that minorities exercise, in the fields concerned, some kind of *self-government*—usually through representative bodies, the members of which are elected by and from members of the minority concerned. In this context, I should like to stress that the success of such models seems to depend, on the one hand, on the degree to which such bodies truly represent the minorities concerned and, on the other hand, on the availability of sufficient financial means and the power to decide how to spend such monies. It should be mentioned, however, that models of such 'functional autonomy' might also be successfully implemented within the framework of systems of territorial autonomy—

10 See, for example, first opinion on Denmark, para. 36; first opinion on Finland, para. 47; first opinion on Italy, paras. 61-62; first opinion on Moldova, para. 91; first opinion on Serbia and Montenegro, paras. 111-112; first opinion on Spain, para. 75; and first opinion on Switzerland, para. 74.

11 See, for example, second opinion on Denmark, paras. 158-168.

12 Marko, *op.cit.* note 4, 4.

13 Weller, *op.cit.* note 3, 435 *et seq.*

14 For the following, see *ibid.*, 439.

as an example, one might mention the case of the Danish-language schools in Schleswig-Holstein, Germany.

2. Territorial Autonomy or Territorial Layering of Public Authority

In contrast thereto, the concepts of territorial autonomy or territorial layering of public authority may be usefully applied in situations where a minority constitutes the majority or a sizeable minority of the population in a given region of a state.[15] Depending on the constitutional traditions and/or the present political situation, states have opted for the establishment of different kinds of territorial autonomy, ranging from a truly federal system to regional structures or a system in which certain territories in which groups of persons that do not constitute a state-wide majority but a majority in that region—which might be relatively small and in some instances only comprising a few municipalities—are given the power to regulate and run regional or local affairs. From a substantive point of view, such regional or local affairs will include, as a rule, cultural affairs, education, language policies and media, but might also comprise economic and social matters.

Again, experience seems to show that the actual success of such models depends, to quite a considerable extent, on the existence of mechanisms that guarantee both genuine representation of all groups concerned (including, in particular, 'minorities in a minority') in the regional or local authorities and sufficient financial autonomy, which, in my opinion, should include competences to raise public incomes by means of taxation and to spend such incomes on the basis of a budget approved by such regional or local authorities. I find it important to note that these preconditions seem to be fulfilled in the cases of the Åland Islands, the Eastern cantons of Belgium and South Tyrol; on the other hand, the—what I consider—persistent and persisting failure of the system of territorial autonomy established in Bosnia and Herzegovina as a result of the Dayton Agreements shows that all such systems do only work if implemented in good faith and on the basis of the common resolve of all actors concerned to work together in a constructive way.

B. Effective Political Participation and Electoral Representation

In any democratic society, effective political participation depends, to a large extent, on the mechanisms available to ensure the adequate representation of minorities in elected legislative bodies.[16] Issues to be discussed under this heading include freedom of association and the right to vote and to stand as a candidate; electoral mechanisms, such as exemptions from threshold requirements in proportional representation systems or the drawing of boundaries in majority vote systems or reserved seats in the legislature; and proportional representation or ethnic quotas in the respective legislative bodies.

15 For the following, see *ibid.*, 435 *et seq.*

16 For the following, see *ibid.*, 440 *et seq.*; and Hine, *op.cit.* note 6, 4 *et seq.*

1. Freedom of Association and Electoral Rights

Freedom of association—in particular, the right to form political parties representing the interests of minorities in public life—is a *conditio sine qua non* to enable dialogue not only among individuals but also between groups of persons. It is, therefore, important to note that the Advisory Committee followed the same approach as the ECtHR in its judgments in the *United Communist Party*,[17] *Sidiropoulos*[18] and *Ilinden*[19] cases and held that the activities of political organizations aimed at the promotion of the distinct identity of minorities do not *per se* constitute a threat to national security and must, therefore, not be prohibited unless there are additional reasons, such as indications that such aims shall be achieved by non-democratic means.[20] Of particular relevance is the view that domestic legislation, as in the Russian Federation, prohibiting the formation of political parties of minorities raises most considerable problems as to its compatibility with Article 7, FCNM.[21] Moreover, the Advisory Committee criticized, in the case of Moldova and the Russian Federation,[22] regulations on the registration of political parties requiring a certain number of members in at least half of the territorial districts of the respective country as hampering, in particular, the opportunities of territorially concentrated minorities to be represented in public life.

As concerns electoral rights, it goes without saying that every citizen—irrespective of his or her ethnic affiliation—must be entitled to vote and to stand as a candidate. This means, in particular, that language proficiency requirements for electoral candidates must be carefully limited to situations where they are truly necessary to protect a specific public interest; in this context, I should like to mention the fact that Estonia abolished such requirements, which had been strongly criticized by the Advisory Committee.[23]

2. Electoral Mechanisms

At the outset,[24] it should be stressed that the Advisory Committee has been consistently of the opinion that equal voting rights and the integration of persons

---

17 ECtHR, Appl. No. 19392/92, *United Communist Party and Others v. Turkey*, judgment of 30 January 1998.

18 ECtHR, Appl. No. 26695/95, *Sidiropoulos and Others v. Greece*, judgment of 10 July 1998.

19 ECtHR, Appl. Nos. 29221/95 and 29225/95, *Stankov and the United Macedonian Organisation Ilinden v. Bulgaria*, judgment of 2 October 2001.

20 See, for example, first opinion on Azerbaijan, paras. 43-45; and first opinion on Moldova, para. 49.

21 See first opinion on the Russian Federation, paras. 68-70.

22 See first opinion on Moldova, para. 49; second opinion on Moldova, paras. 74-77; and first opinion on the Russian Federation, para. 105.

23 See first opinion on Estonia, paras. 55-60; and second opinion on Estonia, paras. 163-166.

24 For the following, see Marko, *op.cit.* note 4, 6.

belonging to national minorities in general party lists are not sufficient means to ensure effective participation in elected bodies. In many instances, it called upon states parties to consider the adoption of "special measures", without, however, recommending specific legal instruments. In any case, it might be concluded that a seat in elected bodies is seen as a necessary requirement for effective political participation. In my opinion, this means that there are good arguments to consider the mere existence of consultative mechanisms—which I shall discuss later—without representation in elected bodies as not sufficient for effective political participation.

Whenever national legal systems provide for such "special measures"—such as exemptions from threshold requirements, benign gerrymandering through the drawing of boundaries of electoral districts in favour of minorities, reserved seats or even quotas—the Advisory Committee welcomed, as a rule, such measures as a means to enhance effective participation. It must be stressed that such instruments and their implementation did not raise any concerns with respect to their compatibility with the principle of equality. In view of the present discussion in Bosnia and Herzegovina (and possibly elsewhere), it is important to note that the Advisory Committee recommended the introduction of such mechanisms on all territorial levels—and not only on the national level.[25] I should also like to stress that the Advisory Committee, while being reluctant to recommend the first-time introduction of such special measures,[26] was quite critical when states parties withdrew such measures.[27]

As concerns proportional representation or quota mechanisms in elected bodies, the Advisory Committee welcomed such instruments as a means to achieve effective participation but raised some concerns with regard to certain aspects of their implementation in view of Article 3, FCNM.[28] This provision guarantees to every person belonging to a national minority the right freely to choose to be treated or not to be treated as such and that no disadvantage shall result from such choice or the exercise of the rights connected with such choice. Therefore, the Advisory Committee criticized electoral rules in Bosnia and Herzegovina that oblige candidates to declare their ethnic affiliation in advance for reserved quotas[29] and the legal regime here in South Tyrol that requires a language affiliation declaration from everyone and recommended less restrictive measures to achieve

25 See first opinion on Bosnia and Herzegovina, para. 104.

26 But see, for example, first opinion on Slovenia, paras. 69-75; and second opinion on Slovenia, paras. 165-174 (welcoming the level of participation accorded to the Italian and Hungarian minorities in the former but calling for increased efforts to improve the actual participation of Roma in the latter).

27 See, for example, first opinion on Lithuania, para. 75; and first opinion on Ukraine, paras. 69-70.

28 See, for example, first opinion on Bosnia and Herzegovina, para. 104; and first opinion on UNMIK-administered Kosovo, paras. 110-113.

29 See first opinion on Bosnia and Herzegovina, para. 105.

minority representation.[30] I am aware of the sensitivity of this issue and do understand that such measures might indeed contribute to improving or even securing effective participation; I am also convinced that such rigid regulations might, under certain historical circumstances, even be necessary. I am, however, equally convinced that all such rigid measures should be held under constant review as to whether they are still necessary to achieve the legitimate aim for which they were introduced and, if this is no longer the case, they should be repealed.

C. Effective Political Participation and Consultative Mechanisms

Marc Weller has convincingly shown[31] that there are two forms of truly consultative mechanisms, namely 'mechanisms of co-decision' and 'mechanisms of consultation *stricto sensu*', whereas 'mechanisms of coordination', such as inter-ministerial working groups or expert bodies that call on representatives of minorities to comment upon legislative proposals or policy issues relevant for minorities, do not constitute genuine consultative mechanisms. I shall, therefore, focus on the two former mechanisms.

Before doing so, I shall, however, briefly touch upon one issue that is relevant for both types of mechanisms and that has been frequently addressed by the Advisory Committee:[32] the composition of the bodies involved in such consultative mechanisms, insofar the Advisory Committee has stressed that at least 50% of the members of such bodies must be selected by the minorities themselves, whereas the remaining 50% may be appointed by the state authorities. Moreover, the Advisory Committee has stressed that governmental authorities, when appointing persons as members of such bodies, must ensure democratic pluralism by not favouring one or some minority organization(s) and must seek to ensure that also numerically smaller minorities will not be left outside the consultation process.[33]

1. Mechanisms of Co-decision

Co-decision[34] occurs where minority consultative councils must be heard before decisions can be taken or where such bodies have original decision-making powers. Co-decision in the former sense will take place mostly where such consultative councils are attached to national or regional parliaments; usually, they will have the right to review draft legislation of special interest to them and to offer their views. Where such legislation cannot be adopted without such views having been obtained and considered, one may speak of a soft form of co-decision. In some instances, however, minority members of parliament or even minority consultative bodies will have some kind of blocking power (veto rights) as concerns the

30 See first opinion on Italy, paras. 18-21.

31 Weller, *op.cit.* note 3, 6 *et seq.*

32 Marko, *op.cit.* note 4, 7.

33 See, for example, first opinion on Austria, para. 69.

34 Weller, *op.cit.* note 3, 6.

adoption of sensitive legislation specifically affecting their genuine interests. This constitutes a hard form of co-decision.

It is obvious that such blocking powers (veto rights), as foreseen, for example, in Bosnia and Herzegovina, Slovenia and UNMIK-administered Kosovo, raise considerable concern from a democratic perspective, since they might result in a situation where a parliamentary minority (or even a consultative body) might dominate the political majority. So, in ethnically divided societies, ethnic quota mechanisms combined with such veto powers might block the entire political process and turn, to quote Joseph Marko, "democracy into ethnocracy".[35] In this context, I should only like to remind you of the judgment rendered in 2000 by the Constitutional Court of Bosnia and Herzegovina, where it ruled that ethnic quotas in combination with absolute veto powers were incompatible with the Constitution.[36]

2. Mechanisms of Consultation *Stricto Sensu*

There are several ways of organizing mechanisms of consultation, both at the level of central or regional/local government.[37] First, there are consultative bodies principally composed and organized by minority representative organizations. They will usually serve to articulate minority interests and present them to government or parliament and will mainly be self-organizing. While sometimes established by legislation, minority representative groups themselves usually arrange for membership, working methods and activities.

The second model consists of a minority consultative council attached to a high-ranking governmental official, or a government contact office for minority issues. This kind of consultative mechanism gives minorities access to government at a high level.

The third type of minority consultative council would be led by governmental representatives and comprise both representatives of government and minority representative organizations. Depending on the role of such bodies in the process of decision-making, they might be considered as genuine consultative bodies or rather as mechanisms of coordination.

While it is, of course, impossible to give a general assessment as to the effectiveness of these three forms of consultative mechanisms, it seems that the first type would best ensure effective participation of minorities provided that all minorities are represented in an adequate manner and that such bodies are thoroughly integrated in the decision-making process.

---

35 Marko, *op.cit.* note 4, 8.

36 Constitutional Court of Bosnia and Herzegovina, Case No. U-5/98, *Re Alija Izetbegović, Chair of Presidency of Bosnia and Herzegovina*, partial decision of 1 July 2000 (cited in first opinion on Bosnia and Herzegovina, para. 28).

37 Weller, *op.cit.* note 3, 6.

D. Effective Political Participation and 'New' Minorities

Before I conclude, I should like to very briefly touch upon the issue of effective political participation of 'new' minorities. In light of recent developments in many states with a sizable immigrant population, I find it convincing to argue that an improved social integration of persons belonging to such groups might be achieved by means of a more effective political participation. Obviously, one has to distinguish between those immigrants who have acquired the citizenship of their country of residence and those who have not.

As concerns the former group, it is clear that they have the same political rights, starting with the right to vote and to stand as a candidate, as any other citizen of the state concerned. This means that they would also have the right to form political parties with a focus on improving the situation of such immigrants—I should like to raise some doubts, however, whether such an action would indeed contribute to the improved integration of these persons into the society of their country of residence and citizenship.

The main question to be raised is, of course, whether persons belonging to such 'new' minorities are equally interested in maintaining their distinct identity, as is expected from members of 'old' minorities. If that is the case, then I think the most appropriate way to achieve this goal, as regards effective political participation, would be by means of consultative mechanisms. In particular, in the field of educational affairs, organizations representing such 'new' minorities could provide important input into efforts directed towards the goal of improving integration by means of improving education.

As concerns the latter group—i.e., persons who have not acquired the citizenship of their country of residence and are, therefore, from a legal point of view to be treated as aliens—the situation is, of course, fundamentally different: if they are citizens of EU member states and have migrated to EU member states, they have at least the right to vote and to stand as a candidate in local elections. If not, they do not have this right. Moreover, aliens do not have the right to vote (or stand as a candidate) in regional or state-wide elections and, in many countries, they face considerable limitations as regards their exercise of political rights. In my opinion, it would be worthwhile to consider the question of whether the extension of the right to vote and to stand as a candidate to all non-citizens, subject to certain conditions, would result in the improved integration of such persons into the societies of their country of residence.

Apart from that, it seems to me that the most viable option would consist in the setting-up of specific consultative councils, starting from the bottom (local level) to pass through the regional level and to end at the central state level, the members of which would be elected from among resident foreigners and who might constitute an appropriate body to make the voices of these groups of persons heard. Obviously, such consultations should take place in the context of legislative work on aliens' legislation, educational affairs and other matters of particular relevance to such groups.

V. Concluding Remarks

In order to allow for as much time as possible for the ensuing discussion, I shall refrain from attempting to come up with any conclusion. I should like to stress, however, a few points that, although they do constitute truisms, are of particular relevance for our topic tonight.

First, I am deeply convinced that all minorities, be they 'old' or 'new', need to feel that the state in which they live also 'belongs to them'—obviously in varying degrees, but in principle this feeling of ownership must prevail over any feeling of exclusion. If not, there will be no integration and, most obviously, without integration there will be no social and political stability. I do not think that, in front of this audience, I have to stress that integration does not mean assimilation—by no means!

Second, I am equally deeply convinced that effective political participation is one of the most powerful and important tools to achieve—or contribute to the achievement of—this goal of social integration. Such effective political participation presupposes the implementation of the fundamental principle of equality and should encompass measures of electoral representation and consultation.

Third, and I think this is—notwithstanding that I am preaching the obvious—most important, that every society should find its own specific way to deal successfully with the challenge of integrating minorities without assimilating them. This way will depend on a number of factors, such as history, constitutional and other legal and political traditions, the numerical strength of minorities, their way of settlement, their traditions, historical experiences and present expectations. Therefore, it is obviously impossible to simply export systems that have proved to be effective solutions to the problems of majority–minority relations in one country to other countries—one might learn from them, but not more. This is also the reason why the drafters of the Framework Convention rightly chose to draft a *Framework* Convention,[38] which, on the basis of some common and shared values, translated into legal norms, allows for a variety of specific solutions adapted to the specific needs of a specific situation.

And it is in this sense that I should like to invite you to join us in our common goal to seek and find solutions adapted to a specific situation and compatible with the fundamental values that are shared by all of us.

38 On this specific character of the Framework Convention, see Rainer Hofmann, "The Framework Convention for the Protection of National Minorities: An Introduction", in Weller, *op.cit.* note 3, 1-24, at 5.

*Sia Spiliopoulou Åkermark**

Shifts in the Multiple Justifications of Minority Protection

I. Why Speak Again of the Justifications of Minority Protection? Justificatory Chains and the 'Deep Structure of Law'

In social sciences in general and in the science of law in particular, it is almost impossible to describe the causal paths that resulted in the adoption of a particular piece of legislation, and even more difficult to discern shifts in perceptions of a legal system or of a society. The usual methodological approach of social scientists is therefore to look at the multiplicity of factors and variables affecting a social phenomenon and to try to create an explanatory model for such phenomena. Indeed, in law in particular it is crucial to be able to account for the justifications underpinning a piece of legislation or a legal reasoning in a court decision. The formal legality of a legal product is linked to its substantive legitimacy as well as to its sociopolitical embeddedness. Formal legality relies upon the processes of adoption of a court decision or a piece of legislation, whereas substantive legitimacy is concerned with the accordance and coherence between the different rules of a legal system and their respect for the core principles and values of that system.

Finally, the sociopolitical embeddedness of a legal act is concerned with the understanding and acceptance of that rule or legal product by core groups affected by it (as objects or as implementers) and by the broader society as a whole. So each time a legal rule or set of rules is questioned, or even attacked rhetorically or empirically (through non-observance), the need to reformulate, reexplain and reassess the justification behind the rule(s) is triggered. We are confronted with "the obstinacy of the legitimacy issue".[1] Such obstinacy seems particularly acute with regard to minority protection in international law because there are a number of states, even within the limited geographic boundaries of Europe, that completely refuse to accept minority-related obligations, while the argument is frequently made that minority-protection regimes are concerned with and are adapted only

* Jur. Dr., Associate Professor, Director, The Åland Islands Peace Institute.

1 Kaarlo Tuori, *Critical Legal Positivism* (Ashgate, Helsinki, 2002), 243.

Minority Governance in and beyond Europe, ISBN 978-90-04-27648-2. pp. 119-134.

to the continent of Europe. Meanwhile, social scientists from different disciplines and theoretical strands continue to analyze minority rights and their institutional regimes from their various preferred angles, whether that may be security, multiculturalism, individual human dignity or democratic participation.

If we continue to use Kaarlo Tuori's writings and his understanding of a 'deep structure of law' and of the discursiveness of legal practices, then understanding and being able to account for this 'deep structure of law' is necessary to establish the normative as well as the empirical legitimacy of law.[2] In a similar vein, Thomas Franck has argued that the legitimacy of international law relies upon the *coherence*, *validation* and *determinacy* of international decisions and rules.[3] For Tuori, legitimacy is twofold: it is formal and it is substantive (or normative). For the latter, Tuori requires justification in "the light of the morally- and ethically-laden principles of the law's subsurface layers".[4]

Joseph Raz argues that "lawyers commonly conceive of the law as made of sets of nested rules linked by justificatory chains".[5] On the basis of this it has been argued that international law, as a structure of authority, forms such a justificatory hierarchy and that new rules are developed through old rules existing in treaties, customs, general principles, etc. This is not simply a question of the hierarchical relation of rules and of formal legislative procedures but, equally, of the goals aspired to by the adoption of the rules.[6] The importance in Raz's formulation lies, however, in his use of the plural form when writing of "nested rules linked by justificatory chains". Thus, one rule, or one set of rules, does not necessarily rely simply on a single clear-cut justificatory chain. At times, the justificatory chains may converge and reinforce each other, but at other times they might diverge, creating the internal dynamics of the legal process.

In this article, many elements of the argument will be well known and have been analyzed previously by various authors. The effort here is to draw together these different lines of argument and thinking about minority protection and to demonstrate ways in which they coexist and interact. Instead of simply trying to respond to questions like, "Why is minority protection neglected?" with pragmatic answers such as, "Because states do not want to limit their sovereignty" or "Because minority situations vary greatly and do not render themselves suitable to international regulation", it might be more useful to reflect upon the basis and the basics of minority protection. Why is minority protection part of international law, and why is it still controversial? It is so because even though many states have ratified many of the international instruments protecting minorities and indigenous peoples, there is no doubt that minority questions are still perceived in many

2 *Ibid.*, 244-281.

3 Thomas Franck, *The Power of Legitimacy* (Oxford University Press, New York, 1990).

4 Tuori, *op.cit.* note 1, 276.

5 Joseph Raz, "Legal Rights", 4 *Oxford Journal of Legal Studies* (1984), 1-21, at 4.

6 Athanasia Spiliopoulou Åkermark, *Justifications of Minority Protection in International Law* (Kluwer Law International, The Hague, 1997), 55.

states as highly explosive, non-legitimate and therefore not a part of what could be called 'the hard core' of international law. But why?

For the reasons given above, it is argued that it is crucial to be able to formulate, discuss and regularly reevaluate the basic understandings or justifications that make a rule or a legal system legitimate. Although at first sight the above discussion may appear overly theoretical, it does of course have immense importance for the understanding and, thus, the interpretation and implementation of the law. The tools used and the answers given to concrete legal questions will differ greatly depending upon the justificatory chain dominating minority thinking at a given moment. For instance, if individual human dignity is at the centre of attention then we may expect firm non-discrimination and equality-oriented measures and legislation with strong elements of legal avenues of redress and supervision. If, on the other hand, peace and security is the dominating core thinking, we can expect the prevalence of political negotiation tools and presumably group-oriented solutions addressing concrete 'security threats'. These two examples are of course simplified descriptions of reality—caricatures perhaps—but are based on real experiences even if they do not reflect future solutions in a deterministic manner.

A. The Main Justificatory Grounds of Minority Protection

It is argued hereby that the justifications for minority protection over time can be arranged into four main categories:

- peace and security
- human dignity
- protection of culture(s) and cultural diversity
- democratic participation and democratic pluralism

These justificatory blocks have evolved over time but are not isolated from each other. Although one can observe a chronological line of evolution in which the sequencing of human dignity versus culture is not easy to establish, these four lines of thinking and arguing about minority rights influence and complement each other. They are simultaneously polemic and mutually reinforcing.

B. Minority Protection as the Precondition of Peace and Security

Minority protection in its current form in international law—i.e., as international commitments made by states—has been justified in the above-mentioned ways (peace, human dignity, culture and democracy). Chronologically, the first line of justification was that of preserving 'peace and security'. Not only was this justificatory ground found in the historical background of the Treaty of Westphalia (1648), which tried to establish a religious, political and military balance in Europe, but it was also distinctly apparent in the post–World War I setting. This setting consisted of the two following main elements:

The first is that minority provisions were introduced in peace treaties. Minority protection provisions never became part of a generalized system within the Covenant of the League, but were limited to those states in which minority issues were considered an important element of the effort towards enduring peace. These minority-protection provisions took three different forms: as special minority treaties negotiated and concluded within the framework of the Paris Peace Conference; as provisions in chapters concerning minority provisions incorporated in wider peace treaties; and as unilateral declarations of states before the League of Nations, often as part of the admission process to the League of Nations and confirmed unilaterally by the Council of the League of Nations.[7]

The second is that minority protection was institutionally internationalized through the role of the League of Nations in the implementation of minority treaties. For instance, Article 12 of the Polish Treaty placed it "under the guarantee of the League of Nations", something which was taken to incorporate an external as well as in international element.[8] Whereas the internal element concerned the placement of the treaty within the hierarchy of the relevant domestic legal system, the external element meant that the provisions of the treaties could be modified only with the approval of the majority of the Council of the League of Nations and that the Council and the Permanent Court of International Justice (PCIJ) were the organs, respectively, of a political and a judicial nature that controlled implementation of the treaty. The League Council appointed committees to examine minority petitions, and most of the work of the League of Nations in minority issues was in fact done within these committees as opposed to the alternative, the PCIJ.

The system created after World War I was a system extending guarantees primarily at the *interstate level*, even though minorities themselves were given the right to alert the Council of the League of Nations without such action giving rise to any corresponding obligation of the Council to actually take up the question. As US President Wilson had explained, "nothing [...] is more likely to disturb the peace of the world than the treatment which might, in certain circumstances, be meted out to the minorities".[9]

Moreover, at that time, there was often a clear and explicit link drawn between a particular territory or territories and the minority protection envisaged, as illustrated by the letter of the President of the Paris Peace Conference

7 Pablo de Azcárate, *League of Nations and National Minorities: An Experiment* (Carnegie Endowment for International Peace, Washington, DC, 1945). de Azcárate was for several years the director of the minorities section of the Secretariat of the League of Nations.

8 Patrick Thornberry, *International Law and the Rights of Minorities* (Oxford University Press, Oxford, 1991), 44.

9 As cited in Jacob Robinson *et al.*, *Were the Minorities Treaties a Failure?* (New York : Institute of Jewish Affairs of the American Jewish Congress and the World Jewish Congress, 1943), 21.

Clemenceau to Polish Prime Minister Paderewski presenting the Treaty to be signed by Poland:

> The territories now being transferred both to Poland and to other States inevitably include a large population speaking languages and belonging to races differently from that of the people with whom they will be incorporated. Unfortunately, the races have been estranged by the long years of bitter hostility.[10]

According to this understanding, minority protection regimes were *interstate obligations* pertaining to the circumstances in *specific territories* within the concerned state, concerning *specific groups* and being *internationally monitored* to secure peace and security. Political tools were given preference over legal tools, and the regime was essentially built upon the idea of interstate reciprocity, evidenced also by the nature of several of the minority treaties, which were constructed as agreements between the allied powers and a number of different states.[11]

Although other justificatory grounds entered the discourse of minority rights after World War II, the above characteristics never completely abandoned the field of minority protection. There are two main reasons for this. First, bilateral treaties have remained an important tool of minority protection, thereby retaining the requirement of reciprocity as an element of minority protection.[12] Although the bilateral and reciprocal conceptualization of minority protection is particularly striking in Central and Eastern Europe, it is not exclusive to the region. Shortly after the end of World War II, the South Tyrol dispute resulted in the so-called Paris Agreement of 1946 between Italy and Austria. However, it was followed by several steps and controversies, and the dispute between the two countries was not fully resolved until the UN declaration in 1992.[13] During the same period, the question of the minorities on either side of the Danish–German border was resolved in a similar bilateral manner through the Bonn–Copenhagen Declarations of 1955 guaranteeing similar rights for the Germans in the south

10 The text of the letter is reproduced in Harold William Temperley (ed.), *A History of the Peace Conference of Paris*, Vol. V (Frowde and Hodder & Stoughton, London, 1921), 432 (letter dated 24 June 1919—i.e., four days before the Treaty with Poland was signed).

11 Special minority treaties were signed as part of the outcome of the Paris Peace Conference between the Allied and Associated Powers and Poland; the Kingdom of Serbs, Croats and Slovenes; Czechoslovakia; Romania; and Greece (in chronological order). See Spiliopoulou Åkermark, *op.cit.* note 6, 105.

12 Kinga Gál, *Bilateral Agreements in Central and Eastern Europe: A New Inter-State Framework for Minority Protection?*, ECMI Working Paper No. 4, May 1999; Emma Lantschner and Roberta Medda, "Protection of National Minorities through Bilateral Agreements in South-Eastern Europe", paper presented at the 8th Meeting of Government Offices for National Minorities, 21-22 May 2001, Strasbourg, France.

13 Jens Woelk, Francesco Palermo and Joseph Marko (eds.), *Tolerance Through Law—Self Governance and Group Rights in South Tyrol* (Brill, Leiden, 2008).

of Denmark and the Danish minority in the north of Germany. *Bilateralism* and *reciprocity* form part of the peace and security justification and logic of minority protection but have, of course, been modified and have evolved under the influence of another of the justificatory grounds of minority protection, that of human dignity. So, for instance, in recent times new issues have been raised in discussions about bilateral treaties, such as the participation of minorities themselves in the management of bilateral regimes.[14]

Secondly, the institutional response of the OSCE in Europe (at that time, still the Conference on Security and Co-operation in Europe) in the aftermath of the collapse of the Soviet Union, tensions in the Baltic states and the war in the former Yugoslavia was to establish the High Commissioner on National Minorities (HCNM), a post which became effective as of January 1993. The participating states stressed at the outset that the HCNM was not envisaged as an ombudsman for minorities. It was seen as a tool of preventive, silent diplomacy, requiring involvement as early as possible before a minority problem has turned into violent armed conflict. The working methods of the HCNM require close interaction with the chairman-in-office of the OSCE, and the outcome of HCNM involvement may take the form of non-binding recommendations to the parties or on thematic issues.

Since 1996, the HCNM has issued several thematic recommendations. In this sense, there is no doubt that the HCNM has indeed acted as a *normative intermediary* by spreading existing binding norms (derived from other international legal documents outside the OSCE, which may, formally, not be binding for specific concerned states or actors), but also in evolving and explaining such norms through the interpretative tool of thematic recommendations.[15] Whereas the first of these all concerned various types of minority rights, such as linguistic rights in education or the media and participatory rights in public life and electoral processes, the two most recent recommendations are closer to the peace and security logic of minority protection.[16]

In 2006, the HCNM issued the *Recommendations on Policing in Multi-Ethnic Societies*, and in June 2008 the Office of the High Commissioner launched *The Bolzano/Bozen Recommendations on National Minorities in Inter-State Relations*

14 See for example Lantschner and Medda, *op.cit.* note 12.

15 The idea of the HCNM as a 'normative intermediary' has been introduced by Steven Ratner, "Does International Law Matter in Preventing Ethnic Conflict?", 32 *New York University Journal of International Law and Politics* (2000), 591-698.

16 The Hague Recommendations regarding the Education Rights of National Minorities (1996); the Oslo Recommendations regarding the Linguistic Rights of National Minorities (1998); the Lund Recommendations on the Effective Participation of National Minorities in Public Life (1999); and the Guidelines on the Use of Minority Languages in the Broadcast Media (2003), which can be found at <http://www.osce.org/hcnm>.

together with an explanatory note.[17] The final section of the Recommendations on Policing, which follows sections based on human rights principles of fair and multiethnic recruitment, representation of minorities and non-discrimination, is entitled "Prevention and Management of Conflict" and outlines the potential role of the police in situations of interethnic tensions and as a mediator. In the 2008 Recommendations on Inter-State Relations, the peace and security theme can be traced even more clearly. The main goal of the document was to tackle the problem of so-called 'kin-state support'. The recommendations encourage states "to co-operate across international frontiers within the framework of friendly bilateral and multilateral relations and on a territorial rather than an ethnic basis" (para. 16). Again, minority protection is perceived primarily as an issue of interstate relations rather than as a system of entitlements on the basis of universal values and the equality of all human beings.[18] Furthermore, this shift can be seen as evidence of the fact that the use of bilateral, interstate and primarily political tools beyond the requirements and quasi-judicial monitoring of human rights law has never been outdated and is still seen by some states and by some experts as a better model of minority protection.

The problem with the requirement of paragraph 16 of the Recommendations on Inter-State Relations is, of course, the background of the League of Nations outlined above. The idea of minority protection in the League of Nations was premised on the assumption of an overlap of a dominant ethnicity—or rather race—in a specific territory. A second more general problem of the re-securitization of minority protection, as evidenced, *inter alia*, in the renewed interest in bilateral models, methods of policing and efforts to regulate kin-state support, is the fact that they are seen to reflect and support what has been called the 'multiculturalism of fear'.[19] This gives scholars of international relations the opportunity to continue discussing the preconditions for de-securitization of minority rights.[20]

17 The document can be found at <http://www.osce.org/publications/hcnm/2008/10/33388_1189_en.pdf>.

18 Of course, all along, Article 18 of the Framework Convention on National Minorities has consistently encouraged bilateral agreements, in particular between neighbouring states.

19 Jacob T. Levy, *The Multiculturalism of Fear* (Oxford University Press, New York, 2000).

20 For an example, see Paul Roe, "Securitization of Minority Rights: Conditions of Desecuritization", 35(3) *Security Dialogue* (2004), 279-294; comments by Matti Jutila, "Desecuritizing Minority Rights: Against Determinism" 37(2) *Security Dialogue* (2006), 167-185, and the response of Roe in "Reconstructing Identities or Managing Minorities? Desecuritizing Minority Rights: A Response to Jutila", 37(3) *Security Dialogue* (2006), 425-438.

However, as argued recently, by this understanding international law effectively values minority protection, not for reasons of universal value, but because it mitigates dangers of violence, cruelty and political humiliation.[21]

C. Minority Protection as a Part of Human Rights

Today, the omnipresent rhetoric of peace and security is balanced by reference to the justification of individual human dignity. To say that minority protection is at present part of international human rights law may be perceived as a truism. In all documents concerning minority protection that have been adopted in recent years there is an obligatory reference to minority protection being understood as an integral part of human rights. As an example, one might mention the Framework Convention on National Minorities, which in its very first operative paragraph clarifies that

> The protection of national minorities and of the rights and freedoms of persons belonging to those minorities forms an integral part of the international protection of human rights, and as such falls within the scope of international co-operation.

The function of such a pronouncement is firstly to ensure the (re-)internationalization and the de-bilateralization of the issue of minority protection. Minority protection is, according to this understanding, not solely an issue of bilateral relations and the relations between minorities and their possible kin-states. Minority protection is a legitimate concern of all states in the Council of Europe (in this particular case) and a legitimate concern of all states that engage in the implementation of international human rights norms—that is, more or less all the states around the world. In this way, the distinction between, on the one hand, states that subscribe to and abide by minority-specific obligations and, on the other hand, states that reject such obligations is blurred by the existence of other human rights obligations of relevance and importance for minorities. Almost all states subscribe, at least on paper, to the obligation not to discriminate against members of minorities and to respect general human rights rules.[22]

However, the scope of this obligation of non-discrimination is still quite controversial, and there is extensive debate on the relationship between equality and the special measures needed to protect minority cultures. This is so both

21 Patrick Macklem, "Minority Rights in International Law", University of Toronto, Legal Studies Research Series No. 8-19, July 2008.

22 For a critical assessment of some of these questions, see Asbjørn Eide, "Towards a Pan-European Instrument?", in Annelies Verstichel, André *Alen*, Bruno *De Witte* and Paul *Lemmens* (eds.), *The Framework Convention for the Protection of National Minorities: A Useful Pan-European Instrument* (Intersentia, Antwerp, 2008), 5-17.

in the field of law and in political theory.[23] Many theorists of multiculturalism would argue that because non-discrimination and libertarian egalitarianism have failed to address the concerns and needs of minorities, indigenous peoples and immigrants, leading to increased reliance on ethnic origin, language, culture or religion as the common space of continuity and comfort, efforts have been made to introduce some form of 'multiculturalism' in many societies.[24] One of these efforts involves introducing individually based minority rights such as all the international legal provisions and case law referring to "persons belonging to minorities".[25] It would be wrong to assume that elements of human rights did not exist prior to World War II. As Lauterpacht has argued, there was "occasional recognition of some fundamental human rights in treaties providing for religious freedom and the cultural and political rights of minorities".[26] So, in fact, the recognition of cultures and collective identities came prior to the affirmation of individual human rights.

Much of the current discussion on the relationship between human rights and multiculturalism theories touches upon the tension between defending the autonomy of individuals while simultaneously recognizing the importance of the

23 Within law, one line of thinking focuses on the synergies between general human rights law and the need for special measures for minorities. See, for example, Kristin Henrard, "The Added Value of the Framework Convention for the Protection of National Minorities (II). The Two Pillars of an Adequate System of Minority Protection Revisited", in *ibid.*, 91-117. A critical analysis argues that in most cases general human rights law has not been able to meet the specific conditions and circumstances of minority groups and of persons belonging to minorities. See, for example, Sia Spiliopoulou Åkermark, "The Limits of Pluralism—Recent Jurisprudence of the European Court of Human Rights with Regard to Minorities: Does the Prohibition of Discrimination Add Anything?", 3 *JEMIE* (2002), available at <http://www.ecmi.de>; and *id.*, "Att vilja göra rätt men ändå göra fel: Om domstolsgranskningen av romsk utbildning I Tjeckien", in Ulla Börestam, Satu Gröndahl and Boglárka Straszer (eds.), *Revitalisera mera! En artikelsamling om den språkliga mångfalden i Norden tillägnad Leena Huss*, Uppsala Multiethnic Papers 50 (Uppsala University, Uppsala, 2008), 169-178. For a review of many of the positions within political theory, see Paul Kelly (ed.), *Multiculturalism Reconsidered* (Polity Press, Oxford, 2002); and, in the field of language rights, Will Kymlicka and Alan Patten (eds.), *Language Rights and Political Theory* (Oxford University Press, Oxford, 2003).

24 See the discussions in the Review symposium on Brian Barry, "Culture and Equality: An Egalitarian Critique of Multiculturalism", 2(2) *Ethnicities* (2002), 261-287.

25 There is a vast literature on the subject of minority human rights. Among them one may mention Patrick Thornberry and Maria Amor Martin Estébanez, *Minority Rights in Europe: A Review of the Work and Standards of the Council of Europe* (Council of Europe, Strasbourg, 2004); Gaetano Pentassuglia, *Minorities in International Law: An Introductory Study* (Council of Europe, Strasbourg, 2002); and Marc Weller, *Universal Minority Rights: A Commentary on the Jurisprudence of International Courts and Treaty Bodies* (Oxford University Press, Oxford, 2008).

26 Hersch Lauterpacht, *International Law and Human Rights* (Frederick A. Praeger, New York, 1950), 33.

collective embeddedness of identity. This idea of a common humanity is also a core underpinning of the entire human rights project. It is not a coincidence that John Stuart Mill used the vocabulary of human rights in the context precisely of the abolition movement. Slaves are like us; slaves are "human beings, entitled to human rights".[27]

By contrast, multiculturalists start from the position of difference and, in most cases, assume that complete equality is by definition impossible.[28] The struggle between ideas of similitude and ideas of difference is, I would argue, the main reason why there is perceived tension between multiculturalism and human rights. The universalist similitude of human rights does not easily accept the fundamental otherness intrinsic to multiculturalism. Human rights universalism assumes, further, that there is a universal truth—that is, a common, albeit minimal—understanding of human dignity. Multiculturalism can be seen as an outcome of the post-Enlightenment rejection of a single truth. Its rise coincided historically with, and drew strength from, the anti-colonial movement. Once again, the fate of minority protection was tied to the fate of territories and interstate disputes over territories.

The concrete results of the struggle between similitude and difference can also be seen in the diverging responses given by states, as well as international human rights organizations, to the headscarf problem. Some European countries do not introduce any legal restrictions, whereas others introduce restrictions only in primary education; some countries only limit headscarves covering the entire face, and other states prohibit any kind of religiously tainted symbols.[29] The fact that so many different solutions are provided for what can be perceived as a rather simple human rights question—the right to dress as you please, providing you do not provocatively disturb or harm people around you—is problematic for a legal system of individual human rights that claims universal applicability. However, as McGoldrick has argued, the advantage of using individual human rights rules as a starting point for discussion is that they offer a platform for analysis and debate that would otherwise be perceived either as falling entirely within the private domain or as being completely within the sphere of competence of collective identities, including religious groups.[30] This brings us to the third justification for minority protection: culture.

27 As cited in Kwame Appiah, *The Ethics of Identity* (Princeton University Press, Princeton, 2005), 145.

28 Sia Spiliopoulou Åkermark, "Multiculturalism in Crisis?", in Eduardo Ruiz Vieytez and Robert Dunbar (eds.), *Human Rights and Diversity: New Challenges for Plural Societies* (University of Deusto, Bilbao, 2007), 35-50.

29 Dominic McGoldrick, *Human Rights and Religion. The Islamic Headscarf Debate in Europe* (Hart Publishers, Oxford, 2006).

30 *Ibid.*

D. Minority Protection as Affirmation and Promotion of Culture

That groups are recognized—or even constructed by and promoted through—the tools of minority protection, is beyond doubt. As we saw earlier, in the League of Nations era, minority protection was indeed group oriented and was intended as a tool to safeguard the needs and survival of 'populations' or 'races' that may have been at risk because of "long years of bitter hostility" (see the above-mentioned letter of Clemenceau to Paderewski). We have also seen that, even at this early stage in the evolution of minority protection, minority groups were intimately linked to particular territories. In addition, the assumption has always been that a person can only belong to one collective identity, at least as far as ethnicity, language and religion is concerned. This is still a feature of human rights provisions concerning persons belonging to minorities. For instance, the Framework Convention on National Minorities refers consistently to "the minority language" of persons belonging to minorities, thereby making the implicit assumption that each person belongs to one minority and has one—and only one—minority language that he or she wishes to use in all contexts and for all purposes. However, as beautifully elaborated by Amartya Sen:

> The illusion of unique identity is much more divisive than the universe of plural and diverse classifications that characterize the world in which we actually live. The descriptive weakness of choiceless singularity has the effect of momentously impoverishing the power and reach of our social and political reasoning. The illusion of destiny exacts a remarkably heavy price.[31]

Diminishing history and identity to a single tie to a specific territory neglects the extreme difficulties faced by groups and individuals that lack such links, such as the Roma in Europe or nomads living in Europe, Africa, the Arabian Peninsula and many other parts of the world.

What then is this minority culture that is to be preserved and protected? Article 5 of the Framework Convention for the Protection of National Minorities does not explicitly define what a minority is, but speaks of the 'essential elements' of the *identity* of minority members, "namely their religion, language, *tradition and cultural heritage*".[32] Of those elements, language has been granted a privileged position in law as marker of identity.[33] Perhaps this is to bypass the obvious risks of defining ethnicity and minority on the basis of blood-transmitted common ancestry, while not falling prey to the ambiguity of a reference to 'culture'. After all, although some of us could imagine a perfectly happy life without practicing

31 Amartya Sen, *Identity and Violence—The Illusion of Destiny* (W.W. Norton, New York, 2006), 17.

32 Emphasis added.

33 See, for instance, The European Charter for Regional or Minority Languages adopted within the Council of Europe (entered into force the same year as the Framework Convention for the Protection of National Minorities—i.e., in 1998).

any religion or claiming any particular ethnicity, we all need to use a language both in the private sphere as well as in public affairs.

Culture can be perceived as an evolving system of values, beliefs, attitudes and practices for "making sense of the world".[34] But it can also be perceived as a constant, homogenous and rigid set of such values and practices. The trickiest argument surrounding culture and identity is that relating to the (often) unbearable weight of history. As we saw above, there is a link in the logic of the Framework Convention on National Minorities—and, indeed, of most minority debates—between culture and tradition or heritage. However, minorities also have the right to evolve, as has in fact been argued by the UN Human Rights Committee (HRC), starting with its reasoning in the case of *Länsman et al. v. Finland*, in which it emphasized that Article 27 of the International Covenant on Civil and Political Rights does not only protect 'traditional' ways of livelihood of minorities.[35] In fact the very tension between individual human rights and the affirmation of group rights could only be resolved in a concrete situation and, in the long run, if both sides are prepared for at least some change and evolution. This does not mean that individual human rights should always adapt to requirements of cultural specificity, or *vice versa*. It means that the balancing between the two is a continuous debate in our societies and part of what we referred to earlier as "the deep structure of law".

But even so, the discussion of minority protection as protection of cultures and of cultural diversity gives rise to some of the really difficult questions. If we protect minorities primarily for cultural reasons, why then is the culture of old minorities more valuable and deserving of protection than the culture of recent—and perhaps more-vulnerable—immigrants? The argument of consent proposed by Will Kymlicka does not seem sufficient here, nor does it appear politically correct.[36] Often, migrants feel forced to move to another country for a variety of reasons, and many do not consent at all to the abandonment of their original identities. So why should they have lesser rights? Why do our liberal democracies, or at least most of them, readily accept the obligations of the FCNM but reject the obligations of the International Convention on the Protection of the Rights of All Migrant Workers and Members of Their Families (1990), which, *inter alia*, requires respect for their cultural identity (Art. 17(1))?

One possibility would be to argue that history matters. But if history matters, how does it matter? I believe that this is one point on which further thinking is required: are we proposing an argument for the special responsibility of states

---

34 As inspired by Ulf Hannerz, *Cultural Complexity, Studies in the Social Organization of Meaning* (Columbia University Press, New York, 1992).

35 Communication 511/1992, *Ilmari Länsman* et al. *v. Finland*, views adopted 26 October 1994, Report of the Human Rights Committee, Vol. II, GAOR, Fiftieth Session, Suppl. No. 40 (A/50/40).

36 Will Kymlicka, *Multicultural Citizenship: A Liberal Theory of Minority Rights* (Oxford University Press, Oxford, 1995); *id.*, *The Rights of Minority Cultures* (Oxford University Press, Oxford, 1995).

toward those that have lived within its boundaries for a long time? But most of our states have not existed for all that long! Are we proposing that there should be a compensatory element? This argument suggests that because states have suppressed minorities for many years they now need to make up for past injustices. Of course, there exists the risk that this compensatory spiral can reach far back into history and touch all kinds of groups claiming to be native and autochthonous.

We also need to be aware of the thorny issue of previous usage of the term 'culture'. In 19th-century writings, when the Western colonizing powers wished to describe themselves they used the term 'civilized nations', as we all know from the provision on the sources of international law in the Statute of the International Court of Justice and its predecessor the Permanent Court of International Justice.[37] By contrast, 'culture' or 'cultures' were the terms used to describe the colonized groups and territories, the savages: we, civilization; you, culture. So the term 'culture' can also be used in a way that emphasizes difference, and perhaps even inferiority.

In addition to the diverging connotations of individual human rights and protection of culture, there is also a difference with regard to the epistemic communities that support and develop them. Whereas culture is the domain primarily of anthropologists, ethnographers and linguists, the domain of human rights is largely dominated by lawyers and a few political scientists. Many in the first category, which we can call 'the culture people', are seen by some of the 'rights people' as advocating a museum-like agenda of protecting at any price all 'endangered cultural species', which are to be retained pure and unspoiled. This is in stark contrast to human rights thinking, which assumes the development of individual human personality in its social and dialectical relations with its environment, both at the level of interpersonal relations and collective dynamics.

E. Minority Protection as Democratic Participation

The most recent of the justificatory chains of minority protection is that of democratic participation. Through the writings of Jürgen Habermas, Charles Taylor, Iris Marion Young, James Tully, Will Kymlicka and many others, we see that the need to reconstruct the idea and the bonding links of citizenship in increasingly complex and multiethnic societies have become one of the dominant themes arguing in favour of minority protection. In law, this line of thinking is strongest among constitutional lawyers.[38] It has a lot in common with both the human rights arguments and those advocating the protection of culture. The themes of suppression and exclusion, either as discrimination, segregation or political subordination, appear in all three of these justificatory chains.[39] There are two dif-

37 Article 38 of the ICJ refers to "the general principles of law recognised by civilised nations" among the sources of international law.

38 Christina Johnsson, *Nation States and Minority Rights—A Constitutional Law Analysis* (Uppsala University, Uppsala, 2002).

39 Iris Marion Young, *Inclusion and Democracy* (Oxford University Press, Oxford, 2000).

ferent strands among proponents of democratic participation. On the one hand, there are those who argue primarily from the perspective of individual citizenship. All individual members of a society have to be given a fair chance to participate in political debates and decision making, to influence the outcome of elections and to stand for elections. By this logic, the goal of minority protection is thus the empowerment of persons belonging to minority groups so that they are or may become active citizens in the countries in which they live. The idea of the citizen is at the heart of such writings.[40] The other line of argument focuses on the political system and the process of decision making itself and emphasizes the need to ensure political pluralism and the representation of a wide range of views in societal debates. Whereas the first line of argument appears in various recent documents concerning participatory rights of persons belonging to minorities, the second line of thinking is perhaps most clearly represented in the jurisprudence of the European Court of Human Rights. Even when, for various reasons, the court has not found a violation in concrete cases, and even though in general the European Court of Human Rights cannot be considered a proactive proponent of minority rights, the Court has always discussed the issue of political participation of minorities under the banner of the primacy of political pluralism.[41]

The participatory justification of minority protection has seen a strong upsurge in recent times. It may be that the theme of participation is one of the dominant themes of international law and relations at present, with a strong presence in various sub-fields, such as the participation of non-governmental organizations in the workings of international organizations and in the discourse on participatory development processes. In the field of minority protection, the aforementioned Lund Recommendations on the Effective Participation of National Minorities in Public Life launched by the HCNM in 1999 have been recently followed up by a thematic commentary of the Advisory Committee of the FCNM on this topic—i.e., spelling out the requirements under Article 15 of the FCNM.[42] Article 15 of the FCNM requires the "effective participation of persons belonging to national minorities in cultural, social and economic life and in public affairs". Similarly,

40 See in this regard several of the works of Pierre Rosanvallon, such as *Le nouvel âge des inégalités* (Éditions du Seuil, Paris, 1996; with Jean-Paul Fitoussi); and *id.*, *Le peuple introuvable: histoire de la representation démocratique en France* (Gallimard, Paris, 1998).

41 This case law is analyzed in Sia Spiliopoulou Åkermark, "The Limits of Pluralism—Recent Jurisprudence of the European Court of Human Rights with Regard to Minorities: Does the Prohibition of Discrimination Add Anything?" 3 *JEMIE* (2002), available at <http://www.ecmi.de>.

42 ACFC, Commentary on the effective participation of persons belonging to national minorities in cultural, social and economic life and in public affairs, ACFC/31DOC(2008)001, adopted 27 February 2008.

in legal writings, the theme of participation in democratic decision making has moved to centre stage.[43]

Of course, there are many challenges that stem from this strand of thinking. I shall only mention two of them briefly. One such challenge is the ultimate vulnerability and powerlessness of many smaller minority groups lacking financial and other resources or the powerful support of a kin-state. At a very basic level, many minority groups cannot attend all the meetings necessary to ensure effective participation and cannot produce the documentary evidence needed or requested by the authorities prior to a decision-making process. Another such challenge is that limited participation may be used to legitimize curtailment of the other substantive rights of minorities. Extensive proceduralization may therefore run the risk of leading to renewed disempowerment, rather than to the empowerment of minorities and their members. In its interaction with the other justificatory grounds, democratic participation may fall into a number of traps and conflicts. Majority decisions may curtail the human rights of individuals, and majority decisions may lend support to one or a few minority groups and cultures. As with democracy and democratic participation in general, the effective participation of minorities requires not only the institutions (organizations, political parties, etc.) but a number of other preconditions, such as education, information and freedom of expression.

II. Conclusion

I have argued above that, today, minority protection rests upon four supporting pillars that serve as its justificatory chains. These are peace and security, individual human dignity (which includes equality), protection of cultures and democratic participation. The multiplicity of justificatory claims does not call into question the role and importance of minority protection. On the contrary, the fact that there are several justifications for minority protection indicates that minority protection remains a crucial part of international law. The latest of these grounds is democratic participation, which has become one of the dominant themes of current international law. The relative weight of the four justificatory grounds varies over time and space. Some observers, especially human rights lawyers, may be tempted to believe that the human rights perspective is the dominant one or the most important one, at least here and now. My argument has been that this may be so only in some parts of the world or only during a particular period of time in the development of international law. The interplay of the justificatory grounds is likely to continue for decades to come. The fact that minority protection is based

43 A number of reports and conference papers have been written by Marc Weller on this topic, but there are also several other studies, such as Yash Ghai, *Public Participation and Minorities* (Minority Rights Group, London, 2003); Annelies Verstichel, *Representation and Identity: The Right of Persons Belonging to Minorities to Effective Participation in Public Affairs: Content, Justification and Limits* (European University Institute, Florence, 2007).

upon such multiple, partially converging and occasionally divergent justificatory chains increases the need to reflect continuously upon the rationale behind minority protection measures and to take them into account during the interpretation and implementation of the relevant legal norms. Although some may argue that this is a Sisyphean task, I would argue that this is the very process that gives minority protection its constant relevance and its potential for renewal.

Roberta Medda-Windischer *

The European Convention on Human Rights and Language Rights: Is the Glass Half Empty or Half Full?

Language rights are an essential component of the right to identity, which represents in many ways the essence of the case for minorities within the corpus of human rights—the claim to distinctiveness and the contribution of a culture on its own terms to the cultural heritage of mankind. The identity to be protected and promoted may be composed of different factors: linguistic, ethnic, cultural, religious, or all of these altogether. The concept of identity is a broad and important concept for individuals and communities because it concerns their belonging; their way of thinking, feeling, and acting. Consequently, respect for and protection of identity, including the linguistic aspects therein, can be considered as constitutive elements of respect for human dignity.

The 1950 European Convention for the Protection of Human Rights and Fundamental Freedoms, known as the "European Convention on Human Rights" (ECHR, hereafter "the Convention")[1] neither guarantees specific language rights, at least as such, nor rights that are peculiar to minorities.[2] The only reference to minorities in the Convention is contained in Article 14 that guarantees the right

* Senior Researcher at the European Academy of Bolzano/Bozen, Institute for Minority Rights, LL.M (University of Essex), PhD (Law–University of Graz). From 1999 to 2000, she worked at the Registry of the European Court of Human Rights.

1 Convention for the Protection of Human Rights and Fundamental Freedoms, CETS No.177, adopted on 4 November 2000, entered into force on 1 April 2005.

2 In 1993, the Parliamentary Assembly of the Council of Europe recommended the addition to the Convention of a Protocol on the rights of minorities. Art. 8 of the draft protocol provides that each member of a national minority "shall have the right to learn his/her mother tongue at an appropriate number of schools and state educational and training establishments located in accordance with the geographic distribution of the minority". Commentary to the protocol made clear the right to learn the mother language did not automatically include a right that such language be the principal medium of instruction. PACE, Recommendation 1201 (1993) on an additional protocol on the rights of national minorities to the European Convention on Human Rights, 1 February 1993. See, among others, Mark W. Janis, Richard S.

Minority Governance in and beyond Europe, ISBN 978-90-04-27648-2. pp. 135-163.

not to be discriminated on the grounds, *inter alia,* of language and of belonging to a national minority, but only in the enjoyment of other Convention rights.[3] Accordingly, for any individual to challenge discriminatory treatment under Article 14 ECHR, they must first establish that it falls "within the ambit" of one of the other rights and freedoms guaranteed by the Convention. The Strasbourg Court has sought to alleviate this burden by accepting that there is no need for a finding of a violation of another right of the Convention; rather, merely requiring that the issue in question falls in the scope of another convention right.[4] The limited, accessory nature of Article 14 means that frequently the Court will not examine potential issues of discrimination, also on the ground of language, if it has already found a violation of a substantive right extended elsewhere in the Convention.

To counteract the 'parasitic' nature of Article 14, which left the Convention provisions short of recognizing an independent 'right to equality' or a right to non-discrimination applicable beyond the confines of the other enumerated rights in the Convention, in November 2000, the Council of Europe promulgated Protocol No. 12 to the Convention that, for the first time, provided a right to non-discrimination separate from the other substantive articles and including, like Article 14 ECHR, the grounds of language and of belonging to a national minority.[5]

Kay, Anthony W. Bradley, *European Human Rights Law: Text and Materials* (Oxford University Press, New York, Oxford, 3rd ed. 2008), 256.

3 According to Schokkenbroek (Head of the Human Rights Development Department–DG Human Rights and Legal Affairs, CoE): "The reasons why a more restrictive approach was followed in Article 14 do not appear clearly from the *travaux preparatoires* of the ECHR, but it has been suggested that, as a matter of international law, the principles of equality and of non-discrimination were still very much in their infancy at the time the ECHR was drafted and indeed for a considerable period of time thereafter. For example, it was certainly not self-evident at the time that any guarantee of equality and non-discrimination would extend to nonnationals. Neither was it clear then that not every difference of treatment amounted to a discrimination." Jeroen Schokkenbroek, "A New European Standard against Discrimination: Negotiating Protocol No. 12 to the ECHR", in Jan Niessen and Isabelle Chopin (eds.), *The Development of Legal Instruments to Combat Racism in a Diverse Europe* (Martinus Nijhoff, Leiden, Boston, 2004), 61-79, at 62-63.

4 See, among others, Pieter van Dijk and G. J. H. van Hoof, *Theory and Practice of the ECHR* (Kluwer Law International, The Hague, London, Boston, 3rd ed. 1998), 711-716; David J. Harris, Michael O'Boyle and Colin Warbrick, *Law of the ECHR* (Butterworths, London, 1995), 464-469.

5 Protocol No. 12 to the ECHR, CETS No.177, adopted on 4 November 2000, entered into force on 1 April 2005. The list of discrimination grounds included in Protocol 12 is identical to that in Art. 14. Art. 1(1) states: "The enjoyment of any right set forth by law shall be secured without discrimination on any ground such as sex, *race, colour, language, religion*, political or other opinion, national or social origin, *association with a national minority*, property, birth or other status" (emphasis added). As of 1 February 2010, 17 states had ratified Protocol No. 12, at <http://www.conventions.coe.int>.

Despite the formulations, apparently promising, contained in the Convention and its protocols, the Strasbourg organs[6] have consistently held that the Convention does not provide for any right of a linguistic minority as such, and that the protection of individual members of such a minority is limited to the right not to be discriminated against in the enjoyment of the Convention rights on the grounds of their belonging to the minority. This principle was formulated by the then European Commission on Human Rights (hereafter "the Commission") in the case *X. v. Austria*,[7] in which it was not found to be degrading treatment that the applicant, who belonged to the Slovene minority, although her mother tongue was German, could not express her allegiance to the minority in the specific context of a linguistic census. The applicant claimed that this census amounted to degrading treatment because it put her in a situation in which she had to choose between making a false declaration regarding her mother tongue or deny her allegiance to the Slovene minority. The Commission considered it as relevant that she was not otherwise prevented from stating that she considered herself as a member of the Slovene minority: "She only could not do this at the special mother-tongue census which was limited to finding out the language spoken by Austrian citizens."[8]

Despite the absence of a specific provision on minority rights, since their early activities, the Strasbourg organs have reviewed several cases concerning minority rights as well as language rights by referring to various provisions of the Convention. The best guidance on the interpretation of the meaning and implementation of language rights within the Convention's provisions is found in the case law of the Strasbourg Court that concern areas pertaining to the lives of minorities: from the use of minority languages in dealing with administrative or judicial authorities to the effective participation in public life; from education to printed media and radio and TV broadcasting; from the acquisition of citizenship to the use of personal names in the minority language according to minority traditions and linguistic systems.

I. Use of Minority Language(s) in Judicial Proceedings

Regarding the choice of language before judicial authorities, the European Convention on Human Rights contains several special provisions on the use of language in the context of judicial proceedings: the right to be informed in a language which one understands of the grounds of detention and of any criminal charge (Art. 5, para. 2 and, Art. 6, para. 3 (a)), and the right of everyone charged with a criminal offence to the free assistance of an interpreter if he or she cannot understand or speak the language used in court (Art. 6, para. 3 (e)). The principle

6 To ensure the observance of the Convention, the European Court of Human Rights was set up in 1959. On 1 November 1998, a full-time Court was established, replacing the two original enforcement institutions, the part-time Court and the European Commission of Human Rights.

7 ECommHR, *X v. Austria*, decision on the admissibility of 10 October 1978, D.R.18.

8 *Ibid.*, 92.

of fair hearing (Art. 6, para. 1) may make it a requirement that translations or interpreters are made available in civil cases too.[9]

The principle that the assistance of an interpreter has to be understood as 'free of charge' has been spelled out by the European Court of Human Rights (hereafter "the Court") in the case of *Luedicke, Belkacen and Koç v. Germany*,[10] in which the three applicants were charged before the German courts with the commission of various criminal offences and because they were not sufficiently familiar with the language of the country, they were assisted by an interpreter in accordance with German law. After conviction, they were ordered to pay the costs of the proceedings, including the interpretation costs. The Court clarified that the right protected by Article 6, paragraph 3 (e) entails, for anyone who cannot speak or understand the language used in court, the right to receive the *free* assistance of an interpreter, without subsequently having claimed back from him or her payment of the costs thereby incurred.[11]

The specific Convention's provisions concerning the use of language in the context of judicial proceedings, which at first sight might afford some protection to minorities, have proved in many cases to be not so relevant in practice. Those who have tried to read into Article 5, paragraph 2 and Article 6, paragraph 3 (a) and (e) a right to use one's *minority language* in court proceedings have been disillusioned by the Commission and the Court.

According to the established case law, the judicial authorities are not obliged to take steps to comply with requests for translations or the assistance of interpreters, as long as they are in a position to establish that the applicant has sufficient knowledge of the official language used in court. The assessment by the judicial authorities of the level of knowledge of the official language on the part of the applicant, on which the availability of free translations or the assistance of interpreters depend, has been the object of several cases before the Strasbourg organs and also before the UN bodies.[12]

---

9 ECommHR, *X. v. Austria*, Appl. No. 9099/80, D.R.27.

10 ECtHR, *Luedicke, Belkacen and Koç v. Germany*, Appl. Nos. 6210/73, 6877/75, 7132/75, judgment of 28 November 1978.

11 *Ibid.*, para. 46.

12 See, among others, UN Human Rights Committee, *Dominique Guesdon v. France*, Communication No. 219/1986, 25 July 1990, 1990–GAOR (A/45/40) (Part II), at 67-68. See also, ECJ, Bickel and Franz case (case C-274/96, Criminal Proceedings against Bickel (1998) ECR I-7637) for the extension of free translation in judicial proceedings, otherwise only provided to members of officially recognized minorities as to cover individuals not belonging to 'protected' groups but speaking the same language (the specific case referred to two German-speaking persons of Austrian and German citizenship being prosecuted in South Tyrol to have the criminal proceedings conducted in the German language on the same basis of the German-speaking officially recognized minority living in South Tyrol).

The *Kamasinski* case[13] illustrates the approach taken by the Court in this regard. In this case, the Court rejected the applicant's complaint that he had not been supplied with certain information relating to the charges against him in a language he understood. Although the applicant had not in fact received a written translation on the indictment, the Court inferred from the evidence, including the applicant's behaviour, that as a result of the oral explanations he had been sufficiently informed of the accusations against him. The Court held that the state's provision of a *defence counsel capable of communicating in both the language of the court and the language of the applicant* fulfilled the requirements of Article 6, paragraph 3 (a). Another example in this sense is the case of *K. v. France*,[14] in which the Commission held that a French court had lawfully denied the applicant the services of an interpreter to conduct his defence in the Breton language because the record showed that the applicant was *born* in France and had *no difficulty* understanding and speaking the French language in which the proceedings were conducted.

The Court followed the same line of reasoning in the case of *Lagerblom v. Sweden*,[15] in which the applicant, who settled in Sweden and whose mother tongue was Finnish, complained that he was not allowed to be defended by a counsel with whom he could have spoken Finnish and whose pleadings he would have fully understood. He also complained that he was able to communicate with the counsel appointed for him only via an interpreter. The applicant maintained that, belonging to a large Finnish minority in Sweden, the courts should have appointed a Finnish-speaking public defence counsel for him. At the outset, the Court stated that the right for an accused person who cannot understand or speak the language used in court to have the free assistance of an interpreter extends to all those documents or statements in the criminal proceedings which it is necessary for the accused to understand or to have rendered into the court's language to have *the benefit of a fair trial*.[16] As for the interpreting assistance provided in criminal proceedings, the Court noted that it should enable the accused to have knowledge of the case against him or her and to defend himself or herself, notably by being able to put before the court his or her version of the events.[17] The Court

13 ECtHR, *Kamasinski v. Austria*, judgment of 19 December 1989, Series A, No.168, at 35-38.

14 ECommHR, *K. v. France*, Appl. No. 10210/82, 7 December 1983, D.R. 35, at 207; see also ECommHR, *X and Y v. Belgium*, Appl. No. 2332/64, decision of 7 October 1966, concerning the use of the Flemish language in a civil court procedure; ECommHR, *Bideault v. France*, Appl. No. 11261/84, decision of 6 October 1986, D.R.48, at 235-236 concerning the refusal to criminal court to hear witnesses in the Breton language. These cases closely resemble the approach adopted by the UN Human Rights Committee in similar cases; see, *Dominique Guesdon v. France*, *op.cit.* note 12.

15 ECtHR, *Lagerblom v. Sweden*, Appl. No. 26891/95, decision on the admissibility of 15 February 2000.

16 *Ibid.*, para. 61.

17 *Ibid.*

accepted that, in this specific case, the applicant's knowledge of Swedish might have been somewhat limited despite his lengthy stay in Sweden. However, noting that the applicant described his proficiency as "street Swedish" and that he thus had a *certain command of the language*, the Court could not find that he was so handicapped that he could not communicate at all with his counsel or understand him. The Court further observed that interpreting between Finnish and Swedish was arranged at the national court's hearings and that the applicant made oral submissions in Finnish during those hearings. Furthermore, in accordance with the Nordic Language Convention, he was allowed to make written submissions in Finnish to the domestic courts which were translated and entered into the case file. In these circumstances, the Court considered that the interpretation assistance provided for the applicant was *adequate* and that the applicant was able to *participate effectively in his trial*. Consequently, the criminal proceedings, taken as a whole, could not be regarded as unfair and accordingly there was no breach of Articles 6 (1) and (3) of the Convention.

To understand the reasoning of the Court in cases relating to the free assistance of interpreters in judicial proceedings, it is worth referring to a case that although it does not refer to persons belonging to minorities, it sheds light on the arguments followed by the Court in these types of cases. In the case of *Brozjcek v. Italy*[18] the applicant, a German national, claimed that he had not been informed, "in a language which he understood", of the institution of criminal proceedings against him despite the fact that he had informed the Italian authorities that he had difficulty in understanding the contents of the communications for linguistic reasons. According to the Strasbourg Court, the Italian authorities did not take steps to verify that the applicant understood Italian, but *merely presumed* that he understood the substance of the judicial notification. For the Court, unless the Italian authorities were in a position to establish, beyond a mere presumption, that the applicant had *sufficient knowledge* of Italian to understand the charges brought against him, then the Italian judicial authorities should have taken steps to comply with the applicant's request regarding the use of his mother tongue. As no such evidence appeared from the documents in the file, the Court concluded that there had therefore been a violation of Article 6, paragraph 3 (a).

From the cases analyzed in this section, it is clear that for the Court 'belonging to a national, linguistic minority' is not *per se* an element entailing automatically the free assistance of an interpreter. In case of refusal by the national authorities to provide free translation in a judicial proceeding, the Court would apply a presumption of '(in)sufficient knowledge' of the official language(s) on the basis of 'hard' evidences of the case—origin or place of birth and residence. The burden of proof would then shift onto the government to whom it falls to show that the applicant has an *effective knowledge* of the language used in the proceedings.

An additional principle illustrated by the case law of the Strasbourg organs concerns the time in which documents and other material submitted by the appli-

18 ECtHR, *Brozjcek v. Italy*, Appl. No. 10964/84, judgment of 19 December 1989.

cants charged before judicial authorities must be translated: for the Court, this work cannot exceed the *'reasonable time'* requirement necessary to guarantee a fair trial according to Article 6, paragraph 1 unless convincing explanations for the delay are provided.[19] For the Commission, it is for the member states to organize their legal systems in a way that enables them to comply with the requirements of Article 6 paragraph 1, including that of trial within a reasonable time.[20]

II. Effective Participation in Public Life and Political Representation

In areas not covered by the special judicial provisions, the Convention organs have consistently held that no right to the use of a particular language is guaranteed by the Convention to citizens in their contacts with the authorities.[21] The right to use minority languages in relation with administrative authorities is perhaps the most challenging and controversial among the catalogue of minority rights because it raises the question of whether an official language must necessarily be favoured and used by state's apparatus and officials underlying the tension between the state's official language(s) and the minority language.[22]

In cases concerning political representation and linguistic minorities, the Strasbourg organs have also followed a rather restrictive approach. The following cases illustrate some principles articulated in their pronouncements by the Strasbourg bodies. In the case of *Fryske Nasjonale Partij and others v. the Netherlands*,[23] the Commission reiterated that *the Convention does not guarantee the right to use the language of one's choice in dealing with the authorities.* The applicants were a Frisian political party and two candidates to the provincial elections in

19 ECommHR, *Samo Pahor v. Italy*, Appl. No. 19927/92, report of 29 November 1995.

20 ECtHR, *Baggetta v. Italy*, judgment of 25 June 1987, Series A No. 119-B, at 32, para. 23.

21 See ECommHR, *Inhabitants of Leeuw-St-Pierre v. Belgium*, Appl. No. 2333/64, decision of 15 July 1965, Yearbook 8, at 338 for administrative proceedings in general. The Strasbourg Court has dealt with many cases concerning political participation and minority groups, such as *Sidiropoulos v. Greece* (1998), *Stankov and the United Macedonian Organisation Ilinden v. Bulgaria* (2001), *United Communist Party of Turkey and Others v. Turkey* (1998), *Socialist Party and Others v. Turkey* (1998), *Freedom and Democracy Party (ÖZDEP) v. Turkey* (1999), *Yazar, Karatas, Aksoy and the People's Labour Party (HEP) v. Turkey* (2002) and *Görzelik v. Poland* (2004). As the focus of the present article is limited to linguistic rights, those cases fall outside the ambit of this article as they do not refer specifically to questions related to linguistic rights. For an analysis of the Strasbourg case law, see EYMI, International Developments, ECHR, Vol. 1-8, 2001-2009.

22 Fernand De Varennes, "Article 10", in Marc Weller (ed.), *The Rights of Minorities. A Commentary on the European Framework for the Protection of National Minorities* (Oxford University Press, New York, Oxford, 2005).

23 ECommHR, *Fryske Nasjonale Partij and others v. the Netherlands*, Appl. No. 11100/84, decision of 12 December 1985, D.R. 45, at 240.

Frisland. They complained that their candidatures had been struck off the list because their names and addresses were not listed in Dutch. The Commission held that the applicants were not as such prevented from standing as candidates because nothing prevented them from submitting a translation of their request for registration into Dutch. The Commission held that the Convention does not guarantee the right to use a particular language for electoral purposes. The applicants had further complained that the refusal to allow them to use the Frisian language for administrative and political purposes constituted a violation of their right to freedom of expression. By declaring the application inadmissible, the Commission recalled that the Convention does not guarantee 'linguistic freedom' as such. In particular, it does not guarantee the right to use the language of one's choice in administrative matters.

In the case *Clerfayt, Legros and others v. Belgium,*[24] the Commission pointed out again that *no article of the Convention or its Protocols explicitly guarantees 'linguistic freedom' as such.* In particular, it was held that *the Convention does not guarantee elected representatives the right to use the language of their choice in statements and votes made in their capacity as members of public bodies.* In this case, the applicants were members of the municipal councils and public social assistance centres of six "peripheral municipalities" of Bruxelles. Following the 1970 reform, these municipalities were included in a Dutch-language region. Alongside a Dutch-speaking population, there were a large number of French-speaking residents. They had, thus, a special status providing for the use of the French language in the relations between the administration and the public and in the field of education. In 1983, the Council of State ruled that in and for the Dutch-language region, the official language was Dutch and that, except when required to deal with French-speaking members of the public, the administrators had to use Dutch. Consequently, at the meetings of municipal assemblies, the language of deliberation was Dutch and votes could be cast only in Dutch. By relying on Article 3 of Protocol No.1 (right to free elections), the applicants complained, *inter alia,* that any statement in French was not recorded in the minutes and any vote cast in French was devoid of legal effect. The Commission held that municipal councils and public social assistance centres, organs of local authorities with power to make rules and by-laws but not laws, do not form part of the 'legislature' within the meaning of Article 3 of Protocol No. 1 and, consequently, no question of discrimination could arise.[25]

24 ECommHR, *Clerfayt, Legros and others v. Belgium*, Appl. No. 10650/83, decision of 17 May 1985, D.R. 42, at 212.

25 In September 2008, the case of *Birk-Levy v. France* concerning the obligation to use the French language in the French Polynesian Assembly was communicated to the French Government. The applicant, an elected member of the French Polynesian Assembly, was challenging the French Conseil d'Etat's decision to render void a part of an internal rule of the assembly that allowed the possibility for members of the assembly to use the Tahitian language or one of the Polynesian languages. The case was communicated under Arts. 10, 11 and 14 of the Convention. At the time of writing, no decision on the admissibility had been adopted yet.

The leading case on the applicability of the Convention in relation to the political representation of minority groups is the case of *Mathieu-Mohin and Clerfayt v. Belgium.*[26] In this case, the Commission considered that non-representation of a minority constituted a breach of the Convention (Article 3 of Protocol No. 1),[27] but the Court did not confirm this view. The case concerned the elections to legislative bodies established according to linguistic criteria. The context in this case was particularly relevant: it concerned a regional body, the Flemish Council, that had legislative autonomy in regional and community matters and consisted of members of the Dutch-language groups in the Belgian House of Representatives and Senate. To belong to one of these groups, a Representative or Senator elected in Brussels had to have taken his or her parliamentary oath in Dutch. It followed that French-speaking voters in Brussels could elect to the Flemish Council only Dutch speakers, or French speakers who agreed to join the Dutch-language group. The two applicants in this case had been elected in Brussels and taken their oaths in French. They were, thus, not entitled to sit on the Flemish Council and claimed that this discrimination violated the Convention.

The Court considered that the legislation establishing the Flemish Council was part of the general institutional system of Belgium, which was based on the *territoriality principle* and covered the various administrative and political institutions and the distribution of their powers. It was a stage in a reform, which was not yet complete, designed to achieve an equilibrium between regions and communities through a pattern of checks and balances. The aim was to *defuse language disputes* in the country by establishing more stable and decentralized organizational structures. Holding that this aim was legitimate and widely supported, the Court pointed out that the obligation on linguistic minorities to vote for candidates able and willing to use the language of their region was found in several other states and need not threaten the minorities' interests, especially when, as here, there were safeguards against inopportune or arbitrary changes.[28]

Regarding the specific electoral model, the Court recalled that *the Convention does not create any obligation to introduce a specific electoral system* such as proportional representation or majority voting.[29] Considering that the legislation of the member states on the matter varies from place to place and time to time, they are allowed a wide margin of appreciation. The Court made the point that: "Electoral systems seek to fulfil objectives which are sometimes scarcely compatible with each other: on the one hand, to reflect fairly faithfully the opinions of the people, and on the other, to channel currents of thought so as to promote the emergence of a sufficiently clear and coherent political will".[30] The Court took into consideration the

26 ECtHR, *Mathieu-Mohin and Clerfayt v. Belgium*, Appl. No. 9267/81, judgment of 2 March 1987, Series A, No. 113.

27 ECommHR, *Mathieu-Mohin and Clerfayt v. Belgium*, Appl. No. 9267/81, report of 15 March 1985.

28 ECtHR, *Mathieu-Mohin and Clerfayt v. Belgium*, *op.cit.* note 26, para. 57.

29 *Ibid.*, para. 54.

30 *Ibid.*

particular cultural and constitutional context and noted that "any electoral system must be assessed in the light of the political evolution of the country concerned".[31] As a result, "features that would be unacceptable in the context of one system may accordingly be justified in the context of another".[32] It then held that the reference in Article 3 of Protocol No.1 to the free expression of opinion implies two things: freedom of expression, which is already protected by Article 10, and the principle of equality of treatment of all citizens in the exercise of their right to vote and their right to stand for election. The Court added, however, that the principle of equal treatment does not mean "that all votes must necessarily have equal weight as regards the outcome of the election or that all candidates must have equal chances of victory".[33] In the present case, the Court considered thus that French-speaking electors in the Brussels region enjoyed the right to vote and to stand for election on the *same legal footing* as the Dutch-speaking electors and thus no violation aroused. In a joint dissenting opinion, five members of the Court expressed their disagreement with this ruling.[34] In their view the pressure on electors to vote for Dutch-speaking candidates was so great as to deprive them of the free expression of their opinion in the choice of the legislature and the arguments relied on by the Court's majority were unpersuasive.

In this case, as in many other areas of the Convention, the states' margin of appreciation represents an important element in determining the legitimacy of a practice. The scope of the margin of appreciation is a difficult issue, especially when the justification for a certain practice must be sought in conditions peculiar to the respondent state. In this regard, the Strasbourg Court has taken the line that by reason of their direct and continuous contact with the vital forces of their countries, state authorities, including national courts, are in principle in a better position than the international judge to give an opinion on the exact content and necessity of these restrictions, leaving to the international courts the competence to provide general guidelines and a framework of reference.[35] The 'residual' role

31 *Ibid.*

32 *Ibid.*

33 *Ibid.*

34 *Ibid.*, Judges Cremona, Bindschedler-Robert, Bernhardt, Spielmann and Valticos.

35 See among others, ECtHR, *Golder v. the United Kingdom*, judgment of 21 February 1975, Series A, No. 18, 21 para. 45; ECtHR, *Silver and Others v. the United Kingdom*, judgment of 25 March 1983, Series A, No. 61, 38, para. 98; ECtHR, *Dudgeon v. the United Kingdom*, judgment of 22 October 1981, Series A, No. 45. The permissible restrictions, included in various Convention rights such as privacy, family life, conscience, expression, and association (Articles 8-11) are in addition to the 'protection of the rights and freedoms of others' and 'protection of public order', 'public safety', 'protection of health or morals', 'national security' and 'territorial integrity'. These restrictions can be invoked by a state as grounds to restrict the individual's exercise of a given right, but they also serve to protect the individual against arbitrary state restrictions of rights. Considering the breadth of the permissible restrictions, the Court has established a rule of 'strict interpretation' to ensure protection of the individual against possible abuses by the state. Therefore, the permissible restrictions can

of the Court is thus to review state actions against principles and limits set forth under the restriction invoked.[36]

Linguistic minority representation and electoral laws was also the subject of *Silvius Magnago and Südtiroler Volkspartei (SVP) v. Italy* case,[37] in which the applicants were a political leader and a political party from the autonomous Province of Bolzano/Bozen, where more than 70% of the inhabitants belong to the German-speaking and Ladin-speaking population. The applicants complained that, as representatives of a national minority, that is, the German-speaking majority in the region of Trentino-Alto Adige, they were prevented under the Italian electoral law from having a seat in the Chamber of Deputies in Rome, insofar as these seats were allocated by a system of proportional representation. They complained, in particular, of the 4% threshold of the votes cast on the national level required for the election of 25% of the members of the Chamber of Deputies to be elected under the system of proportional representation. The Commission considered that this system was intended to *promote the emergence of sufficiently representative currents of thought* and that this was a legitimate aim under the terms of Article 3 of Protocol No. 1. The Commission, recalling that the electoral law in issue applied to all candidates and that *the Convention does not compel the member states to provide for "positive discrimination" in favour of minorities*,[38] concluded that the present application did not disclose a violation of the Convention.

Regarding the right to stand for election, the Court has ruled more recently in the case *Podkolzina v. Latvia*,[39] concerning a Latvian national, a member of the Russian-speaking minority in Latvia, who complained that her candidature in the election to the Latvian Parliament was struck off the list because her language

---

only be applied for the purposes for which they have been prescribed and not beyond. Article 18 of the Convention reads: "The restrictions permitted under this Convention to the said rights and freedoms shall not be applied for any purpose other than those for which they have been prescribed". By establishing the principle of 'strict interpretation' of restrictions, the Court has helped to ensure that the individual's rights and freedoms in borderline cases will be favourably balanced against states' claims of overriding interests.

36 The Court clarified this point in *Klass and Others v. Germany*, ECtHR, judgment of 6 September 1978, Series A, No. 28, 23, para. 49: "It is certainly not for the Court to substitute for the assessment of the national authorities any other assessment of what might be the best policy in this field [...] Nevertheless [...] this does not mean that the Contracting Parties enjoy an unlimited discretion [...] the Contracting States may not [...] adopt whatever measures they deem appropriate".

37 ECommHR, *Silvius Magnago and Südtiroler Volkspartei (SVP) v. Italy*, Appl. No. 25035/94, decision on the admissibility of 15 April 1996.

38 *Ibid.*, 5.

39 ECtHR, *Podkolzina v. Latvia*, Appl. No. 46726/99, judgment of 9 April 2002. See on the same subject, UN, Human Rights Committee, Communication No. 884/1999, *Antonina Ignatane v. Latvia*, Views of 25 July 2001. Ms Ignatane did not submit a petition to the ECtHR because, at that time, Latvia had not yet ratified the Convention.

proficiency certificate attesting her knowledge of Latvian, the state's official language, was withdrawn following an examination conducted by the state Language Centre. The possession of a language certificate was at that time a precondition for registration on the list of candidates for persons who had not completed their studies in Latvian. In this case, the Court made the following statement:

> regard being had to the principle of respect for national characteristics [...] the Court is not required to adopt a position on the choice of a national parliament's working language. That decision, which is determined by historical and political considerations specific to each country, is in principle one which the State alone has the power to make. Accordingly, regard being had to the respondent State's margin of appreciation, the Court concludes that *requiring a candidate for election to the national parliament to have sufficient knowledge of the official language pursues a legitimate aim.*[40]

However, under the specific circumstances of the case, in particular the fact that the Latvian authorities decided to subject the applicant to a new language examination despite the fact that she had a valid, lawful certificate and that the procedure followed differed fundamentally from the normal procedure for certification of linguistic competence—in the second examination, the full responsibility for assessing the applicant's linguistic knowledge was left to a single civil servant, who had exorbitant power in the matter—the Court found a violation of Article 3 of Protocol No. 1 due to the *irregular procedure* followed by the national authorities during the language exam that was *incompatible with the requirements of procedural fairness and legal certainty* to be satisfied in relation to candidates' eligibility.[41]

The violation of the rights of a minority political party was denounced by the Court in its judgment *Ouranio Toxo and Others v. Greece*.[42] Ouranio Toxo is a lawfully established political party defending the interests of the Macedonian minority living in Greece. In September 1995, the party established its headquarters in Florina and affixed a sign with the party's name in the two languages spoken in the region, Greek and Macedonian, to the balcony of the premises. It included the word "*vino-zito*", written in the "Slav alphabet", which means "rainbow" in Macedonian but was also the rallying cry of forces who had sought to take the town of Florina during the civil war in Macedonia. With the aim of removing the sign, the local municipality called on the population to march "against the enemies of Greece". The police removed the sign but the applicants promptly replaced it. During the following night, the party's offices were attacked by a crowd that broke into the premises and assaulted those inside, demanding that they deliver up the sign, which the applicants did; equipment and furniture on the premises were then thrown out of the window and set on fire. The applicants called the police

40 *Ibid.*, para. 34. Emphasis added.

41 *Ibid.*, paras. 36-38.

42 ECtHR, *Case of Ouranio Toxo and others v. Greece*, Appl. No. 74989/01, judgment of 20 October 2005.

station repeatedly, but were told that no officers were available to assist them. The investigation into the events never led to the prosecution of the attackers.

On the specific aspect of the case concerning the sign in the minority language—Macedonian—the government justified the removal of the sign by the negative historical connotation of the word *vino-zito* written on the sign in Macedonian. In the government's view, reference to this term in itself was capable of provoking feelings of discord among the inhabitants of Florina.[43] By finding a violation of Article 11 (freedom of association) of the Convention, the Court stated:

> Affixing a sign to the front of its headquarters with the party's name written in Macedonian cannot be regarded as reprehensible or considered to constitute in itself a present and imminent threat to public order. The Court accepts that the use of the term *vino-zito* certainly aroused hostile sentiment among the local population. Its ambiguous connotations were liable to offend the political or patriotic views of the majority of the population of Florina. However, the risk of causing tension within the community by using political terms in public does not suffice, by itself, to justify interference with freedom of association.[44]

III. Education 'in' and 'of' Minority Language(s)

A powerful means to achieve the protection of minorities' language rights is the education of children belonging to the group. In the Strasbourg system, the right to education was one of the most controversial rights when the Convention was drafted, in particular as far as the parents' right to influence the education of their children is concerned. The right to education is included in a separate protocol to the Convention—Protocol No. 1[45]—whose Article 2 is composed of three main elements. First, the state shall not deny anyone the right to education, thus, the state may not interfere with a person's exercise of the right to education, for

43 *Ibid.*, para. 39.

44 *Ibid.*, para. 41. For an analogous case concerning the use of an Albanian flag in the Former Yugoslav Republic of Macedonia, see *Rufi Osman and Others v. FYROM*, Appl. No. 50841/99, decision on the admissibility of 11 October 2001. In this case, the Court did not consider as disproportionate the conviction of the applicant to one year and three months spent in prison for having organized a meeting with the citizens of Albanian ethnic origin calling on them to protect the flag of the Republic of Albania at the cost of their lives, for having executed, as a mayor, in breach of a Constitutional Court's order, the decision of the municipal council to put the flag of the Republic of Albania in front of the Town Hall, and for having subsequently being actively involved in planning and setting up crises headquarters and armed shifts for the protection of the flag of the Republic of Albania.

45 Art. 2 of Protocol No. 1 to the ECHR reads: "No person shall be denied the right to education. In the exercise of any function which it assumes in relation to education and to teaching, the State shall respect the right of parents to ensure such education and teaching in conformity with their own religions and philosophical convictions".

instance by preventing him or her from availing himself or herself of the educational opportunities provided by the state. Second, it gives total discretion to the state to determine the nature and scope of its involvement with education and teaching; in general, this means that the state is under no obligation to provide certain kinds of educational opportunities or to guarantee that every individual receives the education he or she desires. Third, it guarantees the rights of parents to have their convictions and beliefs respected in relation to their children's education.

In their early activities, the Strasbourg organs have reviewed the interpretation of this article in a leading case concerning language rights and education: the case "*Relating to Certain Aspects of the Laws on the Use of Languages in Education in Belgium*" (the Belgian Linguistics case).[46] In this case, the applicants were a group of French-speaking parents whose children were denied access to the French-language schools in some predominantly Dutch-speaking suburbs of Brussels on the grounds that the French-speaking families did not live in those districts. The Dutch-language schools in the same districts, however, were open to anyone irrespective of his or her place of residence. In finding a violation of Article 2 of Protocol No. 1 in conjunction with Article 14, the Court articulated a number of principles.

At the outset, the Court held that, as a general principle, the primary obligation of the member states is to ensure that persons under their jurisdiction can avail themselves, in principle, of the means of instruction existing at a given time and obtain official recognition of the studies which they have completed.[47] The Court also noted that the Convention does not specify *the language* in which education must be conducted in order that the right to education should be respected. However, it added: "*the right to education would be meaningless if it did not imply in favour of its beneficiaries, the right to be educated in the national language or in one of the national languages, as the case may be*".[48] The Court then stressed that Article 2 of Protocol No. 1 *does not require of states that they should, in the sphere of education or teaching, respect parents' linguistic preferences.*[49] The preparatory work of Protocol No. 1 confirms that the object of the second sentence of Article 2 was in no way to secure respect by the state of a right for parents to have education conducted in a language other than that of the country in question; indeed in June 1951 the Committee of Experts which had the task of drafting the Protocol set aside a proposal put forward in this sense. Several members of the Committee believed that it concerned an aspect of the problem of ethnic minorities and that it consequently fell outside the scope of the Convention.[50] The Court also noted that:

---

46 ECtHR, *Case Relating to Certain Aspects of the Laws on the Use of Languages in Education in Belgium* (Merits), judgment of 23 July 1968, Series A, No. 6.

47 *Ibid.*, 31, para. 4.

48 *Ibid.*, 30, para. 3.

49 *Ibid.*, 33-34, para. 11.

50 See, Doc. CM (51) 33 final, at 3.

> persons subject to the jurisdiction of a Contracting State cannot draw from the Convention the right to obtain from the public authorities the creation of a particular kind of educational establishment; *nevertheless, a State which had set up such an establishment could not, in laying down entrance requirements, take discriminatory measures within the meaning of Article 14.*[51]

By applying the above principle to the specific circumstances of the *Belgian linguistics* case, the Court established discrimination in respect of the linguistically mixed region of Belgium in which there was *a clear and disproportionate disadvantage for children of one linguistic group* finding thus a violation of the right to education taken together with Article 14 (non-discrimination clause). However, it recognized as *legitimate* the purpose of the contested legislation to achieve *linguistic unity* in the regions of Belgium in which the large majority of the population speaks only one of the national languages (i.e., unilingual regions).[52]

In addition to the principles established by the Strasbourg organs in the *Belgian linguistic case*, a number of other findings on education can be found in a series of cases concerning private schooling that are also relevant for the education 'in' and 'of' minority languages. The Strasbourg institutions have held that the primary obligation on education devolving on a member state is applicable both to state and private teaching.[53] However, if states must allow private schools and can regulate their establishment to ensure in particular the quality of the education,[54] there is no state's obligation to subsidize private educational establishments.[55] Yet, when providing subsidies, the state may not discriminate between types of schools

51 ECtHR, *Case Relating to Certain Aspects of the Laws on the Use of Languages in Education in Belgium* (Merits), judgment of 23 July 1968, Series A, No. 6, at 32, para. 9. Emphasis added.

52 On the right to education in the minority language and the requirement of the place of residence see, ECtHR, *Fatmir Skender v. FYROM*, Appl. No. 62059/00, decision on the admissibility of 10 March 2005, in which the applicant complained under Art. 14 of the Convention in conjunction with Art. 2 of Protocol No. 1 (right to education) about the impossibility of sending his daughter to school in another district where education in the Turkish language was provided (there being no such schools in his own district). The application was eventually rejected due to lack of 'victim' requirement and (non)exhaustion of domestic remedies.

53 See, ECtHR, *Kjeldsen, Busk Madsen and Pedersen v. Denmark*, judgment of 7 December 1976, Series A, No. 23, at 25-26, para. 52.

54 ECommHR, *Jordebo Foundation of Christian Schools v. Sweden*, Appl. No. 11533/85, decision of 6 March 1987, D.R.51, at 125.

55 *Ibid.*, ECommHR, Appl. No. 6853/74 *v. Sweden*, decision of 9 March 1977, D.R. 9, at 27; ECommHR, Appl. No. 10476/74 *v. Sweden*, decision of 11 December 1985, D.R. 45, at 143. Likewise, there is no obligation for the state to create or subsidize schools which are in conformity with particular religious or philosophical convictions as derived from the second sentence of Art. 2 of Protocol No. 1; ECommHR, Appl. No. 9461/81 *v. the United Kingdom*, decision of 7 December 1982, D.R. 31, at 210.

as clarified by the Commission in a case concerning nondenominational private schools in Northern Ireland.[56]

As is clearly stated in the *Belgian Linguistic Case*, under the Convention there is no *right to mother-tongue education*. However, in the recent case of *Cyprus v. Turkey*[57] the Court made an interesting pronouncement concerning secondary educational facilities for children of Greek Cypriots living in northern Cyprus.[58] At the outset, it has to be noted that these educational facilities were formerly available to children of Greek Cypriots and were then abolished by the Turkish-Cypriot authorities. The legitimate wish of Greek Cypriots living in northern Cyprus to have their children educated in accordance with their cultural and ethnic tradition, and in particular through the medium of the Greek language, could no longer be met. In this situation, children of Greek-Cypriot parents in northern Cyprus wishing to pursue a secondary education through the medium of the Greek language were obliged to transfer to schools in the south. Taking into consideration the fact that the Convention does not specify the language in which education must be conducted for the right to education to be respected, the Court first noted that, in the strict sense, there was no denial of the right to education because it was open to children, on reaching the age of 12, to continue their education at a Turkish or English-language school in the north. However, the Court considered the option available to Greek-Cypriot parents to continue their children's education in the north as *unrealistic* in view of the fact that the children in question had already received their primary education in a Greek-Cypriot school there.[59] The authorities had to be aware that it was the wish of Greek-Cypriot parents that the schooling of their children be completed through the medium of the Greek language. The Court held:

> Having assumed responsibility for the provision of Greek-language primary schooling, the failure of the "TRNC" ("*Turkish Republic of Northern Cyprus*") authorities to make continuing provision for it at the secondary-school level must be considered in effect to be a denial of the substance of the right at issue. It could not be maintained that the provision of secondary education in the south in keeping with the linguistic tradition of the enclaved Greek Cypriots suffices to fulfil the obligation laid down in Article 2 of Protocol No. 1, having regard to the impact of that option on family life.[60]

The Court concluded that there had been a violation of Article 2 of Protocol No. 1 in respect of Greek Cypriots living in northern Cyprus in so far as no appropriate

56 ECommHR, Appl. No. 7782/77 *v. the United Kingdom*, decision of 2 May 1978, D.R. 14, at 179.

57 ECtHR, *Cyprus v, Turkey,* Appl. No. 25781/94, judgment of 10 May 2001.

58 *Ibid.*, paras. 275-280.

59 *Ibid.*, para. 278.

60 *Ibid.* Emphasis added.

secondary-school facilities were available to them. Although the specific circumstances of the case were particularly relevant in deciding on this application, the pronouncement is rather promising as it might be transposed to other situations in which minority groups are denied education in their mother tongue that they had formerly enjoyed.

Despite the fact that the *D. H. and Others v. the Czech Republic* case,[61] concerning the assignment of Romani pupils to the so-called 'special schools' for the (mildly) mentally disabled regardless of their actual intellectual abilities did not center around the typology of test used to place Romany children to substandard schools, the issue of the test, as not specifically designed for minorities, has been raised and widely discussed in the final Grand Chamber's decision. One of the main problems arising from the *D.H.* case was in fact that whatever the merits of separate education for children with genuine mental disabilities, the decision to place Roma children in special schools was in the majority of cases not based on any actual mental disability but rather on *language and cultural differences* which were not taken into account in the testing process.[62] In the *D.H.* case, the tests used to place the Roma children in the 'special schools' were the same for all children who were examined, irrespective of their ethnic origin. Even the Czech authorities acknowledged in 1999 that Romany children placed in special schools displayed an average or above-average intellect and were placed in those schools solely on the basis of the results of psychological tests that were conceived for

61 ECtHR, *D.H. and Others v. the Czech Republic*, Appl. No. 57325/00, judgment (Grand Chamber) of 13 November 2007. Along the same lines, see, ECtHR, *Sampanis and Others v. Greece*, Appl. No. 32526/05, judgment (Chamber - First Section) of 5 June 2008, adopted unanimously by the Strasbourg Court seven months after the Grand Chamber's ruling in the *D.H.* case. The *Sampanis* case concerned a number of Romani children who, due to enrolment difficulties, missed a full year of primary school education and, subsequently, were placed in preparatory classes in a separate building attended only by Roma and located five kilometres from the primary school main premises. For more details on these cases see, Roberta Medda-Windischer, "Dismantling Segregating Education and the European Court of Human Rights: D.H. and Others vs. Czech Republic. Towards an Inclusive Education?", 7 *EYMI* (2009).

62 See, ECHR, D.H. (Grand Chamber) sc. *Ibid.*, "Third Party Intervention by Minority Rights Group International, the European Network against Racism and the European Roma Information Office", para. 167. The recent UN Recommendations on Minorities and the Right to Education affirm: "State or local policies of educational segregation through special classes or special schools for minority pupils, including policies leading to overrepresentation of minority pupils in such, are strongly discouraged and in no case should minority pupils be assigned to special classes or schools simply on the basis of their ethnicity". See, UN Human Rights Council, *Recommendations on Minorities and the Right to Education*, UN Forum on Minority Issues, Geneva, 15-16 December 2008, A/HRC/FMI/2008/2, 11 December 2008, para. 21, at <http://www2.ohchr.org/english/bodies/hrcouncil/minority/forum.htm>.

the majority population without *taking Roma specifics into consideration*.[63] In this regard, the Court noted that various independent bodies, such as the FCNM Advisory Committee,[64] the ECRI and the CoE Commissioner for Human Rights have expressed doubts over the adequacy of the tests.[65] The Court concluded that, at the least, there was a danger that the tests were biased and that the results were not analyzed in the light of the particularities and special characteristics of the Roma children who sat them.[66]

A further relevant reasoning that can be inferred from the Court's decision in the *D.H.* case is that the right to education means not only the individual's obligation to attend school and the state's duty to provide schooling, but also the duty to *reasonably accommodate specific Romani needs in public education*.[67] This deductive conclusion, however, has not been fully elaborated in the *D.H.* judgment and it is hoped that the Strasbourg Court will have the opportunity in the near future to take a more explicit stance in this regard and to clarify whether and under which circumstances the Convention requires a duty of reasonable accommodation or affirmative action in cases of minority education.[68]

The line of reasoning followed by the Court in the *D.H.* case against racial segregation in education was confirmed in the Grand Chamber's judgment *Oršuš and Others v. Croatia*, in which the Court, reversing a negative unanimous judg-

63 ECtHR, *D.H.*(Grand Chamber), *ibid.*, para. 200.

64 In its opinion on the Czech Republic, adopted on 6 April 2001, the FCNM Advisory Committee noted that although the special schools were designed for mentally handicapped children, many Roma children who were not mentally handicapped were placed in these schools due to real or perceived language and cultural differences between Roma and the majority. Advisory Committee on the FCNM, *Opinion on the Czech Republic*, 6 April 2001, ACFC/INF/OP/I(2002)002, para. 61, at 12.

65 ECtHR, *D.H.*(Grand Chamber), *op.cit.* note 61, para. 200.

66 *Ibid.*, para. 201.

67 Lilla Farkas, "The Scene After Battle: What is the Victory in *D.H.* Worth and Where to Go From Here?", 1 *Journal of the European Roma Rights Centre, Issue on "Roma Education: The Promise of* D.H.*"* (2008), 51-65, at 62.

68 De Schutter distinguishes between 'reasonable accommodation' and 'special measures' for minorities. Reasonable accommodation consists of an obligation to identify solutions which, in the specific context in which the individual faces certain obstacles in his or her social or professional integration may remove these obstacles to facilitate that integration. Reasonable accommodation, therefore, is seen in principle as possessing an individualized character, whereas 'special measures' are conceived in a broader perspective of equality as a means to achieve more structural solutions. Olivier De Schutter and Annelies Verstichel, "The Role of the Union in Integrating the Roma: Present and Possible Future", *European Diversity and Autonomy Papers* (2005) No.2, at 20. See also, Lisa Waddington and Aart Hendriks, "The Expanding Concept of Employment Discrimination in Europe: From Direct and Indirect Discrimination to Reasonable Accommodation Discrimination", 18(3) *International Journal of Comparative Labour Law and Industrial Relations* (2002), 403-427, at 410.

ment by the Chamber in 2008,[69] decided by nine votes to eight that Croatia's segregating schooling of Roma children breached the Convention's antidiscrimination provision (Art. 14) in conjunction with the right to education (Art. 2 of Protocol No. 1).[70] The *Oršuš* case concerned the assignment of Romani pupils to segregated Roma-only classes in what are otherwise mainstream primary schools in various Croatian villages.[71] The applicants contended that the placement was made on the basis of ethnic criteria, whereas for the government, the applicants had been placed in separate classes simply on account of their 'inadequate command' of the Croatian language. Because it was not contested that at their enrolment in primary school, the pupils concerned lacked the required level of language proficiency, the central question of the case was whether *adequate steps* were taken by the school authorities to ensure the applicants' speedy progress in acquiring an adequate command of Croatian and, once this was achieved, their immediate integration in mixed classes.[72]

The relevance of the *Oršuš* case is that, in comparison to the *D.H.* case, the segregation of Romani children into separate classes materialized in the *ordinary schools* and not in separated *special schools*: a circumstance that is quite common in European countries, at least in practice if not in official, blatant policies.[73]

On the practice of separate classes, the Court clearly stated that "temporary placement of children in a separate class on the grounds that they lack an adequate command of the language is not, as such, automatically contrary to Article 14 of

69 ECtHR, *Oršuš and Others v. Croatia*, Appl. No.15766/03, judgment (Chamber – First Section) of 17 July 2008.

70 ECtHR, *Oršuš and Others v. Croatia*, Appl. No.15766/03, judgment (Grand Chamber) of 16 March 2010. In their Joint Partly Dissenting Opinion annexed to the judgment, the dissenting judges emphasized, among others, the margin of appreciation for the state, the responsibilities of the parents and the interests of the non-Roma children. More generally, the dissenters stressed that in a situation in which the Court is overruling a "well-reasoned judgment by a Constitutional Court", as well as a unanimous judgment by one of its Chambers, by adopting a Grand Chamber judgment with a nine to eight vote, it should have presented "more convincing arguments" to justify its decisions. Ibid., Joint Partly Dissenting Opinion, para. 19.

71 Similar to the *D.H.* case, the applicants turned to the Strasbourg Court claiming that their placement in the segregated Roma-only classes, in which the curriculum was significantly reduced in scope and volume as compared with the officially prescribed teaching plan, stemmed from a practice of discrimination based on their ethnicity by the schools concerned, reinforced by pervasive anti-Romani sentiment of the local non-Romani community.

72 ECtHR, *Oršuš and Others v. Croatia, op.cit.* note 70, para. 145.

73 In the *D.H.* judgment, the Court emphasized that, because it was apparent from the documentation produced by ECRI and the CoE Commissioner for Human Rights, "the Czech Republic *is not alone* in having encountered difficulties in providing schooling for Roma children: other European States had had similar difficulties". ECtHR, *D.H.* (Grand Chamber), *op.cit.* note 61, para. 205.

the Convention".[74] Thus, in the specific case, if the aim of placing Romani pupils in Roma-only classes were to serve the purpose of bringing their command of the Croatian language up to an adequate level and then securing their immediate transfer to a mixed class, the Court would not have considered it necessarily as illegitimate.[75] However, despite that the Croatian authorities have adopted a number of measures to address some of the difficulties in providing adequate schooling for Roma children—individual parent-teacher meetings, assistance by mediators, special activities for all pupils to improve non-Roma children's understanding of Roma traditions and culture—once assigned to Roma-only classes, the Romani pupils were not provided with any specific programme to address their alleged linguistic insufficiencies, including a timeframe for the various phases of acquisition of the necessary language skills that would have ensured their immediate and automatic transfer as soon as adequate language proficiency was attained.[76]

For the Court, the main deficiency in the case was the lack of adequate safeguards as prescribed and transparent monitoring procedure ensuring that in the exercise of its margin of appreciation in the education sphere the state had sufficient regard to the special needs of Romani pupils as members of a disadvantaged group: in other words, the system left too much room for arbitrariness on the part of the national authorities.[77]

IV. Media: Printed Media and Radio and TV Broadcasting

Media rights are of essential relevance for the protection and promotion of the distinct identity of minorities as well as for the promotion of tolerance and cultural pluralism.[78] The use of a minority language in private or among members of a minority group is also protected by the right to freedom of expression guaranteed under Article 10 ECHR. Thus, minorities have a right to publish their own newspapers or use other media, without interference by the state or others.

A relevant case on the subject of printed media is the case of *Ekin v. France*[79] concerning the banning of a book on historical, cultural, linguistic and sociopo-

74 ECtHR, *Oršuš and Others v. Croatia, op.cit.* note 70, para. 157 (Emphasis added).

75 In this regard, the Court referred to the Opinion on Croatia of the Advisory Committee on the Framework Convention for the Protection of National Minorities, adopted on 1 October 2004 (para. 129), according to which "pupils should not be placed in such separate remedial classes on the basis of their affiliation with a national minority but *rather on the basis of the skills and needs of the individuals concerned*, and where such placing is found necessary, it should be for a *limited period only*". *Ibid.*, para. 174 (Emphasis added).

76 *Ibid.*, paras. 166 and 173.

77 Ibid., paras. 182-184.

78 See, in particular, OSCE HCNM, *Guidelines on the use of Minority Languages in the Broadcast Media*, 10 October 2003.

79 ECtHR, *Association Ekin v. France*, Appl. 39288/98, judgment of 17 July 2001.

litical aspects of the Basque conflict. The application was brought by a French Basque organization set up to protect Basque culture and the Basque way of life. The ban was permitted under an 1881 French law that differentiated between books published in French, those published in other languages, and books in which the authors were not French nationals. The ban referred to the circulation, distribution and sale of the book in France on the grounds that it promoted separatism, vindicated recourse to violent action and, accordingly, represented a potential danger for public order. The applicant complained that the law concerned was discriminatory and violated Articles 10 and 14 of the Convention on the ground of language or national origin. The Court held that in this case there was a violation of Article 10 because the nature of the publication *did not represent a danger for security and public order* as to justify the important limitation to the freedom of expression imposed on the applicant's rights.

The allocation of radio and television licences connected with the manifestation of culture and identity through the use of minority languages is clearly of primary importance for minorities. The case of *Informationsverein Lentia and Others v. Austria*[80] concerns, *inter alia,* the allocation of radio frequencies and elements of alleged discrimination against the Slovene minority in Austria. The five applicants, all of whom wished to establish private radio or television broadcasting businesses in Austria, claimed that the operation of a broadcasting monopoly by the Austrian Broadcasting Corporation violated their rights to freedom of expression under Article 10 of the Convention by rendering it impossible to establish and run private radio or television stations in Austria. Two of the applicants also claimed a violation of Article 14 in conjunction with Article 10, one of them on the ground that they wished to broadcast in part in Slovenian, especially in the bilingual area of Southern Carinthia. They also claimed that in their programmes, particular efforts would have been made for the promotion of the Slovenian language and culture and that cooperation with other radio stations in Yugoslavia and Italy would reflect the multilinguistic identity of the region (Alpen-Adra-Raum). The Court found a violation of Article 10 regarding the applicants' complaints that they were unable to set up radio and television stations due to the broadcasting monopoly of the Austrian Broadcasting Corporation; however, unfortunately, as in many cases concerning Article 14 ECHR, the Court declared it unnecessary to review the discrimination claim.

As in our modern age, media are subject to rapid developments due to the introduction of new technologies and instruments, such as the internet, it can be expected that in addition to cases regarding traditional print media and radio and TV broadcasting, future cases before the Strasbourg Court regarding media rights and minorities will more frequently concern the emergence of new technological means.

80 ECtHR, *Informationsverein Lentia and Others v. Austria,* judgment of 24 November 1993, Series A, no. 276.

V. Citizenship: Obstacles to the Acquisition of and Connected Problems for Linguistic Minorities

Effective participation in large sectors of life by persons belonging to linguistic minorities can be hampered by various requirements states have imposed, such as language proficiency, citizenship and residency. Minorities without citizenship are, for instance, many Roma or persons belonging to the Russian-speaking communities in the Baltic States who have become noncitizens as a consequence of state succession or state restoration. In particular, since the ratification of the Convention by Latvia, the Court has reviewed several cases concerning the Russian-speaking minority and their problems in obtaining the certificates attesting knowledge of the Latvian language as well as in acquiring Latvian citizenship. As seen in the aforementioned case of *Podkolzina v. Latvia*, language proficiency attestation can be difficult to obtain, and often this is an insurmountable obstacle for the acquisition of citizenship, especially for elderly persons for whom acquiring a sufficient knowledge of a language other than their mother tongue may be extremely arduous.

Although neither the Convention nor its Protocols contain a 'right to nationality' similar to Article 15 of the Universal Declaration of Human Rights, for the Court an arbitrary denial of nationality may, under certain circumstances, amount to an interference with the rights under Article 8 of the Convention (right to respect for private and family life).[81] The case of *Slivenko and others v. Latvia*[82] illustrates this point: the case concerns a soviet military officer and his family members who, following the independency of Latvia from the USSR in 1991, were required to leave Latvia under the terms of the Latvian-Russian treaty on the withdrawal of the Russian troops. The applicants, following their failure to comply with the expulsion orders, were detained in a centre for illegal immigrants and subsequently, moved to Russia, where they adopted Russian citizenship as former nationals of the USSR. The Latvian Government maintained that the expulsion orders were justified as the removal of the foreign military forces and their families from the territory of independent Latvia was essential for the protection of national security and for the prevention of disorder and crime. Moreover, for the Latvian authorities, the applicants had not been sufficiently integrated into

81 ECtHR, *Slivenko and others v. Latvia*, Appl. No. 48321/99, decision on the admissibility of 23 January 2002, para.77.

82 ECtHR, *Slivenko and others v. Latvia*, Appl. No. 48321/99, judgment (Grand Chamber) of 23 October 2003. An analogous case concerning the refusal by the Latvian authorities to regularize the residence of a former soldier of the Soviet Army and his family members and their consequent expulsion from Latvia is ECtHR, *Sisojeva and others v. Latvia*, Appl. No. 60654/00, judgment (Grand Chamber) of 15 January 2007.

Latvian society, particularly considering the *level of the applicants' proficiency in the Latvian language*.[83]

In this regard, the Court observed that it had not been shown that the degree of the applicants' fluency in the language—although the precise level was in dispute—was insufficient for them to pursue a normal everyday life in Latvia so that they were unable to obtain the status of "ex-USSR citizens" and remain in Latvia on a permanent basis.[84] For the Court, the applicants' removal from the territory of Latvia could not be regarded as having been "necessary in a democratic society" because the Latvian authorities overstepped the margin of appreciation enjoyed by the member states in such a matter and by doing so, they failed to strike a fair balance between the legitimate aim of the protection of national security and the protection of the applicants' rights under Article 8.

As has previously been noted, citizenship and residency requirements may have a negative impact on the access of a series of rights, such as the access to the labour market and health service, for persons belonging to linguistic minorities.[85] Persons belonging to linguistic minorities do not necessarily have to fulfil different requirements than do members of the majority to qualify for certain benefits or forms of assistance, such as public housing. However, this does not mean that they have access to public housing on an equal basis. For example, some public housing may accept only a limited number of minorities regardless of how many minorities qualify for public housing.

The vulnerability of stateless persons belonging to minorities to discrimination in different areas of life is well-illustrated in the recent case of *Andrejeva v. Latvia*.[86] The case involved the pension award of Ms. Andrejeva—belonging to the Russian-speaking group in Latvia—that was considerably reduced due to a narrow interpretation of the law by the Latvian authorities resulting in the exclusion from the pension calculation of a period in which her work formally did not constitute "employment in the territory of Latvia". In reality, the applicant had physically been working in Latvia throughout her employment; she was nominally employed by Soviet but non-Latvian agencies and had social tax paid on her behalf on the same basis as Latvian citizens. The applicant, who came to live in Latvia as a child, spent her entire working life there and became stateless as a result of the dissolution of the Soviet Union in December 1991. She complained of the fact that this interpretation was applied only to noncitizens, including stateless people, and that the discriminatory treatment in comparison with Latvian citizens in a similar position amounted to a violation of Article 14 of the Convention

83 ECtHR, *Slivenko and others v. Latvia*, Appl. No. 48321/99, judgment (Grand Chamber) of 23 October 2003, paras. 88 and 123-125.

84 *Ibid.*, para. 124.

85 ACFC, *Commentary on the Effective Participation of Persons Belonging to National Minorities in Cultural, Social and Economic Life and in Public Affairs*, 5 May 2008.

86 ECtHR, *Andrejeva v. Latvia*, Appl. No. 55707/00, judgment (Grand Chamber) of 18 February 2009.

taken in conjunction with Article 1 of Protocol No. 1 (right to peaceful enjoyment of possessions).

In the Grand Chamber's decision, the Court did not accept the government's argument that it would be sufficient for the applicant to become a naturalized Latvian citizen to receive the full amount of the pension claimed. In this regard, the applicant stated that in her opinion the naturalization requirements in Latvia were too strict and had already been severely criticized by the Council of Europe's Parliamentary Assembly and Commissioner for Human Rights.[87] For the Court, the prohibition of discrimination enshrined in Article 14 of the Convention is meaningful only if, in each particular case, the applicant's personal situation in relation to the criteria listed in that provision is taken into account *exactly as it stands*. To proceed otherwise in dismissing the victim's claims on the ground that he or she could have avoided the discrimination by altering one of the factors in question—for example, by acquiring a nationality—would render Article 14 devoid of substance.[88] Considering the particular disadvantage in Ms Andrejeva's situation as a 'permanently resident non-citizen' of Latvia, and the fact that Latvia was "the only State with which she has any stable legal ties and thus the only State which, objectively, can assume responsibility for her in terms of social security",[89] while also being mindful of the broad margin of appreciation enjoyed by member states in the field of social security, the arguments submitted by the government were not sufficient to satisfy the Court that there was a "reasonable relationship of proportionality" that rendered the impugned difference of treatment compatible with the requirements of Article 14 of the Convention.

VI. Identity-Related Issues: Names and Lifestyle

Important elements linked to identity and minority language are personal names and names of the environment in which the person lives.[90] Along the lines of the Framework Convention, the OSCE Oslo Recommendations likewise affirms that persons belonging to minorities have the right to use their personal names in their language according to their traditions and linguistic systems.[91]

The Strasbourg Court has reviewed a significant case concerning the issue of names and identities of minority groups: in the case of *Kuharec v. Latvia*,[92] the applicant, Russian by ethnic origin and a 'noncitizen' of Latvia—a specific legal

87 *Ibid.*, para. 64.

88 *Ibid.*, para. 91.

89 *Ibid.*, para. 88.

90 The ECJ recognized the linkage between the use of personal names and the right of identity in the case *Garcia Avello v. Belgium*, Case C-148/02, judgment of 2 October 2003.

91 OSCE HCNM, *The Oslo Recommendations Regarding the Linguistic Rights of National Minorities*, 1 February 1998, Recommendation 1.

92 ECtHR, *Lidija Kuharec alias Kuhareca v. Latvia*, Appl. No.71557/01, decision on the admissibility of 7 December 2004.

status for persons who came to Latvia between 1940 and 1991 and their descendants, if they have not yet been naturalized—complained about the 'Latvianization' of her name when issued her passport. The Court recalled that there is no common policy among the member states about the recognition and use of personal names, which largely depend on historical, linguistic, religious and cultural factors and that, as a consequence, *states enjoy a broad margin of appreciation regarding the use of the official language(s) in personal documents and other official documents.*[93] In particular, regarding the relevance of the official language, the Court noted:

> The official language is one of the basic constitutional values along with national territory, the way the state is organized and the national flag. The language is not an abstract value; it cannot be dissociated from its real use by the users. Consequently, by defining a language as official, in principle the state commits itself to guarantee to the citizens the right to use it without hindrances not only in their private life, but also in their relations with the public authorities, when communicating or receiving information in this language. For the Court, it is necessary to consider the measures aimed at protecting a given language primarily from this perspective. In other words, the existence of an official language implies the existence of certain subjective rights for the users.[94]

Under the specific circumstances of the case, in striking a balance between individual rights and state interests, the Court noted that the adaptation of the applicant's name ('*Kuharec*' instead of '*Kuhareca*') and the consequences in her life were *minimal.*[95] Therefore, by taking a rather conservative approach toward minority rights, the Court declared the change of the applicant's name as not discriminatory and the application inadmissible.[96]

In a number of cases the Strasbourg organs have recognized that a particular lifestyle of a minority is protected by Article 8 as part of 'private life', 'family life' or 'home'. In addition to the so-called 'UK Gypsies cases', concerning Roma, Gypsy and Travellers,[97] the Court has made several determinations in which it has

93 *Ibid.*, at 16-17.

94 *Ibid.*, at 15-16. Unofficial translation by the author. At the time of writing, the judgment was available only in French.

95 *Ibid.*, at 17.

96 *Ibid.*,at 17-18. See, in particular, Art 11(1) FCNM that reads: "The Parties undertake to recognise that every person belonging to a national minority has the right to use his or her surname (patronym) and first names in the minority language and the right to official recognition of them, according to modalities provided for in their legal system".

97 ECtHR, *Chapman v. the United Kingdom,* Appl. No. 27238/95; *Beard v. the United Kingdom,* Appl. No. 24882/94; *Coster v. the United Kingdom,* Appl. No. 24876/94; *Lee v. the United Kingdom,* Appl. No. 25289/94; *Jane Smith v. the United Kingdom,* Appl. No. 25154/94, judgments (Grand Chamber) of 18 January 2001.

recognized that the identity of a minority, in which the language is an essential element, is relevant within Convention jurisprudence.

The Court has reviewed a variation on the aforementioned theme in the case *Noack and others v. Germany*,[98] in which part of the Court's reasoning was that the Sorb identity, including the linguistic aspect, would not be destroyed despite the villagers being displaced by a mining venture. Regarding the protection of the linguistic identity of the community, the Court stated:

> Even though the transfer means a move and reorganising life in the resettlement area, the inhabitants will continue to live in the same region and the same cultural environment, where the protection of the rights of the Sorbs is guaranteed by Article 25 of the Constitution of the Land of Brandenburg, *where their language is taught in the schools and used by the administrative authorities,* and where they will be able to carry on their customs and in particular to attend religious services in the Sorbian language".[99]

Although the complaint was eventually declared inadmissible, it provided the opportunity for the Court to underline the principle according to which the language of a minority is an essential part of its identity and consequently, it is of relevance when assessing facts and claims of specific applications brought before it.

VII. Concluding Remarks

Although the European Convention on Human Rights does not provide specific provisions on minority rights coupled with the failure to adopt an additional Protocol to the Convention on the rights of minorities,[100] the Convention and its Protocols have been frequently used by minorities to vindicate their rights from different perspectives and grounds and, as a consequence, the Strasbourg Court has become one of the most authoritative judicial mechanisms of redress in the field of minority rights. It is indeed acknowledged that the strength of the Convention and its Protocols is based on the fact that their observance is subject to the judicial control of the Court that can pronounce legally binding decisions, rather than on the content of their provisions.[101]

98 ECtHR, *Noack and others v. Germany*, Appl. No. 46346/99, judgment of 25 May 2000.

99 *Ibid.*, 11 (Emphasis added).

100 PACE, Recommendation 1201 (1993), *op.cit.* note 2.

101 Schokkenbroek noted that it was precisely this feature of supranational judicial control, not the substantive norm as such (virtually all states concerned are indeed already bound by Article 26 ICCPR) which made negotiations during the preparation of Protocol 12 so difficult and which indeed led to the failure of the earlier attempts to include a free-standing provision on equality and non-discrimination in the ECHR system. Jeroen Schokkenbroek, *op.cit.* note 3, 78.

With its several decades of interpretative jurisprudence, the European Convention on Human Rights has engendered the most sophisticated jurisprudence of any of the international judicial instruments promulgated to protect human rights. However, the Strasbourg system is not devoid of criticisms: common criticisms when applying the European Convention on Human Rights as a tool to protect human rights in general, and more specifically minority rights, are that few specific cases are decided by the Strasbourg Court in comparison with the numerous issues arising from minority claims; its provisions are formulated at a high level of abstraction leaving much room for interpretation, and the state's margin of appreciation in the implementation of the Convention's provisions is often considered to be too broad.

Through the annals of the Strasbourg's judgments, which represent the veritable 'life-blood' of the Convention mechanism, it emerges clearly that since its early activity the Court (and earlier the Commission) has made several determinations concerning minority rights, and language rights in particular. This has been possible through the 'creative' use of the Convention's provisions, such as those referring to the rights to private life, home, freedom of expression and association which were not originally conceived for minorities. The main actors of this steadily progressing development of the Strasbourg case-law toward minority rights under the Convention have been the victims themselves, direct or indirect, especially family members, but particularly NGOs, human rights lawyers and various associations representing minority groups before the Court. Organizations such as the European Roma Rights Centre, the Aire Centre, and the Kurdish Human Rights Project, as well as individual lawyers committed to the cause of human and minority rights who have defended applicants in Strasbourg or submitted third-party comments have acted as a 'catalyst' in this steady and irreversible process.

Yet, the high number of cases cannot, in itself, lead us necessarily to a positive appraisal of the Convention system *vis-á-vis* minority protection. Despite the panoply of cases of the Strasbourg Court on language rights, minorities have been left quite disillusioned for the rather conservative approach taken by the Court, especially in the case of the use of minority language(s) in contact with administrative powers, the use of one's name in the form of the minority language, the use of minority languages in assemblies of elected persons, such as municipal or provincial councils or assemblies. In these cases, the Court seemed reluctant to recognize the linguistic claims of the applicants and it has thus often left a wide margin of appreciation to the states, especially as long as the recognition of these claims amounts to positive actions or additional financial burdens for the member state and not simply a negative obligation to refrain from performing certain acts or practices. The Court has taken a positive stance toward minority rights only when, under the specific circumstances of the case, a given practice or omission by the state constitutes, 'a clear and disproportionate disadvantage' or an 'excessive burden' for certain groups. Otherwise, the state's margin of appreciation has been broadly recognized.

Often, the most effective way to protect and promote linguistic minority rights would be to introduce specific legislative or administrative measures imposing a duty of reasonable accommodation or even a duty of affirmative action. Yet, an obligation to adopt positive action is still controversial within the Convention system as it has not yet been formulated in clear terms by the Strasbourg Court, although other organs of the Council of Europe, such as the European Committee of Social Rights and the CoE Parliamentary Assembly have been much more progressive in this respect.[102] The Court's position in this regard is rather ambiguous and half-hearted: the Convention does not compel the member states to provide for positive actions in favour of minorities; however, it does not automatically prohibit them as long as the difference in treatment is justified in each case.[103] Clarifications as to whether and under which circumstances affirmative actions are expected on the part of the state, especially when language rights are concerned, would certainly be required in future cases from the Strasbourg Court.[104]

Despite the aforementioned pessimistic picture, some positive, although uneven signs can still be detected in the more recent Strasbourg case law, such as, the *Cyprus v. Turkey* case, *Podkolzina, Ouranio Toxo, D.H., Ekin,* and partly in the *Latvian* cases. Moreover, the ever-increasing tendency by the Court to refer in its case law to international treaties on minority rights, such as the CoE Framework Convention for the protection of National Minorities, which reflect for the Court an evolutionary process in favour of minority rights among the member states, it is worth praising.[105] The Strasbourg Court has indeed often stressed that the Convention is a 'living instrument' which must be interpreted in the light of present-day conditions: this means that as society and attitudes change, the Court will change and develop the way in which it interprets the Convention. The reference to minority treaties is particularly relevant for the interpretation of the Convention because in deciding whether a difference of treatment has an objective and reasonable justification, the Strasbourg Court gives particular importance to the *trends* which may be discernible in the practice of the contracting states as

102 In favour of an obligation to positive action for minorities see, European Committee of Social Rights, Collective Complaint No. 31/2005, *European Roma Rights Center (ERRC) v. Bulgaria*, Decision on the merits of 30 November 2006; CoE, Parliamentary Assembly, *The legal situation of Roma in Europe*, Recommendation 1557 (2002) adopted on 25 April 2002 (15th Sitting). See also, UN CESCR, Bosnia and Herzegovina, E/C.12/BIH/CO/1 (2006), para. 51; UN CESCR, Serbia and Montenegro, E/C.12/1/Add.108 (2005), para. 64.

103 See, among others, ECtHR, *Lindsay v. United Kingdom*, Appl. No. 11089/84, decision of 11 November 1986, 49 DR 1986, p. 181.

104 For a thorough analysis on positive obligations under the Strasbourg system see, Alastair Mowbray, *The Development of Positive Obligations under the European Convention on Human Rights by the European Court of Human Rights* (Hart Publishing, Oxford, Portland Oregon, 2004).

105 See, among others, the so-called 'UK Gypsy cases', *op.cit.* note 97; ECtHR, *Sidiropoulos v. Greece*, judgment of 10 July 1998, D.R. 98.

reflected, among others, by the commitments undertaken by them through the signatures and ratifications of international instruments.[106]

Finally, the entry into force of Protocol No. 12 to the Convention, which provides a general non-discrimination clause complementing Article 14 ECHR with its limited accessory nature, will give new breath and strength and new opportunities to challenge minority rights before the Strasbourg Court.[107]

In conclusion, the European Convention on Human Rights, with its rather conservative but evolving case law on minority rights, together with the Framework Convention for the Protection of National Minorities and some important EU instruments, primarily the Charter of Fundamental Rights, constitute the 'armoury' of European instruments that, by imposing important obligations on national public authorities, represents the emergence of a veritable 'regional framework' on minority rights in Europe. It remains to be seen whether this new European system of minority protection will evolve in symbiosis, complementing each other to create a significant impact on the protection of minorities.[108] Along with the European Court of Human Rights, the role of national courts in the enforcement of minority rights law cannot be underestimated. Indeed, domestic courts remain pivotal in monitoring and implementing minority rights because, as a general rule, the route to international remedies remains blocked until the rule of full "exhaustion of domestic remedies" is complied.[109] Only a genuine and effective cooperation between international bodies but also between international and national bodies on the implementation of common principles emerging from the minority rights instruments and jurisprudence can truly contribute to provide an effective protection to minority rights.[110]

106 See, among other authorities, the following judgments: ECtHR, *Tyrer v. UK*, judgment of 25 April 1978, Series A No. 26, at 15, para. 31; ECtHR, *Soering v. UK*, judgment of 7 July 1989, Series A No. 161, at 40, para. 102; ECtHR, *Loizidou v. Turkey*, judgment of 23 March 1995, Series A No. 310, at 26, para. 71.

107 The first successful application brought before the Strasbourg Court on the basis of Protocol No. 12 is ECtHR, *Sejdović and Finci v. BiH*, Appl. Nos. 27996/06 and 34836/06, judgment of 22 December 2009 on the ineligibility to stand for election to the House of Peoples and the Presidency of Bosnia and Herzegovina for Romani and Jews.

108 See, among others, Kristine Henrard and Robert Dunbar (eds.), *Synergies in Minority Protection* (Cambridge University Press, Cambridge, 2008).

109 Art. 35(1) ECHR.

110 For an enhanced cooperation between international courts and national constitutional courts see, among others, Louis Favoreau, *Corti Costituzionali e Corte europea dei diritti dell'uomo*, in *Rivista di Diritto Costituzionale* (2004) 3-24, at 23.

Gulara Guliyeva *

Defining the Indefinable: A Definition of 'Minority' in EU Law

I. Introduction

Originally, the European Community (the predecessor of the EU) did not concern itself with minority rights. In 1993, in the context of the process of democratization in Central and Eastern Europe and the dissolution of the Soviet Union,[1] the EU made membership conditional on respect for and protection of minorities based on the Copenhagen accession criteria.[2] However, EU law contained no corresponding obligation for 'old' member states.[3] As a result, in its monitor-

* Teaching fellow, Birmingham Law School, University of Birmingham.

1 European Council (EC), "Declaration on the Guidelines on Recognition of New States in Eastern Europe and the Soviet Union", EC Bulletin 1991/12, 119.

2 The accession criteria, or 'Copenhagen criteria', were set at the Copenhagen European Council in 1993 and further clarified at the Madrid European Council in 1995. See Copenhagen European Council, Presidency Conclusions of 21-22 June 1993; and Madrid European Council, Presidency Conclusions of 15-16 December 1995, at <http://ec.europa.eu/enlargement/the-policy/conditions-for-enlargement/index en.htm>.

3 These double standards in minority protection towards candidate countries and EU member states have been consistently criticized by commentators: Gráinne de Búrca, "Beyond the Charter: How Enlargement has Enlarged the Human Rights Policy of the European Union", 27 *Fordham International Law Journal* (2004), 679-714, at 699-702; Rainer Hofmann and Erik Friberg, "The Enlarged EU and the Council of Europe: Transfer of Standards and the Quest for Future Cooperation in Minority Protection", in Gabriel Toggenburg (ed.), *Minority Protection and the Enlarged European Union: The Way Forward* (LGI Books, Budapest, 2004), 125-147, at 144; Gabriel Toggenburg, "Minority Protection in a Supranational Context: Limits and Opportunities", ibid. 1-36, at 4; Alexandra Xanthaki, "Hope Dies Last: An EU Directive on Roma Integration", 11(4) *European Public Law* (2005) 515-526, at 525; Gaetano Pentassuglia, "The EU and the Protection of Minorities: The Case of Eastern Europe", 12 *European Journal of International Law (EJIL)* (2001) 3-38, at 38; Gwendolyn Sasse, "Gone with the Wind? Minority Rights in Central and Eastern Europe before and after EU Enlargement", Paper presented at the workshop on "Ethnic Mobilization in

Minority Governance in and beyond Europe, ISBN 978-90-04-27648-2. pp. 165-198.

ing of the 12 new member states' compliance with these criteria, the European Commission relied on the standards developed by the United Nations (UN), the Council of Europe (CoE) and the Organization for Security and Cooperation in Europe (OSCE). Gradually, this external minority conditionality led the EU to create "a higher standard for itself and growing consciousness of and commitment to the need for *self*-transformation in order to better exemplify the union of values it aspires to become".[4]

The necessity of internal minority protection in the EU has finally been addressed with the coming into force of the Lisbon Treaty, which amended the Treaty on European Union (TEU) on 1 December 2009.[5] Article 2 (ex-Art. 6(1)) TEU now asserts that the EU is founded on *inter alia* respect for human rights, including the rights of persons belonging to minorities. In addition, Article 21(1) of the EU Charter of Fundamental Rights (CFR)[6] provides for equality and non-discrimination based on a long list of grounds, including membership of a national minority.

There is however no definition of 'minority' in the EU context. This lack of a definition is further complicated by various adjectives that often precede the term. It is possible to identify some of these 'labels' in the context of EU law. For example, Article 21 CFR refers to "national" minorities. Article 2 TEU follows the wording of Article 27 of the International Covenant on Civil and Political Rights (CCPR)[7] and uses "persons belonging to minorities". Furthermore, under the Directive implementing the principle of equal treatment between persons irrespective of racial or ethnic origin (Race Directive)[8] "racial" and "ethnic" minorities may benefit from rules on non-discrimination in the public and private spheres, while the

the New Europe", Brussels, 21-22 April 2006; Gwendolyn Sasse, "The Politics of EU Conditionality: the Norm of Minority Protection during and beyond EU accession", 15(6) *Journal of European Public Policy* (2008) 842-860, at 843-844; Kyriaki Topidi, "The Limits of EU Conditionality: Minority Rights in Slovakia", 1 *Journal of Ethnopolitics and Minority Issues in Europe (JEMIE)* (2003) 1-35, at 29; Peter Vermeersch, "EU Enlargement and Minority Rights Policies in Central Europe: Explaining Policy Shifts in the Czech Republic, Hungary and Poland", 1 *JEMIE* (2003) 1-30, at 25; Andrew Williams, "EU Human Rights Policy and the Convention on the Future of Europe: A Failure of Design", 28(6) *European Law Review* (2003) 794-813, at 795.

4 Rachel Guglielmo, "Human Rights in the Accession Process: Roma and Muslims in an Enlarging EU", in Gabriel Toggenburg (ed.), op.cit. note 32004), 57 (emphasis in original).

5 Consolidated versions of the Treaty on European Union and the Treaty on the Functioning of the European Union [2010] C 83/01 (TEU).

6 Charter of Fundamental Rights of the European Union, adopted on 7 December 2000 [2010], C 83/391 (CFR).

7 International Covenant on Civil and Political Rights, adopted and opened for signature, ratification and accession 16 December 1966, entered into force 23 March 1976, 999 UNTS 171 (CCPR).

8 Council Directive 2000/43/EC of 29 June 2000 on equal treatment between persons irrespective of racial or ethnic origin: Dir. 2000/43, OJ L180/22 (Race Directive).

Directive on establishing a general framework for equal treatment in employment and occupation (Employment Directive)[9] protects "religious" minorities from discrimination in employment and vocational training. In addition, the European Parliament (EP)'s early (non-legally binding) resolutions referred to "cultural" and "linguistic" minorities;[10] more recently, the EP proposed two motions for resolutions: one concerned traditional "old" minorities and another referred to "new" minorities.[11]

In the light of explicit references to the concept 'minority' in EU law, sooner or later the European Court of Justice (ECJ) may be asked to interpret the term. A generous interpretation by the ECJ may be one concrete way that the EU could contribute to minority protection because, regrettably, despite their symbolic significance, Articles 2 TEU and 21 CFR alone are unlikely to offer minorities any meaningful protection. Thus there are no explicit EU competences and policies to support the good intentions of Article 2 TEU. As to the CFR, its usefulness is limited by the legal effects stemming from Articles 51 and 52(2) CFR, which preclude the EU from acting outside its competences.

This paper will propose a definition of 'minority in the context of EU law. Prior to this, it will examine whether there is in fact a need for such a definition in EU law (Part 1). The paper then investigates whether the various adjectives that often precede the term 'minority' impact on its content. To that end, Part 2 will overview some definitional aspects of 'national', 'indigenous', 'new', 'racial', 'ethnic', 'religious' and 'linguistic' minorities, and aim to establish how these labels affect the content and scope of the definition. Part 3 then deconstructs three influential definitions of 'minority' proposed by Capotorti,[12] Deschenes[13] and the Parliamentary Assembly of the Council of Europe (PACE)[14]. Each of the common elements of these definitions, including both objective and subjective criteria, will be discussed in detail: section III.A assesses the objective existence

9 Council Directive 2000/78/EC of 27 November 2000 establishing a general framework for equal treatment in employment and occupation: Dir. 2000/78, OJ L303/16 (Employment Directive).

10 European Parliament, "Resolution on linguistic and cultural minorities in the European Community", [1994] OJ C061/110.

11 European Parliament, "Motion for a 'Resolution on the protection of traditional national and ethnic minorities within the framework of the European Union'", 2 October 2008; "Motion for a 'Resolution on the new, migrant minorities in the European Union'", 2 October 2008.

12 Francesco Capotorti, *Study on the Rights of Persons Belonging to Ethnic, Religious and Linguistic Minorities* (United Nations, New York, 1979), 96.

13 Jules Deschenes, "Proposal Concerning a Definition of the Term 'Minority'", (1985) E/CN4/Sub2/1985/31, 30.

14 PACE, "Recommendation 1201 (1993) on an additional protocol on the rights of national minorities to the European Convention on Human Rights", Art. 1, at <http://assembly.coe.int/Mainf.asp?link=/Documents/AdoptedText/ta93/EREC1201.htm>.

of a group as a central element of the definition; section III.B analyses the requirement of numerical minority and non-dominant position; section III.C evaluates the necessity of the criterion of citizenship; and section III.D studies the subjective element, namely the collective will of a group to preserve its cultural identity. In conclusion, an EU definition of 'minority' is proposed.

Methodologically, in assessing the elements of the definition, the paper draws on the CCPR and the Framework Convention for the Protection of National Minorities (FCNM), as well as some examples from member state practice. As to the CCPR, according to the jurisprudence of the ECJ,[15] this instrument comprises part of the general principles of EU law and constitutional traditions common to member states (general principles).[16] Therefore, standards of minority protection under Article 27 CCPR may be relevant to an EU definition of 'minority'. The paper also draws on the more recently adopted FCNM which contains a catalogue of minority rights. Admittedly, the FCNM has not been recognized as a part of the general principles of EU law, but arguably it is only a matter of time before this development takes place, as this instrument has already become a significant part of EU enlargement law.[17] Furthermore, even though the FCNM does not contain a definition of 'minority', the practice of the Advisory Committee on the Framework Convention for the Protection of National Minorities (ACFC) provides a useful indication as to the groups protected under the instrument. Conversely, there are only limited references to the European Convention on Human Rights (ECHR), because this instrument lacks minority guarantees, comparable to Article 27 CCPR. Besides, in *Gorzelik v. Poland,* the European Court of Human Rights (ECtHR) refused to get involved in the debates on the definition of a 'national minority',[18] because the concept is not defined in any international treaty and there is no consistent state practice regarding the official recognition of minorities.[19]

As to the examples from member states practice, these are introduced where relevant to explain/justify the relevance of certain elements of the definition of 'minority' in EU law or, alternatively, to show their inappropriateness. For instance, the concepts of numerical threshold and non-dominant position

15 Case 374/87, *Orkem v. Commission* [1989] ECR 3283; Joined Cases C-297/88 and C-197/89, *Dzodzi* [1990] ECR I-3763; Case T-315/01, *Yassin Abdullah Kadi v. Council and Commission* [2005] ECR II-3649; Case T-306/01, *Ahmed Ali Yusuf and Al Barakaat International Foundations v. Council and Commission* [2005] ECR II-3533.

16 Art. 6(3) TEU.

17 For discussion see Gulara Guliyeva, "Joining Forces or Reinventing the Wheel? The EU and the Protection of National Minorities", in Gulara Guliyeva and Gaetano Pentassuglia (eds.), "Minority Groups Across Legal Settings: Global and Regional Dimensions", 17(2) *IJMGR* (Special Issue 2010), 287-305.

18 ECtHR, Appl. No. 44158/98, *Görzelik and others v. Poland,* judgment of 17 February 2004.

19 *Ibid.*, para. 67.

are based on the experience of Belgium (III.B), and the criterion of citizenship/nationality is assessed in the context of Latvia (III.C).

II. Is There a Need for an EU Definition of 'Minority'?

Before we delve into defining the term in EU law, it may be appropriate to question whether there is even a need for such a definition. After all, international law adopted a pragmatic approach and the absence of a definition has not prevented even the drafters of the FCNM, the first multilateral legally binding instrument on the rights of minorities in Europe, from elaborating on the rights of minorities. This is so, because for the past 50 years attempts to define the concept of 'minority' have invariably failed, mainly due to states' political resistance and their divergent practices in relation to minorities.

As a result, some commentators question the need to define 'minority', claiming that leaving the term undefined may allow a broader understanding as opposed to a rigid definition, produced as a minimum common denominator inevitably capable of excluding some groups.[20] Moreover, it is precisely because of the lack of a definition that it was possible for bodies monitoring minority provisions within the UN, the CoE and the OSCE to adopt more "comprehensive, progressively expanding [approach] to new minorities under the influence of international law".[21] Furthermore, it may be particularly challenging to define the term in the context of EU law. De Witte argues that because there is "no European nation-state, then there can be no 'national minorities' in the [EU] framework".[22] Indeed, the supranational nature of the EU legal system adds to the confusion over the definition of minorities.

On the other hand, the lack of a definition may arguably lead to a narrow domestic concept designed to "exclude groups 'making trouble'".[23] Åkermark maintains that "the lack of a definition gives States an excuse to refuse the existence of minorities in their own territory".[24] By maintaining the matter within the domestic margin of discretion, states are free to decide which individuals belonging to certain groups may benefit from minority rights mechanisms. As the assessment of minority protection mechanisms demonstrates, it is more difficult to adopt an inclusive approach by the monitoring bodies where states have a wide

20 Ioana Tanase, "Defining National Minorities: Old Criteria and New Minorities", Presentation for Seminar Series "Citizenship and National Minorities in Europe", St Antony's College, University of Oxford, at <http://www.sant.ox.ac.uk/esc/esc-lectures/Tanase.htm>.

21 *Ibid.*

22 Bruno de Witte, "The European Communities and its Minorities", in Catherine Brolmann, Rene Lefeber and Marjoleine Zieck (eds.), *People and Minorities in International Law* (Kluwer Academic Publishers, The Hague, 1993), 168.

23 Athanasia Spiliopoulou Åkermark, *Justifications of Minority Protection in International Law* (Kluwer Law International, The Hague, 1997), 86.

24 *Ibid.*, 87.

margin of appreciation over the definition.[25] Furthermore, as Packer convincingly argues the consideration of legal certainty, clarity, reliability and foreseeability are of particular importance; the identification of bearers of rights and duties is essential for successful operation of a legal regime in practice.[26] Indeed, the lack of a definition "inevitably gives rise to a broad range of interpretations".[27] Therefore, for the purposes of an effective minority protection regime, a "precise definition may serve to minimize controversy by drawing the bounds in a clear fashion".[28] Arguably, the fact that references to 'minority' have found their way into EU primary law will (sooner or later) make it necessary to define the term.

III. Do Labels Matter?

This section assesses the impact of the various adjectives that often precede the term 'minority' on the content of its definition. The discussion begins with an assessment of the term 'national minority' (B.1); it then compares and contrasts 'indigenous people' with 'minority' (B.2). 'New minorities' are then discussed (B.3), before turning to an assessment of which term is broader: 'ethnic minority', 'racial minority' or 'national minority'. The assessment draws on examples from the jurisprudence of English courts, which define the concept of 'race' broadly. This in turn may have implications for the application of the EU Race Directive modelled on the 1976 UK Race Relations Act[29] (B.4). We then consider notions of 'religious' and 'linguistic' minorities (B.5). On the basis of the overall analysis, an assessment is made as to which groups should be included in an EU definition of 'minority.'

A. 'National' Minority

It appears that the concept 'national minority' is a "peculiarly European term".[30] The term 'national' was chosen as a compromise between international and

25 Rianne Letschert, *The Impact of Minority Rights Mechanisms* (TMC Asser, The Hague, 2005), 425.

26 John Packer, "On the Definition of Minorities", in John Packer and Kristian Myntti (eds.) *The Protection of Ethnic and Linguistic Minorities in Europe* (Åbo Akademi University, Åbo, 1993), 23-65, at 26.

27 Jelena Pejic, "Minority Rights in International Law", 19 *Human Rights Quarterly* (1997), 666-685.

28 Malcolm Shaw, "The Definition of Minorities in International Law", in Yoram Dinstein and Mala Tabory (eds.), *The Protection of Minorities and Human Rights* (Kluwer Academic Publishers, The Hague, 1992), 1-32, at 1.

29 UK Race Relations Act 1976 (c. 74) as amended in 2000 (the Race Relations Amendment Act) and in 2003 (to give effect to Race Directive).

30 John Valentine, "Toward a Definition of National Minority", 32 *Denver Journal of International Law and Policy* (2004), 445-474, at 445.

Eastern European terminology.[31] In Eastern Europe, to avoid a negative connotation of the term, the term 'nationality' was substituted for 'minority'.[32] The term is widely used in CoE,[33] OSCE[34] and EU instruments.[35] This practice may be explained by the emergence of the concept in Europe. The broader description of 'national minorities' identifies them as the *historic minorities* that emerged as a result of the territorial divisions after the two world wars. Kymlicka characterizes national minorities as groups created as a result of the incorporation of territories into larger states; usually communities living on those territories wished to maintain their distinctness within the new states.[36] A more restrictive view of national minorities also requires an external kin-state element, i.e., a state with similar ethnic roots. National minorities are only those groups which were separated from their kin states as a result of the redrawing of territorial boundaries.[37]

Another distinct feature of national minority protection is their entitlement to political participation—"a right historically attached to *national* minority regimes".[38] Tomuschat, for example, emphasizes the strong political connotation of the term by describing 'national minorities' as "groups which have become conscious of their own identity to such an extent that they seek to become masters of their own fate at least partially".[39] The author supports the view that this strong political element is the reason for states' opposition to the inclusion of this concept in international instruments. Lerner expresses similar views and explains the absence of the concept 'national minorities' from the text of Article 27 ICCPR as the fear of multinational states to allow secessionist trends.[40] Accordingly, the term 'national minorities' has "an extra dimension [...] namely a certain political

31 Mala Tabory, "Minority Rights in the CSCE Context", in Dinstein and Tabory (eds.) *op.cit.* note 28, 187-211, at 196.

32 *Ibid.*, at 198.

33 Framework Convention for the Protection of National Minorities, adopted on 10 November 1994, CETS No.157 (FCNM).

34 Document of the Copenhagen Meeting of the Conference on the Human Dimension of the CSCE, 29 June 1990, at <http://www.osce.org/docs/english/1990-1999/hd/cope90e.htm>.

35 Art. 21 CFR.

36 Will Kymlicka, "The Internationalization of Minority Rights", 6(1) *International Journal of Constitutional Law* (2008), 1-32.

37 Tove Malloy, "Title and Preamble", in Marc Weller (ed.), *The Rights of Minorities in Europe* (Oxford University Press, Oxford, 2005), 49-74, at 51.

38 Rachel Guglielmo and Tim Waters, "Shifting European Policy Towards Roma", 43(4) *JCMS* (2005), 763-786, 769 (emphasis in original).

39 Nathan Lerner, "The Evolution of Minority Rights in International Law", in Brolmann, Lefeber and Zieck, *op.cit.* note 22, 77-101, at 89.

40 *Ibid.*

aspiration for a degree of autonomy or even independence".[41] Thornberry clarifies that the term 'national' relates to:

> [...] personal rather than legal characteristics, in line with 'ethnic, religious and linguistic' ones, and does not necessarily mean that the standards are confined to those having the nationality or citizenship of a State.[42]

Thus, the concept 'national' does not refer to citizenship; rather, the concept ought to refer to ethnicity. Furthermore, Helgesen argues that the concept 'national' corresponds to the wording of Article 27 CCPR and acts as substitute for 'ethnic, religious or linguistic' minorities.[43] In the EU context, the reference to "national minorities" in Article 21 CFR is in line with Article 14 ECHR, and suggests a similarly broad use of the term.

B. 'Indigenous People' versus 'Minority'

As with the term 'minority', the concept of 'indigenous peoples' remains undefined. Is there a difference between 'indigenous peoples' and 'minorities'? In addressing this question, Kymlicka notes that:

> [...] the term 'indigenous peoples' arose primarily in the context of New World settler states and refers to the descendants of the original non-European inhabitants of lands colonized and settled by European powers [...] 'National minorities,' by contrast, is a term invented in Europe to refer to the European groups that lost out in the tumultuous process of European state formation over the past five centuries, and whose homelands were incorporated (in whole or in part) into larger states dominated by a neighbouring European people.[44]

41 Annelies Verstichel, "Personal Scope of Application: An Open, Inclusive and Dynamic Approach – the FCNM as a Living Instrument", in Annelies Verstichel *et al.* (eds.), *The Framework Convention for the Protection of National Minorities: A Useful Pan-European Instrument?* (Intersentia, Oxford, 2008), 127-157, at 140.

42 Patrick Thornberry, "The UN Declaration on the Rights of Persons Belonging to National or Ethnic, Religious and Linguistic Minorities: Background, Analysis, Observations, and an Update", in Alan Phillips and Allan Rosas (eds.) *Universal Minority Rights* (Abo Akademi, Turku and London, 1995), 13-76, at 30.

43 Jan Helgesen "Protecting Minorities in the Conference on Security and Co-operation in Europe (CSCE) Process", in Allan Rosas and Jan Helgesen (eds.), *The Strength of Diversity: Human Rights and Pluralist Democracy* (Martinus Nijhoff Publishers, Dordrecht/Boston/London, 1992), 159-186, at 164.

44 Kymlicka, *op.cit.* note 36, 8.

In explaining the difference in the degree of protection granted to indigenous peoples (who have, for example, an explicit right to autonomy)[45] and national minorities, Kymlicka observes that, because the subjugation of indigenous peoples was more disruptive to those societies compared to the treatment of national minorities in Europe, the international community gave priority to the protection of the former.[46] As a result, in the context of UN standard-setting, a dual track has emerged to deal with these two groups.[47] It is generally perceived that the approach adopted for minority rights has been influenced by European experiences, while rules on indigenous rights have been formulated against developments in the Americas and the Pacific region.[48] Furthermore, persons belonging to minorities:

> [...] often have several identities and participate actively in the common domain. Indigenous rights, on the other hand, tend to consolidate and strengthen the separateness of these peoples from other groups in society.[49]

Despite the different contexts and needs of these groups, it is debatable whether a clear cut distinction between indigenous people and minorities is useful.[50] For example, if persons of indigenous origin migrate to urban areas they might be better protected under the regime of minority protection, while minorities who live compactly together in a certain region of a country may benefit from the degree of self-government usually accorded to indigenous people.[51] This distinction is even less pertinent in the context of European minorities and indigenous peoples protected under the umbrella concept of 'national minorities'. For example, the ACFC confirmed that indigenous groups, such as the Sami in Norway, can benefit from protection under the FCNM,[52] in addition to other instruments

45 Declaration on the Rights of Indigenous Peoples (2007) UNGA Resolution 61/295, Art. 4.

46 Kymlicka, *op.cit.* note 36, 10.

47 Asbjørn Eide, "Working Paper on the Relationship and Distinction between the Rights of Persons Belonging to Minorities and those of Indigenous Peoples", (2000) E/CN.4/Sub.2/2000/10, para. 22.

48 *Ibid.*, para. 25.

49 *Ibid.*, para. 23.

50 After considering the defining elements of the terms 'minority' and 'indigenous people', Daes concludes that the main legal distinction between these two groups is the degree of internal self-determination granted to the latter: Erica-Irene Daes, "Working Paper on the Relationship and Distinction between the Rights of Persons Belonging to Minorities and those of Indigenous Peoples", (2000) E/CN.4/Sub.2/2000/10, para. 43.

51 Eide, *op.cit.* note 47, para. 26.

52 Advisory Committee on the Framework Convention for the Protection of National Minorities (hereinafter ACFC), First Opinion on Norway (adopted on 12 September 2002), para. 19.

that specifically apply to indigenous people. Consequently, an EU definition of 'minority' should not draw a distinction between indigenous people and minorities. The degree of protection accorded should depend, not on a label, but on the needs and specific circumstances of a group.

C. 'New' Minorities

One of the stumbling blocks in defining the concept 'minority' is whether the so-called 'new' minorities should be included. Given the controversy surrounding this matter, this section assesses whether a definition of 'minority' in EU law should extend to 'new' minorities. A useful starting point for such an assessment is to refer to a working distinction between 'old' and 'new' minorities. Thus:

> Old minorities are composed of persons who lived, or whose ancestors lived, in the country or a part of it before the state became independent or before the boundaries were drawn in the way they are now. New minorities are composed of persons who have come in after the state became independent.[53]

This latter category includes migrant workers, as well as new groups of minorities that appeared in the process of state dissolution and succession. As to migrant workers, there is a "broad assumption that since they have decided to immigrate of their own free will, they should generally accept the cultural and linguistic make-up of the country in which they now want to settle".[54] However, the fact that someone left behind their country for economic or political reasons does not mean that they can easily give up their identity.[55] Besides, even though migrants are protected under other international rules,[56] they may still benefit from the pro-

53 Asbjørn Eide, "The Rights of 'Old' versus 'New' Minorities", 2 *EYMI* (2002/03), 365-379, at 365.

54 *Ibid.*, 366.

55 Verstichel, *op.cit.* note 41, 148.

56 For example, the right to education of migrant workers is protected under the International Convention on the Elimination of All Forms of Discrimination (adopted 21 December 1965, entered into force 4 January 1969) UNGA Resolution 2106 (XX), Art. 5; International Convention on the Protection of the Rights of All Migrant Workers and Members of their Families (1990) A/RES/45/158, Art. 30 (children's education), Arts. 43(1)(a) and 45(1)(a) (adult education); ILO Convention 97 on Migration for Employment (adopted 1 July 1949, entered into force 22 January 1952) 120 UNTS 70, Article 6; ILO Convention 143 on Migrant Workers (adopted 24 June 1975, entered into force 09 December 1978) Art. 8(2); European Convention on Establishment (1955) ETS No. 19, Art. 20 (the right to education of migrants' children); European Convention on the Legal Status of Migrant Workers (1977) ETS No. 93, Art. 14 (adult education); and Council Regulation 1612/68/EEC of 15 October 1968 on freedom of movement for workers within the Community: Reg. 1612/68, OJ L 257/2, Art. 12. For discussion see Marianne Van Den Bosch and Willem Van Genugten, "International Legal Protection of Migrant Workers, National Minori-

tection accorded to traditional minorities. Indeed, a certain parallel can be drawn here with indigenous people, protected both under the FCNM and other specialized instruments. As the ACFC emphasizes, "it is not because certain groups can enjoy the protection of other legal regimes, that they cannot enjoy the protection of the FCNM".[57] In addition, international instruments on the protection of migrant workers place increasingly strong emphasis on the protection of their cultural identity.[58] Therefore, groups that constitute a 'new' minority and wish to preserve their distinct cultural identity should be afforded the protection available under relevant international and regional instruments.[59]

In addition, states often rely on the term 'new' minority to avoid granting protection to unwanted groups. For example, Slovenia refuses to offer protection equivalent to that available to the traditional Italian and Hungarian minorities to 'new' minorities originating from other parts of the former Yugoslavia, such as ethnic Serbs, Croats, Bosnians, Kosovo Albanians, and Roma from Kosovo and Albania.[60] The ACFC has strongly criticized such a restrictive interpretation and encouraged Slovenia to adopt a "more inclusive approach in order to better respond to the established reality on the ground".[61] In general, the ACFC adopts a so-called 'article-by-article' approach, where some provisions (for example, Art. 11(3) FCNM) apply to 'old' minorities, while 'new' minorities could benefit from others (Arts. 3, 5, 6, 7 and 8 FCNM).[62] Indeed, before a 'new' minority is firmly established in a state it may have different needs, such as non-discrimination in education and employment. This, however, should not affect the definition of 'minority' as such. After all, the labels 'new' and 'old' are "expressions of a rather relative and arbitrary parameter, namely the lapse of time".[63]

Furthermore, with the process of European integration, which encourages migration and leads to a higher degree of interethnic mixture among Europeans,

---

ties and Indigenous Peoples—Comparing Underlying Concepts", 9 *IJMGR* (2002), 195-233.

57 Verstichel, *op.cit.* note 41, 149.

58 International Convention on the Protection of the Rights of All Migrant Workers and Members of their Families (1990) UN Doc A/Res/45/158, Art. 12 on freedom of religion and Art. 31 on respect for cultural identity.

59 Rudiger Wolfrum, "The Emergence of 'New Minorities' as a Result of Migration", in Brolmann, Lefeber, and Zieck (eds.), *op.cit.* note 22, 165.

60 Julie Ringelheim, "Minority Protection and Constitutional Recognition of Difference: Reflections on the Diversity of European Approaches", in Verstichel *et al.* (eds), *op.cit.* note 41, 33-49, at 42.

61 ACFC Second Opinion on Slovenia (adopted on 26 may 2005, published on 1 December 2005), para. 39.

62 Rianne Letschert, "Successful Integration while Respecting Diversity; 'Old' Minorities versus 'New Minorities'", 1 *Helsinki Monitor* (2007), 46-56, at 50.

63 Gabriel Toggenburg, "Who is Managing Ethnic and Cultural Diversity in the European Condominium? The Moments of Entry, Integration and Preservation", 43(4) *JCMS* (2005), 717-738, at 720.

it is argued that any distinction between 'new' (migrant workers and non-citizens) and 'old' (traditional) minorities should be eliminated.[64] This is so because not only may long-term migrants gradually become 'old' minorities, but also members of 'old' minorities may exercise their right to free movement in the EU and become part of a 'new' minority.[65] Therefore, 'new' minorities require closer examination in the EU context. There are two possible groups that may fall into this category: migrant workers within the EU and Third Country Nationals (TCNs). Let us consider each group in turn.

1. Migrant Workers

As to migrants within the EU, freedom of movement and freedom of establishment encourage EU citizens to reside in member states other than their state of origin. Might these groups of migrants, which are numerically fewer than the majority population, be classified then as possible EU minorities? As discussed above, some commentators argue that migrant workers should benefit from the regime of minority protection.[66] Furthermore, it is suggested that these groups would comprise a minority in a host member state because of their cultural differences from the majority of the population.[67]

However, it is important to note some differences between migration within the EU and from third countries. Often EU migrants are not disadvantaged in comparison to the majority population in a host state, as EU citizenship offers them considerable legal safeguards in accessing, for example, social benefits and education. Moreover, these groups should not suffer discrimination based on their nationality,[68] although they may encounter linguistic barriers as 'tradi-

64 Manfred Nowak, "The Evolution of Minority Rights in International Law, Comments", in Brolmann, Lefeber, Zieck (eds) *op.cit.* note 22, 118; see also, John Packer, "Problems in Defining Minorities", in Deirdre Fottrell and Bill Bowring (eds.), *Minority and Group Rights in the New Millennium* (Martinus Nijhoff Publishers, The Hague, 1999), 223-274, at 264.

65 Gwendolyn Sasse, "Securitization or Securing Rights? Exploring the Conceptual Foundations of Policies towards Minorities and Migrants in Europe", 43(4) *JCMS* (2005) 673-493, at 676; see also, Tawhida Ahmed, "A Critical Appraisal of EU Governance for the Protection of National Minorities", in Guliyeva and Pentassuglia (eds.) *op.cit.* note 17, 265-285, at 269.

66 Wolfrum, *op.cit.* note 59; Gwendolyn Sasse, "Policies towards Minorities and Migrants in Europe", 43(4) *JCMS* (2005) 673-693; Ryszard Cholewinski, "Migrants as Minorities: Integration and Inclusion in the Enlarged European Union", 43(4) *JCMS* (2005), 695-716.

67 Gabriel Toggenburg, "Minorities '...' the European Union: Is the Missing Link an 'Of' or a 'Within'?", 25 (3) *Journal of European Integration* (2003) 273-284, at 276; see also, de Witte, *op.cit.* note 22, 167-185.

68 Art. 18 Treaty on the Functioning of the European Union (TFEU) (ex-Art. 12 Treaty establishing the European Community (TEC)).

tional' minorities sometimes do.[69] Their European citizenship also gives them limited political rights, such as the ability to vote in elections for the European Parliament.[70]

In addition, the EU has offered some protection to preserve migrant workers' cultures by, for example, enacting the Directive on the education of the children of migrant workers,[71] according to which member states are required both to integrate the children of migrant workers into the educational environment and facilities of the host state, and to facilitate their learning of their parents' mother-tongue and culture. However, it has proved difficult to put this Directive into practice and the instrument remains inadequately implemented across the EU.[72]

Overall, this category should be included in an EU minority definition of 'minority'. Even though EU law provides significant guarantees for migrants within the EU, it is desirable that migrant workers—whose needs genuinely shifted from mere economic activity to the preservation of the cultural, religious and linguistic identity of their groups—should not be denied minority status.[73]

2. Third Country Nationals

Another trend in the literature is to identify TCNs as an EU minority.[74] It is argued that because they are numerically fewer than the citizens of the EU and are in underprivileged situation, TCNs are the most logical group to qualify as an EU minority.[75] Staples defines TCNs as:

> [...] nationals from non-Member State countries who have been authorised to take up residence and pursue an economic activity in one of the Member States

69 Case C-379/87, *Anita Gröener v. Minister for Education and City of Dublin Vocational Education Committee* [1989] ECR 3967.

70 For example, Art. 22 TFEU (ex-Art. 19 EC) equipped EU citizens with the right to vote and stand for elections in municipal and European Parliament elections in a host state under the same conditions as nationals of that state. See also, Art. 20(2)(b) TFEU and Arts. 39(1) and 40 CFR. Other political rights include the right to petition the European Parliament, to apply to the European Ombudsman, and to address the institutions and advisory bodies of the Union in any of the Treaty languages and to obtain a reply in the same language. See Art. 20(2)(d) TFEU and Arts. 41(4), 43 and 44 CFR.

71 Council Directive 77/486 on the education of the children of migrant workers, Dir 77/486, OJ L199/32.

72 de Witte, *op.cit.* note 22, 182.

73 Wolfrum argues that immigrant workers may benefit from the protection of Art. 27 CCPR if they can demonstrate that they have preserved their identity on the territory of a host state for a certain time. Wolfrum, *op.cit.* note 59, 163.

74 Steve Peers, "'New' Minorities: What Status for Third Country Nationals in the EU System?", in Toggenburg (ed.), *op.cit.* note 3.

75 Toggenburg, *op.cit.* note 67, 277; see also, de Witte, *op.cit.* note 22, 185.

> of the European Union in accordance with that Member State's immigration legislation and who have benefited from these rights over a period of time.[76]

Thus, unlike migrant workers who come from other EU member states, TCNs are predominantly immigrants and refugees who come from outside of the EU, and thus do not hold EU citizenship. Because under Article 8 of the Treaty on the Function of the European Union (TFEU) (ex-Art. 17(1) Treaty establishing the European Community (TEC)) EU citizenship is additional to national citizenship and does not replace it, the legal status of TCNs depends on national legislation, international arrangements between their country of origin and the EU member states and the Schengen measures.[77] Interestingly, Article 8 TFEU changed a reference to EU citizenship in Article 17(1) TEC from complementary to additional to a member state's citizenship. Even though this wording may prove potent in future ECJ case law, it may still be difficult to offer protection to TCNs as a minority, because this fragmented group lacks a united identity.

Nevertheless, an effort was made to link TCNs with the EU level. The 1999 European Council in Tampere recommended conferring on legally-residing TCNs, who hold long-term residence permits, "a set of uniform rights which are as near as possible to those enjoyed by EU citizens".[78] Based on these recommendations, in 2003, the Long-Term Residents Directive was adopted to address the rights of TCNs.[79] These rights include the rights to residence, education and employment, as well as the right not to be discriminated against *vis-à-vis* the citizens of a host state. TCNs are also entitled to petition the European Parliament and have a right of appeal to the European Ombudsman.[80]

However, one striking feature of the Long-Term Residents Directive is the requirement for TCNs to comply with integration conditions set by member states in their national legislation.[81] Such requirements often aim to assimilate newcomers by demanding knowledge of national language and culture,[82] while

76 Helen Staples, *The Legal Status of Third Country Nationals Resident in the European Union* (Kluwer law International, The Hague, 1999), 12.

77 Protocol (No 19) on the Schengen *acquis* integrated into the framework of the European Union [2010] OJ C 83/290.

78 European Council, Tampere Summit Conclusions, 15-16 October 1999, at <http://www.statewatch.org/ news/2003/sep/tamp.htm>. For criticism see Louise Halleskov, "The Long-Term Residents Directive: A Fulfilment of the Tampere Objective of Near-Equality?", 7 *European Journal of Migration and Law* (2005), 181-201.

79 Council Directive 2003/109 concerning the status of third-country nationals who are long-term residents, Dir 2003/109, OJ L16/44 (hereinafter Long-Term Residents Directive).

80 Arts. 41 and 46 CFR.

81 Long-Term Residents Directive, Art. 5(2).

82 To cope with migration from third countries and protect their values, some member states have resorted to integration requirements, which increasingly demand "explicit reassurances from individual migrants that they are personally committed to liberal

recent approaches to minority rights have been mainly perceived as protection from forced "state-imposed assimilation".[83] Furthermore, the Directive does not grant TCNs political rights, even though TCNs contribute to the economic, cultural and social wellbeing of the EU on an equal footing with EU citizens. Overall, despite the improvement in the legal status of TCNs, significant differences remain between EU citizens and permanent resident TCNs, who are further marginalized by being "pushed to a third-class citizenship status in their host states".[84] The Directive may therefore not be appropriate to ensure protection of TCNs as a 'new' minority.

Another instrument that may indirectly prevent discrimination against TCNs is the Race Directive. However, TCNs may only invoke the Race Directive if they can demonstrate that they were discriminated against on the grounds of their racial or ethnic origin, not their nationality or immigration status.[85] Thus, Article 3(2) of the Race Directive stipulates that the instrument does not cover differences in treatment on the basis of nationality. Moreover, it is without prejudice to provisions and conditions relating to the entry into and residence of TCNs and stateless persons on the territory of member states, and to any treatment which arises from the legal status of the TCNs and stateless persons concerned. Because race and nationality are often intertwined, arguably the Race Directive may perpetuate double standards in relation to TCNs.[86]

Despite some of the similar problems faced by both TCNs and minorities, such as language, citizenship and enjoyment of political rights, it is sometimes argued that the regimes for their protection should be kept separate. For exam-

democratic values". Ronan McCrea, "Limitations on Religion in a Liberal Democratic Polity: Christianity and Islam in the Public Order of the European Union", 18 *LSE Working Papers* (2007) 19, 33-34. Thus, in 2000, 2002, 2003 and 2006, the Netherlands amended its laws to require individuals wishing to naturalize to indicate their integration by passing exams on knowledge of Dutch society and language; if applicants failed to integrate or supposedly were unable to integrate, they would be refused admission or a more secure status, including the equal treatment stemming from that status. *Ibid*, 33-34; see also, "Netherlands Introduces Dutch Language Test for Immigrants", 21 February 2006, at <http://www.workpermit.com/news/2006_02_21/europe/netherlands_introduces_immigrant_test.htm>.

83 Mária Kovács, "Standards of Self-Determination and Standards of Minority Rights in the Post-Communist Era: A Historical Perspective", 9(3) *Nations and Nationalism* (2003), 433-450, 437.

84 Ece Atikcan, "Citizenship or Denizenship: The Treatment of Third Country Nationals in the European Union", 85 *Sussex European Institute Working Paper* (2006), 21.

85 Peers, *op.cit.* note 74, 158.

86 Fernne Brennan, "The Race Directive, Institutional Racism and Third Country Nationals", in Takis Tridimas and Paolisa Nebbia (eds.), *European Union Law for the Twenty-First Century* (Vol. 2) (Hart, Oxford, 2004), 371-386, at 380; see also, Daniela Caruso, "Limits of the Classic Method: Positive Action in the European Union after the New Equality Directives", 44 *Harvard International Law Journal* (2003), 331-386, at 352.

ple, the European Parliament emphasized that, although migrants and overseas minorities may share the disadvantages of linguistic minorities, "their specific problems deserve detailed and separate treatment".[87] However, in some ways such a distinction is artificial. In 2008, the European Parliament adopted two motions for resolution: one concerned traditional 'old' minorities, and the other 'new' minorities.[88] Yet, on closer inspection, similarities can be found in the preamble and some provisions of the resolutions.[89] This is not surprising because in many respects these two groups have to tackle similar issues. Thus, Van Den Bosch and Van Genugten compared the regimes of migrant and minority group protection with an emphasis on citizenship, access to education in mother tongue and voting rights.[90] They conclude that both groups face similar problems.[91] For instance, the right to vote is tied to citizenship, the acquisition of which may be lengthy and equally difficult for both migrants and minorities.

Accordingly, even though TCNs could qualify as an EU minority, their protection at the EU level may prove more controversial than that of migrants from other member states. Nevertheless, because of their vulnerable position in the EU, this group deserves to receive some protection against state-imposed assimilation of their identity.

Arguably, an EU definition should not contain the distinction between 'new' and 'old' minorities based on two arguments. The first argument is pragmatic and advocates the need for consistency in the EU's approach to minorities in both its enlargement policy and in relation to current member states. Indeed, the Copenhagen criteria are silent on what types of minorities are protected; in its accession monitoring the Commission too has adopted a broad approach to the definition by including, for example, migrants.[92] This is not to argue that the EU should offer identical treatment to all minorities. Rather the definition of 'minority' should be consistent, while the required level of protection should be based on a sliding scale of rights stemming from the particular needs of a group.

The second argument is informed by the growing body of academic commentaries which advocate the elimination of this distinction. For example, in Nowak's view in such a multicultural society it will be "difficult to justify why only long-established 'old minorities' should enjoy special protection".[93] Similarly, Arzoz

87 European Parliament, "Resolution on the Languages and Cultures of Regional and Ethnic Minorities in the European Community", [1987] Doc A 2-150/87, para. 16.

88 European Parliament, *op.cit.* note 11.

89 For example, the preambles of both resolutions have regards to Arts. 13 TEC (now Art. 19 TFEU) and 192(2) TEC (now Art. 225 TFEU), Art. 21(1) CFR, the ECHR and the FCNM.

90 Van Den Bosch and Van Genugten, *op.cit.* note 56.

91 *Ibid.*

92 Kristin Henrard and Robert Dunbar, "Introduction", in Kristin Henrard and Robert Dunbar (eds.), *Synergies in Minority Protection: European and International Law Perspectives* (Cambridge University Press, Cambridge, 2008), 1-20, at 12.

93 Nowak, *op.cit.* note 64, 118.

argues that undeniably "it is politically very advantageous that the European Union, in the twenty-first century, commits itself to a basic common standard applicable to every kind of minority, be it 'old' or 'new'".[94] Ultimately, this distinction "drawn between minorities and immigrants", as Kurban maintains, "rests upon an unjustified and arbitrary categorisation, legally explicable as it may be".[95] Indeed, 'new' minorities may also wish not to be assimilated in their host states, but to preserve and cultivate their cultural, linguistic and religious characteristics.

Therefore, an EU definition of 'minority' should not contain the distinction between 'new' and 'old' minorities, even though protection offered to such groups may vary based on the specific needs of a group.

D. 'Ethnic' versus 'Racial' Minorities

This section aims to clarify which of the terms 'ethnic', 'racial' or 'national' is the broadest. In this respect, a generous interpretation of the term 'ethnic' minority in the UN context is contrasted to the equally broad use of 'racial' in the UK. Because the EU Race Directive uses both terms, with an emphasis on 'race', the experience of British courts in defining this term is briefly overviewed.

Until the 1950s, the UN mainly used the term 'racial' minorities, with a subsequent focus on 'ethnic' minorities, because the latter term is "wider in referring to all biological, cultural and historical characteristics, whereas the former term seem[s] to be restricted to inherited physical characteristics".[96] Because in the UN context the term 'ethnic' is the broadest term available,[97] other terms, such as 'racial' and 'national', are subsumed under this umbrella term,[98] without affecting the defining features of 'minority'. Thus, "we witness different uses of terms and not different meanings".[99]

In the EU context, the use of 'racial' and 'ethnic' is combined under the Race Directive, which is preferable, as it may "prevent potentially undesirable

94 Xabier Arzoz, "Article 22 of the EU Charter", in Xabier Arzoz (ed.), *Respecting Linguistic Diversity in the European Union* (John Benjamins Publishing Co, Amsterdam, 2008), 175–190, at 164.

95 Dilek Kurban, "Substantive Challenges to the Protection of Religious Freedom under the Framework Convention", in Verstichel *et al.* (eds.) *op.cit.* note 41, 121.

96 Shaw, *op.cit.* note 28, 17.

97 For various recommendations concerning a definition of 'minority' see the United Nations Sub-Commission on the Prevention of Discrimination and Protection of Minorities (SCPDPM) (1950), UN Doc E/CN.4/Sub.2/119, paras. 31 and 32; see also (1951) UN Doc E/CN.4/Sub.2/140/Annex I/ Draft res 11 and (1952) UN Doc E/CN.4/Sub.2/149, para. 26.

98 Patrick Thornberry, *International Law and the Rights of Minorities* (Clarendon Press, Oxford, 1991), 161.

99 Gaetano Pentassuglia, *Minorities in International Law: an Introductory Study* (Council of Europe Publishing, London, 2002), 63.

gaps regarding the field of application".[100] However, it is not yet clear whether these terms also include 'national minorities', because none are defined in the Race Directive. It is probably only a matter of time before the ECJ is asked to clarify the scope of the instrument's application. Furthermore, the presence of the term 'national minorities' in the CFR may suggest that a different use of the terms might have been intended. Nonetheless, there is nothing to prevent a national minority that shares a common ethnic origin from relying on the provisions of the Race Directive.

Given that the EU Race Directive was modelled on the UK Race Relations Act (RRA)[101] it may be useful to overview briefly the UK's approach to the definition of minorities. In interpreting the concept of 'national' minority under the FCNM, the UK adopted a broad reading of the concept 'racial group' under the RRA, which allowed the inclusion of 'national minorities' in the scope of this instrument.[102] Such a definition is in line with the defining criteria established in *Mandla v. Dowell Lee*.[103] A Sikh boy was refused admission to a school because he did not comply with the school's rules regarding a uniform. In accordance with the Sikh tradition, his father insisted that his son wear a turban over uncut hair, which was contrary to the school uniform rules. The headmaster refused to make an exception, and the applicants claimed indirect discrimination under the RRA. For the RRA to apply, it was essential to establish that Sikhs are a distinct ethnic group. Lord Fraser suggested a test on how to define the concept of 'ethnic origin', which *inter alia* took into account a long shared history of a group and a distinct cultural tradition. It was established that under this test the Sikhs are a distinct ethnic group, because they are a self-conscious community with a common history dating back to the fifteenth century, with a common language, and a common religion. Based on this test, members of the 'traveller' community were also recognized as an ethnic group because they share a common history, geographical origin, customs, folk tales and music.[104]

Accordingly, in interpreting the concepts 'race' and 'ethnic origin', the EU may draw on the experience of the British courts, which have interpreted these terms broadly, and even included the concept of 'national' minority under the FCNM. However, the British experience reveals that this definition has certain deficiencies. For example, it may inevitably exclude religious minorities, as discussed below.

---

100 Kristine Henrard, *Devising an Adequate System of Minority Protection: Individual Human Rights, Minority Rights, and the Right to Self-Determination* (Martinus Nijhoff Publishers, The Hague, 2000), 49; Shaw, *op.cit.* note 28, 17.

101 UK Race Relations Act, see note 29.

102 The UK signed the FCNM on 1 February 1995 and ratified it on 15 January 1998. The FCNM entered into force on 1 May 1998.

103 *Mandla v. Dowell Lee* [1983] AC 548.

104 *CRE v. Dutton* [1989] QB 783.

E. 'Religious' and 'Linguistic' Minorities

This section sheds light on some of the difficulties of defining religious and linguistic minorities. In particular, we draw on the experience of British courts in defining 'racial' groups, which exclude some groups with a common religion from the scope of the RRA. Given that the EU Race Directive was modelled on the RRA, we assess the implications of the EU following this practice. The section concludes with a brief overview of problems in identifying linguistic groups; in addition, ECJ case law on linguistic minorities is reviewed.

At first sight, it may seem easy to identify a 'religious' minority. A 'religious' minority is a group "the members of which are united by a common belief".[105] However, on closer inspection it appears that the lack of a clear dividing line between 'religion' and other spiritual practices causes problems in identifying relevant groups. Furthermore, different denominations may emerge within the main belief system which can cause further controversy.[106]

Moreover, religious minorities "do not fit strictly into the characteristics of spontaneity and permanency. One's religion can be changed by a voluntary act, which is not the case with race, color, language – relatively – and culture."[107] If an individual opts out of belonging to a religious minority, his/her individual freedom of religion is protected under Article 18 CCPR and Article 9 ECHR. By contrast, Article 27 CCPR addresses the problems of minority religious communities, i.e., the "establishment and maintenance of religious institutions and schools and the protection of religious rites and holy places".[108] Furthermore, there is:

> [...] nothing to suggest that the religious rights that are recognized, e.g. under article 27 of the CCPR, are contingent on the prior existence of the religion. The focal point is the existence of persons wishing to profess their religion rather than the types of religions that are professed.[109]

As to the EU context, both the Employment Directive and Race Directive (together referred to as the 'Equality Directives') may be of relevance in ensuring non-discriminatory treatment of religious minorities. The Equality Directives require member states to protect individuals against direct and indirect discrimination, harassment and victimization on the grounds of religion or belief (Employment Directive) and racial or ethnic origin (Race Directive). The scope of the Race Directive is significantly wider, because it applies to employment and occupation, the provision of goods and services, including education in both

105 Henrard, *op.cit.* note 101, 51.

106 *Ibid.*, 51.

107 Nathan Lerner, *Group Rights and Discrimination in International Law* (Kluwer Academic Publishers, Dordrecht, 1991), 32.

108 Shaw, *op.cit.* note 28, 192.

109 Eyassu Gayim, *The Concept of Minority in International Law: A Critical Study of the Vital Elements* (University of Lapland, Rovaniemi, 2001), 49.

public and private spheres. Conversely, the Employment Directive has a somewhat more limited scope, because it applies to employment and occupation in the public sector only.

Recent reforms proposed by the European Commission to expand the scope of the Employment Directive in order to match the Race Directive are significant developments in this respect and may ensure equal treatment of religious minorities who do not share a common ethnic origin, not only in employment, but also in education.[110] However, at present, the EU Race Directive is likely to have more impact on religious minorities with a common ethnic origin. In particular, groups that share a common ethnic origin and a common religion, such as the Sikhs, may benefit from the extensive provisions of this instrument, while groups that share only a common belief may be protected under the Employment Directive only.

To appreciate the effects of exclusion from the scope of the Race Directive, let us turn to another example from the jurisprudence of English courts. In *Crown Suppliers v. Dawkins*,[111] a Rastafarian who wore his hair in dreadlocks was refused employment by a government agency when he did not cut his hair. To establish whether the applicant was discriminated against based on his race, it was essential to decide whether Rastafarians comprise a distinct ethnic group. An industrial tribunal applied the test in the *Mandla* case and concluded that Rastafarians who had shared a common history only for 60 years did not form a distinct ethnic group. The length of the period was relevant here because although Rastarfarians could be regarded as a separate group, they were not identified as distinct by reference to their ethnic origin.[112] Similarly Muslims do not comprise an ethnic group because they have different nationalities, colour and languages.[113]

Religious minorities are often in a vulnerable position in Europe, because they are also 'new' minorities. To prevent discrimination against these groups, it is important to follow the practice of the ACFC, which confirmed that, for the purposes of the FCNM, 'religious' minorities are also 'national' minorities.[114] Accordingly, an EU definition of 'minority' should not be based on differences between racial, ethnic and religious minorities. Rather such protection should be tailored to the specific needs of the group in question.

As to linguistic minorities, they are easily identifiable by a common language. However, problems may arise in identifying and protecting such groups "where multiple languages are spoken and where a variety of dialects exist".[115] In states with multiple languages, if groups satisfy other defining criteria of 'minor-

110 European Commission, "Non-Discrimination and Equal Opportunities: A Renewed Commitment" [2008] COM(2008) 420 final.

111 *Crown Suppliers (Property Services Agency) v. Dawkins* [1993] ICR 517.

112 *Ibid.*

113 *J H Walker Ltd v. Hussain* [1996] IRLR 11.

114 Kurban, *op.cit.* note 96, 120; see also ACFC First Opinion on Cyprus (adopted on 6 April 2001).

115 Shaw, *op.cit.* note 28, 19.

ity' (discussed below in section III), all of these languages may require protection. However, if one of them develops into a *lingua franca* in the public domain, the group may lose the status of a 'linguistic' minority.[116] As to dialects, a pragmatic approach is necessary depending on the particular circumstances of a group and the principle of proportionality.[117]

In the EU context, Article 22 CFR stipulates that the EU will "respect cultural, religious and linguistic diversity". Some commentators argue that Article 22 CFR reflects the second dimension of minority protection.[118] For example, Arzoz claims that, "Article 22 accords to persons belonging to minorities a level of protection equivalent to the one recognised by international human rights law",[119] in particular the one provided by Article 27 CCPR. Conversely, De Witte argues that Article 22 is too vague and does not "translate easily into concrete minority protection standards".[120] Indeed, based on the respect for diversity in Article 22 CFR, it might be difficult to reconcile differences in approaches to minority protection in the constitutional traditions of member states.[121] The term 'respect' entails negative duties, i.e., states must refrain from direct or indirect interference with the enjoyment of a right.[122] Therefore, in the exercise of its competences, a minimum duty of the EU is, for example, not to interfere with the use of minority languages or jeopardize cultural diversity in the member states.[123]

Even though Article 22 does not explicitly refer to linguistic minorities, its aim to preserve linguistic diversity may have a positive impact on the jurisprudence of the ECJ. The ECJ has already offered some protection to 'linguistic' minorities, for example, in access to linguistic facilities in a host member states, albeit relying on EU free movement regimes and citizenship rights, such as in *Mutsch*[124] and *Bickel and Franz*.[125] Both cases concern the right to use a minority language in criminal proceedings in the host member state, a right available to the German

116 Henrard, *op.cit.* note 101, 53.

117 *Ibid.*, 52.

118 EU Network of Independent Experts on Fundamental Rights, "Thematic Comment No 3: The Protection of Minorities in the European Union", 25 April 2005, at <http://ec.europa.eu/justice_home /cfr_cdf/doc/thematic_comments_2005_en.pdf>.

119 Arzoz, *op.cit.* note 95, 164.

120 Bruno de Witte, "The Constitutional Resources for an EU Minority Protection Policy", in Toggenburg (ed.), *op.cit.* note 3, 115.

121 Joseph Marko, "Constitutional Recognition of Ethnic Difference—Towards an Emerging European Minimum Standard?", in Verstichel *et al.* (eds.) *op.cit.* note 41; see also Ringelheim, *op.cit.* note 60, 33-49.

122 Ahmed, *op.cit.* note 65, 267.

123 Arzoz, *op.cit.* note 95, 160; see also Evangelia Psychogiopoulou, "Accessing Culture at the EU Level: An Indirect Contribution to Cultural Rights Protection?", in Francesco Francioni and Martin Scheinin, *Cultural Human Rights* (Martinus Nijhoff Publishers, Leiden/Boston, 2008), 223-245, at 228.

124 Case 137/84, *Ministere Public v. Robert Heinrich Maria Mutsch* [1985] ECR 2681.

125 Case C-274/96, *Bickel and Franz* [1998] ECR I-7637.

minority in Belgium and Italy respectively. The ECJ did not base its reasoning on minority languages *per se*; instead, in *Mutsch*, it relied on the free movement of workers and ruled that it was essential for the integration of migrant workers into the host state to be able to use their language.[126] In *Bickel and Franz*, the ECJ tied the applicants' rights to EU citizenship and reasoned that, although the protection of minorities is a legitimate aim of the state, this aim would not be "undermined if the rules in issue were extended to cover German-speaking nationals of other Member States exercising their right to freedom of movement".[127]

This jurisprudence has significant practical implications. Thus, ECJ case law may allow some 'linguistic' minorities to claim special language rights in other member states, for example, by Slovene citizens in Austria and Italy and by Hungarian citizens in Romania and Slovakia. Moreover, such claims may not necessarily be limited to criminal proceedings but may also apply in other contexts, such as education.

To conclude, as the above overview of various types of minorities illustrates, there are different groups that may be protected under the umbrella concept of 'minority'. Although not all of them require an identical level of protection, this should not lead to different categories of minorities, which might create further confusion in this complicated area of law. In addition, such a categorization of minorities may allow states to evade "their obligations by using different designations for groups that could be considered minorities, such as 'aboriginal', 'immigrant' or whatever".[128] Even the ACFC emphasizes that applicability of the FCNM "does not necessarily mean that the authorities should in their domestic legislation and practice use the term 'national minority' to describe the group concerned".[129] However, the protection accorded to such groups under the regime of minority protection is based on a sliding scale of rights, including the "origin of their situation, length of stay in a particular country, and the reasonableness of a minority preserving and protecting its own culture".[130] Accordingly, this article aims to look beyond labels and focus on the essence of the definition of 'minority'.

126 Niamh Nic Shuibhne, *EC Law and Minority Language Policy: Culture, Citizenship and Fundamental Rights* (Kluwer Law International, The Hague, 2002), 79.

127 *Bickel and Franz*, *op.cit.* note 126, para. 29.

128 Jennifer Jackson Preece, "National Minority Rights vs. State Sovereignty in Europe: Changing Norms in International Relations?", 3(3) *Nations and Nationalism* (1997), 345-364, 348; see also the ACFC's criticism of state practice of narrowing personal and territorial scope of the FCNM's application. See ACFC First Opinion on Denmark (adopted on 22 September 2000); Second Opinion on Denmark (adopted on 9 December 2004, published 11 May 2005); PACE, "Minority Protection in Europe: Best Practices and Deficiencies in Implementation of Common Standards" (2010), Doc. 12109, paras. 69-72.

129 ACFC First Opinion on Norway, *op.cit.* note 52, para. 19.

130 Working Group on Minorities (1996), UN Doc E/CN.4/Sub.2/1996/28, 26.

III. What are the Defining Elements of the Term 'Minority'?

What constitutes a 'minority' for the purposes of EU law? To address this question, this part of the paper first outlines the three most-quoted proposals on the definition of 'minority'.[131] These definitions are then deconstructed and the common elements in all three proposals are discussed in detail, with the aim of defining the term in the EU context.

The most widely quoted definition in the literature[132] was proposed by Capotorti:

> A group numerically inferior to the rest of the population of a state, in a non-dominant position, whose members—being nationals of the state—possess ethnic, religious or linguistic characteristics differing from those of the rest of the population and show, if only implicitly, a sense of solidarity, directed towards preserving their culture, traditions, religion or language.[133]

A less successful, yet quite influential definition,[134] strongly resembling Capotorti's proposal, was suggested by Deschenes:

> A group of citizens of a State, constituting a numerical minority and in a non-dominant position in that state, endowed with ethnic, religious or linguistic characteristics which differ from those of the majority of the population, having a sense of solidarity with one another, motivated, if only implicitly, by a

131 In the Thematic Comment on the Rights of Minorities (*op.cit.* note 119), the EU Network of Independent Experts on Fundamental Rights emphasized that even though they are not legally binding, the definitions proposed by Mr Francesco Capotorti and Mr Jules Deschenes for the UN Sub-Commission on the Prevention of Discrimination and the Protection of Minorities are very influential. A similar importance was attached to a definition suggested by the PACE in Art. 1 of the 1993 Recommendation 1201.

132 Philip Vuciri Ramaga, "The Bases of Minority Identity", 14(3) *HRQ* (1992), 409-428, at 410; Patrick Thornberry, "Self-Determination, Minorities, Human Rights: A Review of International Instruments", 38(4) *ICLQ* (1989), 867-889, at 878; Geoff Gilbert, "The Council of Europe and Minority Rights", 18(1) *HRQ*, 160-189, 164; Thomas Simon, "Minorities in International Law", 2 *Canadian Journal of Law and Jurisprudence* (1997), 507-519, at 512.

133 Capotorti, *op.cit.* note 12, 96.

134 Michael Geroe and Thomas Gump, "Hungary and a New Paradigm for the Protection of Ethnic Minorities in Central and Eastern Europe", 32 *Columbia Journal of Transnational Law* (1995), 673-705, at 674; Jean-Paul Schreuder, "Minority Protection within the Concept of Self-Determination", 8 *LJIL* (1995), 53-80, at 55; Adina Preda, "The Principle of Self-Determination and National Minorities", 27 *Dialectical Anthropology* (2003), 205-226, at 213.

> collective will to survive and whose aim is to achieve equality with the majority in fact and law.[135]

At the European level, PACE's non-legally binding proposal in Recommendation 1201 has been widely cited by commentators:[136]

> [...] the expression 'national minority' refers to a group of persons in a state who:
> - reside on the territory of that state and are citizens thereof;
> - maintain longstanding, firm and lasting ties with that state;
> - display distinctive ethnic, cultural, religious or linguistic characteristics;
> - are sufficiently representative, although smaller in number than the rest of the population of that state or of a region of that state;
> - are motivated by a concern to preserve together that which constitutes their common identity, including their culture, their traditions, their religion or their language.[137]

There are certain common features present in all three definitions. These features may be divided into objective (identified externally) and subjective characteristics (intrinsic to a group). Objective elements include:
- A group
- Non-dominant position
- Numerical minority
- Citizenship/nationality of a state, as well as the requirement of maintaining long-standing, firm and lasting ties with the state.

The subjective element is:
- a sense of solidarity to preserve a minority identity

The following discussion will analyse each element in turn and evaluate its appropriateness for inclusion in an EU definition of 'minority'.

A. The Existence of a Distinct Group

This section deals with the existence of a group as a central element of the definition. In international law, the "notion of group requires the presence of [...] unifying, spontaneous (as opposed to artificial or planned) and permanent factors that

135 Deschenes, *op.cit.* note 13, 30.

136 Stephen Deets, "Reconsidering East European Minority Policy: Liberal Theory and European Norms", 16 *EEPS* (2002) 30-53, at 44; Martin Alexanderson, "The Need for a Generalised Application of the Minorities Regime in Europe", 8 *HM* (1997), 47-58, at 55; Stephen Deets, "Liberal Pluralism: Does the West Have Any to Export?", 4 *JEMIE* (2002), 1-12, at 2.

137 Recommendation 1201, *op.cit.* note 14, Art. 1.

are, as a rule, beyond the control of the members of the group".[138] Accordingly, a minority group can be characterized "by common descent and kinship. It follows that no person can become a member of an ethnic community just by declaring his sympathy or personal liking for that group".[139] At the same time, if group members do not wish to be regarded as a minority, their treatment as a distinct group would be a violation of the individual rights of its members.[140] As Article 3(1) FCNM states:

> Every person belonging to a national minority shall have the right freely to choose to be treated or not to be treated as such and no disadvantage shall result from this choice or from the exercise of the rights which are connected to that choice.

Moreover, the existence of a minority is a matter of fact and is not determined by law, as established by the Permanent Court of International Justice in 1930.[141] The Human Rights Committee (HRC) confirmed this rule in its General Comment on Article 27 CCPR.[142] Even though in practice an official act of recognition of a minority group may significantly facilitate its protection, such an act is not decisive to determine a minority's existence in a state. Otherwise, states could easily undermine provisions of international treaties by "simple legislative inaction".[143]

Accordingly, for the purposes of the present article, a proposed definition of 'minority' should take into consideration the concept that a minority is a group unified on the basis of spontaneous and permanent features. Its existence is determined by fact, not law, although official state recognition may be beneficial for a group's protection.

B. Numerical Minority and Non-Dominant Position

Where a numerical criterion is concerned, the above-discussed definitions by Capotorti, Deschenes and PACE have different ways of identifying a minority. Capotorti refers to a group with ethnic, religious, cultural characteristics which is numerically fewer than *the rest of the population* of a state. Deschenes writes of a numerical minority, while PACE suggests that a minority should be "sufficiently

138 Lerner, *op.cit.* note 108, 107.

139 Kay Hailbronner, "The Legal Status of Population Groups in a Multinational State under Public International Law", in Dinstein and Tabory (eds.), *op.cit.* note 28, 117-144, at 135.

140 Helen O'Nions, *Minority Rights Protection in International Law: The Roma of Europe* (Ashgate, Aldershot, 2007), 60.

141 *Advisory Opinion on the Greco-Bulgarian Community*, 1930 PCIJ Series B, No.17, 22.

142 Human Rights Committee, General Comment No 23: The rights of minorities (Art. 27) (1994) Para. 4, at <http://www.unhchr.ch/tbs/doc.nsf/(Symbol)/fb7fb12c2fb8bb21c12563ed004df111?Opendocum ent>.

143 Thornberry, *op.cit.* note 99, 157.

representative, although smaller in number than the rest of the population of that state or *of a region* of that state", thus adding another defining dimension of the term 'minority.' Based on the example of Belgium, this section aims to demonstrate that PACE's approach may lead to a more coherent definition. A minority in a non-dominant position should be protected both at the state and regional level.

It is a common assumption that a minority group constitutes a numerical minority. However no minimum or maximum threshold is identified, and a context-specific and pragmatic approach to the matter is preferred.[144] Even where a minority is a numerical one, statistics should be used cautiously, because "[a]n ethnic, religious or linguistic group may prove to be a minority in the State as a whole, yet a majority in some districts (where the overall majority is actually in a minority)".[145] Therefore, PACE's approach is more useful.

As to 'non-dominance', the term does "not necessarily imply being subordinate or oppressed, which tends to support the view that in a plural society the several ethnic, religious and linguistic groups could all be considered minorities".[146] Yet the mere coexistence of several minority groups in a country does not automatically suggest a non-dominant position.[147] To qualify for minority protection, a group may need to have a disadvantaged political, economic, social or cultural status.[148]

However, the requirement of non-dominance is complicated by the fact that in some states the country-wide majority may constitute a minority at a regional level and may need the protection afforded to a minority group.[149] This may depend on the degree of autonomy accorded to a district/region where a minority group constitutes an overall majority. Therefore, it may be useful to think of a minority "in the sense that such a group plays a minor role in the affairs of its country"[150] or a region.

Nonetheless, the protection of minorities at the sub-state level is extremely controversial. There is even a significant discrepancy in the approaches of the UN and CoE institutions. Thus, in *Ballantyne, Davidson, McIntyre v. Canada*,[151] concerning the use of English signs in French-speaking Québec, the HRC observed that Article 27 CCPR refers to minorities *in states*.[152] The HRC interpreted Article 27 in light of Article 50 CCPR, which provides that the CCPR applies to all parts

144 Shaw, *op.cit.* note 28, 25.

145 Yoram Dinstein, "Collective Human Rights of Peoples and Minorities", 25(1) *ICLQ* (1976), 102-120, at 112.

146 Henrard, *op.cit.* note 101, 36.

147 Wolfrum, *op.cit.* note 59, 162.

148 Henrard, *op.cit.* note 101, 37.

149 For example, Spaniards in Catalonia, English speakers in Quebec.

150 Dinstein, *op.cit.* note 28, 112.

151 HRC, Communication Nos. 359/1989 and 385/1989, *Ballantyne, Davidson, McIntyre v. Canada*, views of 5 May 1993, CCPR/C/47/D/359/1989.

152 *Ibid.*, para. 11(2).

of federal states. Hence, the English-speaking citizens of Canada could not benefit from the protection under Article 27.[153]

In an individual opinion, Evatt *et al.* rightly criticize this narrow interpretation of the HRC, because it could have the result that:

> [...] a State party would have no obligation under the Covenant to ensure that a minority in an autonomous province had the protection of article 27 where it was not clear that the group in question was a minority in the State considered as a whole entity.[154]

In contrast to the HRC's narrow approach, various CoE bodies consider that national minorities should be protected both at a sub-state and state levels. Recent debates within the CoE concerning Belgium exemplify this tension between a numerical criterion and the requirement of non-dominance at the state or regional levels.[155]

Let us consider the example of Belgium in more detail. Currently, French speakers represent 40% (3.36 million inhabitants) and Dutch speakers 59% (5.9 million inhabitants)[156] of the population of Belgium; a German-speaking minority constitutes a small percentage of the total population. Despite a slight numerical majority of Dutch-speakers as compared to French-speakers, these groups are co-dominant because they are on an equal political footing. Generally, international law does not protect co-dominant majorities in a state, because there is little risk that another language, culture or religion may be imposed on them against their will. The FCNM, however, specifies that if a majority constitutes a minority in the areas populated by another co-dominant nation, they may sometimes be protected as minorities.[157] In its monitoring of state compliance, the ACFC

153 Significantly, Art. 23 of the Canadian Charter of Rights and Freedoms remedies this situation by allowing children of English- and French-speaking citizens of Canada to be educated in their mother tongue in primary and secondary schools where they constitute a minority in a province with another official language. Canadian Charter of Rights and Freedoms (Enacted as Schedule B to the Canada Act) (1982) c. 11, at <http://laws.justice.gc.ca/en/charter/#instruction>.

154 Elisabeth Evatt, Individual opinion co-signed by Nisuke Ando, Marco Tulio Bruni Celli and Vojin Dimitrijevic (concurring and elaborating), in *Ballantyne, Davidson, McIntyre v. Canada*, *op.cit.* note 152.

155 Venice Commission, "Preliminary Observations on Possible Groups of Persons to which the Framework Convention for the Protection of National Minorities could be applied in Belgium" (2001) CDL (2001),121; PACE, "Report on Protection of minorities in Belgium" (2002), Doc. 9536, at <http://assembly.coe.int/ Documents/ WorkingDocs/Doc02/EDOC9536.htm>; Venice Commission, "Opinion on Possible Groups of Persons to which the Framework Convention for the Protection of National Minorities could be applied in Belgium" (2002,) CDL-AD (2002), 1.

156 Patxi Juaristi, Timothy Reagan, and Humphrey Tonkin, "Language Diversity in the European Union: An Overview", in Arzoz (ed.) *op.cit.* note 95, 47-72, at 66.

157 FCNM, Art. 20.

follows the same practice in relation to, for example, Bosnia and Herzegovina, which, as in Belgium, has co-dominant majorities.[158]

In Belgium, even though Dutch speakers constitute a slight numerical majority they feel that they have been treated as a minority for decades. As a result, linguistic boundaries in Belgium have gradually evolved into political frontiers.[159] In particular, Flanders insists that the principle of territoriality should be enforced rigidly in order to protect the Flemish language. Therefore, in their view, French speakers do not constitute a minority at the regional level. In contrast, French speakers residing in Flanders argue that they have the right to preserve their cultural identity. To this end, they have (unsuccessfully) contested a strict application of the territoriality principle in the context of educational and political rights before the ECtHR on numerous occasions.[160]

Consequently, where minority-in-minority situations are present, the correct approach is to take as a frame of reference the internal political composition of the country "insofar as these entities have certain concrete competences which can influence the population groups concerned".[161] As the example of Belgium above, the numerical criterion may not be helpful in defining a minority. Equally, the criterion of non-dominance may be misleading if its application is limited to the state level only. Overall, it is the minor position of a minority that should prevail in defining the term. Thus, for the purposes of an EU definition, a 'minority' is a group which is in a non-dominant position at the state or regional level.

C. Nationality/Citizenship Requirement

There is significant controversy surrounding the requirement of citizenship for the protection of minority rights. All three definitions considered above contain the criterion of citizenship/nationality. The terms citizenship/nationality are often used interchangeably. Indeed, they denote two interlinked aspects of an individual's connection with a state. The concept of 'citizenship' describes the internal dimension of an individual's belonging to a state, where s/he enjoys civil and political rights, while the term 'nationality' is the external aspect of a legal connection between an individual and a state; it is a term of international public

158 ACFC First Opinion on Bosnia and Herzegovina (adopted on 27 May 2004, published on 11 May 2005).

159 Jean-Claude Scholsem, "Belgium: Federalism and Protection of Minorities" (1994) CDL-MIN(94)7, 4-15, para. 1.5 (emphasis omitted), at <http://www.venice.coe.int/docs/1994/CDL-MIN(1994)007-e.pdf> ; Xabier Arzoz, "The Nature of Language Rights" , 6 *JEMIE* (2007), 1-34, at 32.

160 ECtHR, Appl. Nos. 1474/62; 1677/62; 1691/62; 1769/63; 1994/63; 2126/64, *Case relating to Certain Aspects of the Laws on the Use of Languages in Education in Belgium (Belgian Linguistics Case)*, judgment of 23 July 1968; ECtHR, Appl. No. 9267/81, *Mathieu-Mohin and Clerfayt v. Belgium*, judgment of 2 March 1987.

161 Henrard, *op.cit.* note 101, 35.

law.[162] Some commentators support inclusion of this requirement in the definition of 'minority'.[163] This narrow view, however, is increasingly criticized in the literature.[164] This section first contrasts the generous approach of the HRC, which does not require nationality/citizenship as a pre-requisite of minority protection, with the restrictive approach adopted by PACE.

One of the arguments against a citizenship requirement in the definition of 'minority' is that Article 27 CCPR refers to persons, not citizens, as does Article 25 CCPR on political rights.[165] Therefore, a definition of 'minority' under Article 27 should not include the requirement of citizenship. Indeed, the HRC in its comment on Article 27 noted that:

> [...] the individuals designed to be protected need not be citizens of the State party. In this regard, the obligations deriving from article 2.1 [ICCPR] are also relevant, since a State party is required under that article to ensure that the rights protected under the Covenant are available to all individuals within its territory and subject to its jurisdiction, except rights which are expressly made to apply to citizens [...][166]

The HRC's approach is rather generous, because it insists that not only is it unnecessary for minorities to be nationals or citizens, but also they need not be permanent residents: accordingly, "migrant workers or even visitors in a State party constituting such minorities are entitled not to be denied the exercise of those rights".[167]

This is, certainly, a very broad reading of Article 27 CCPR, where the requirement of citizenship is omitted. It is not, however, as broad as the wording may suggest. Scheinin clarifies that:

> [...] contrary to what some ironic commentators have suggested, the HRC did not say that visitors as a group would be a minority in the sense of Article 27. Rather [...] a state must not deny a migrant worker or a visitor membership in

162 John Dugard, "South Africa's 'Independent' Homelands: An Exercise in Denationalization", 10(11) *Denver Journal of International Law and Policy* (1980), 11-36, at 22.

163 Gudmundur Alfredsson, "Minority Rights and the New World Order", in Donna Gomien (ed.), *Broadening the Frontiers of Human Rights: Essays in Honour of Asbjorn Eide* (Scandinavian University Press, Oslo, 1993), 55-77, at 69.

164 Manfred Nowak, "The Evolution of Minority Rights in International Law, Comments", in Brolmann, Lefeber, and Zieck (eds.), *op.cit.* note 22, 116; Wolfrum, *op.cit.* note 59, 161.

165 Shaw, *op.cit.* note 28, 26; Henrard, *op.cit.* note 101, 39.

166 General Comment No 23, op.cit. note 143, para. 5(1).

167 *Ibid.*, para. 5(2).

> an existing minority merely on the basis of the temporary nature of his or her stay.[168]

Consequently, if migrant workers wish to identify with a well-established pre-existing minority group in a state, those workers may "very well claim the same protection as other members of the group, for instance, in the education system".[169] However, a completely new linguistic, religious or ethnic group that arrives in a country may not immediately demand the same level of protection.[170] This is what the requirement of maintaining "longstanding, firm and lasting ties with [the] state" in the definition proposed by PACE emphasizes. It aims to discourage newly arrived groups from claiming rights under the regime of minority protection "since this is perceived to have negative repercussions for national unity".[171] However, as Shaw rightly warns, the requirement of 'long-established' should not be subject to excessive interpretation: "[i]t means that the minority must exist as such. There is no stipulation as to how long this state of affairs has continued, nor any minimum qualification period."[172]

Moreover, the requirement of citizenship should not be a defining criterion of 'minority':

> [...] since the status as non-citizens is not always a result of recent arrival. But lack of citizenship can have serious consequences for members of minorities. In particular, it can seriously undermine their possibilities of effective participation in the political life of the country.[173]

Nevertheless, some commentators express concern that "by abandoning the requirement of citizenship and easing the necessity of a long stay on the territory of the state"[174] international law may weaken the regime of minority protection by opening it to a large number of persons. In particular, if a group meets most of the defining criteria of 'minority' as in the case of traditional ethnocultural groups of non-citizens, it is important to establish whether the lack of citizenship is the result of domestic policies which violate international rules.[175] For example, "unreasonable distinctions in determining citizenship"[176] may breach

168 Martin Scheinin, "The United Nations International Covenant on Civil and Political Rights: Article 27 and Other Provisions", in Henrard and Dunbar (eds.) *op.cit.* note 93, 23-45, at 26.

169 *Ibid.*, 31.

170 *Ibid.*, 31.

171 Henrard, *op.cit.* note 101, 41.

172 Shaw, *op.cit.* note 28, 27.

173 Eide, *op.cit.* note 53, 379.

174 Pentassuglia, *op.cit.* note 100, 59.

175 *Ibid.*, 70.

176 *Ibid.*, 70.

Article 26 CCPR on equal treatment or even Article 25 CCPR on political rights. Furthermore, ethnically motivated deprivation of citizenship may violate Article 5 of the International Convention on the Elimination of All Forms of Racial Discrimination.[177] Therefore, it is argued that, instead of broadening the definition of minorities, it is important to remedy obstacles to the enjoyment of minority rights.[178]

However, states may use the citizenship criterion to limit the enjoyment of minority rights. For example, since 1991 Latvia has denied Latvian citizenship status to a large number of members of its Russian-speaking population, who constitute so-called 'non-citizens' under domestic laws. To acquire Latvian citizenship, Russian-speaking non-citizens, who were mainly Soviet-era immigrants, have to successfully undertake complex naturalization procedures. Lack of Latvian citizenship subjects these minorities to differential treatment in the country, as they are deprived of political rights and barred from access to many professions. Latvia's accession to the EU has aggravated the situation of non-citizens. Russian-speaking non-citizens are now further disadvantaged, because they cannot benefit from EU rights, reserved to nationals of member states only. Despite significant international pressure to alter the situation, Latvia has maintained its restrictive policies for the past 20 years.[179] Even though this situation is indicative of weak enforcement of some international rules, the fact that states are allowed a broad margin of discretion in the matter sometimes results in a restrictive interpretation of the concept 'minority'.

Therefore, the requirement of citizenship/nationality should not feature as a defining criterion of 'minority'. The ACFC, too, warns that "the citizenship criterion may cause problems linked to certain guarantees relating to important areas covered by the Framework Convention".[180] Furthermore, in the context of EU law, the jurisprudence of the ECJ[181] suggests that "it will become increasingly difficult for States to restrict arrangements for linguistic minorities to its own citizens".[182] During its monitoring of the accession process to the EU, the European Commission has also not relied on a citizenship criterion in the definition of minorities. For example, the Commission disagreed with Estonia's "cit-

177 Art. 5(d)(iii).

178 Pentassuglia, *op.cit.* note 100.

179 Gulara Guliyeva, "Lost in Transition: Russian-Speaking Non-Citizens in Latvia and the Protection of Minority Rights in the European Union", 33 *ELR* (2008), 843-869.

180 ACFC Second Opinion on Hungary (adopted on 9 December 2004, published on 14 December 2005), para. 22; ACFC Second Opinion on Italy (adopted on 24 February 2005, published on 25 October 2005), para. 32.

181 *Bickel and Franz*, *op.cit.* note 126; *Ministere Public v. Robert Heinrich Maria Mutsch*, *op.cit.* note 125.

182 Verstichel, *op.cit.* note 41, 146.

izenship-centred definition",[183] introduced in a reservation to the FCNM.[184] In both Estonia and Latvia, the Commission applied minority standards "regardless of the nationality held and difference in personal status arising from nonpossession of Latvian [or Estonian] nationality".[185] Significantly, the European Parliament in its Resolution on the protection of minorities and anti-discrimination policies in an enlarged Europe,[186] while recommending basing an EU definition of minorities on Recommendation 1201(1993) of PACE (quoted above), has deliberately omitted the requirement of citizenship from the list of defining elements.[187]

Accordingly, an EU definition of minorities should not contain the criterion of citizenship. The legal effect of this would be the protection of groups which satisfy all the conditions to qualify for 'minority' status, but who might have been arbitrarily excluded through restrictive citizenship policies in their home state.

D. The Subjective Element

Another important consideration in defining 'minority' is a group's sense of solidarity aimed at preserving their identity. This section briefly outlines the subjective elements of a definition: an implicit intention to maintain a common identity as a group and self-identification of individuals as belonging to a minority.

If there is no sentiment to maintain a distinct identity, Article 27 CCPR would not apply.[188] To qualify as a 'minority' it is not enough that, for instance, a group speaks the same language. The group also needs to decide that exactly those people who share common characteristics should form a group.[189] Such a decision to preserve a minority identity, as the definitions by Capotorti and Deschenes suggest, may be implicit. Otherwise states could pressure a minority so that they would be unable to express their collective wish to survive as a group,[190] in particular, in the case of those minorities which live in undemocratic regimes.[191]

Equally important in this respect is self-identification as a minority. Article 3(1) FCNM leaves this choice with individual members of a group. This choice, however, does not imply a "right for an individual to choose arbitrarily to belong

183 Dimitry Kochenov, "Pre-Accession, Naturalisation and 'Due Regard to Community Law'", 4(2) *Romanian Journal of Political Science* (2004), 71-88, at 71, 80.

184 Estonia, Declaration contained in the instrument of ratification, deposited on 6 January 1997, at <http://www.coe.int/t/e/human rights/minorities/Country specific eng.asp#P263 14100>.

185 Commission, "Agenda 2000—Opinion on Latvia's Application for Membership of the European Union", [1997] DOC/97/14, 18.

186 European Parliament, "Resolution on the Protection of Minorities and Anti-Discrimination Policies in an Enlarged Europe" [2005] 2005/2008(INI), A6-0140/2005.

187 Verstichel, *op.cit.* note 41, 147.

188 Thornberry, *op.cit.* note 99, 165.

189 Marko, *op.cit.* note 123, 22.

190 Shaw, *op.cit.* note 28, 28.

191 Pentassuglia, *op.cit.* note 100, 69.

to any national minority".[192] Self-identification is "inseparably linked [...] to objective criteria relevant to the person's identity".[193] Let us take the example in *Lovelace*,[194] where, under domestic legislation, the female author, who married a non-aboriginal person, was permanently excluded from her aboriginal community. The HRC stressed that Sandra Lovelace "not only identified herself (subjectively) as a Maliseet Indian but also was ethnically (objectively) a Maliseet Indian".[195] Therefore, she had the right to belong with her group and reside on reserve lands belonging to her group. The HRC deemed the state's denial of her rights as unjustifiable and found a violation of Article 27 CCPR.

Accordingly, an implicit will to maintain a common identity should be regarded as a defining element of a 'minority'. Moreover, self-identification with a group is a matter of individual choice and no disadvantage may arise from making such choice. However, the subjective element is linked to the objective elements of the definition—self-identification is not enough to qualify as a minority.

IV. Conclusion

In light of the above discussion and given the presence of diverse minority groups in EU member states, an EU definition of minorities must inevitably be broad. The following elements can be suggested:

- The protection of minorities should focus on their needs, not on their labels. Labels should not affect the content of the definition of 'minority'; rather, the particular needs of a group may inform the degree of required positive state action. For example, a linguistic minority may need mother-tongue education, while a religious one may only require accommodation of its religious practices. If such groups are also protected under other international instruments, this should not detract from their enjoyment of minority guarantees.
- The presence of a well-established group in one or more member states is one of the defining features of 'minority'. A well-established group should regard itself and be regarded in the community as having a particular historic identity of belonging to another group. Such a group possesses certain religious, linguistic, cultural or other characteristics which distinguish them from the majority of the population at the state or regional level.
- To benefit from the regime of minority protection, a group should be in a non-dominant position at the state or regional level. The numerical factor is not necessary as it may limit the scope of the definition.
- The requirement of citizenship should not feature as a defining criterion of 'minority', because states may use this condition to exclude unwanted groups.

192 FCNM and Explanatory Report, *op.cit.* note 33, para. 35.

193 Verstichel, *op.cit.* note 41, 130.

194 HRC, Communication No. R 6/24, *Sandra Lovelace v. Canada*, views of 30 July 1981, UN Doc. Supp. No. 40 (A/36/40) at 166 (1981).

195 Scheinin, *op.cit.* note 169, 29.

- The subjective element of the definition is closely linked to the objective criteria—it is not sufficient to self-identify as a minority.

Accordingly, this paper advocates a broad definition of 'minority'. This definition is preferable because it is more inclusive in that it emphasizes the needs of minorities, as opposed to 'labels'. Such a broad definition may prevent states from excluding unwanted minority groups from the enjoyment of rights at the domestic and EU levels.

Summing up the proposed features, the following working EU definition of 'minority' may be suggested:

> A 'minority' is a well-established group in one or more EU member states. Such a group identifies itself and is identified by others as different from the rest of the population of a state or a region, on the basis of its language, religion, common culture, history and/or geographic origin. Only groups in a non-dominant position at the state or regional level may benefit from the regime of minority protection. The existence of a minority is determined by fact, not law. The choice of belonging to a 'minority' lies with the individual. Citizenship/nationality is not a defining criterion of a minority as such. The scope of protection, entailing different rights, depends on particular needs of a group.

*Peter Vermeersch**

The European Union and the Roma: An Analysis of Recent Institutional and Policy Developments

I. Introduction

Although traditionally limited in its influence over how national governments protect ethnic minorities and vulnerable social groups, the European Union (EU) has, over the last decade, significantly stepped up its efforts to bring the situation facing the Roma onto the policy agenda, both on the European level and that of the member states. In one respect, this move is the logical outcome of larger EU concerns for building better social policies across Europe, protecting minority citizens more effectively, combating poverty, and eradicating discrimination; but it also indicates a growing recognition of the specific challenges facing many Romani communities throughout the continent. This European policy attention is the type of consideration for which many Romani advocacy groups have worked. Although some authors have noted that a severe lack of data still hampers an accurate assessment of the situation,[1] continued reporting[2] by NGOs and international

* Peter Vermeersch is professor of political science at the University of Leuven in Belgium where he is affiliated with the Institute for International and European Policy and the Centre for Research on Peace and Development. In 2006, he published the book *The Romani Movement: Minority Politics and Ethnic Mobilization in Contemporary Central Europe* (Berghahn Books).

1 Christina McDonald and Katy Negrin, *No Data – No Progress. Data Collection in Countries Participating in the Decade of Roma Inclusion 2005-2015* (Open Society Institute, New York, 2010).

2 From the broad range of reports that have appeared in recent years, high-profile examples include: EU Agency for Fundamental Rights (FRA), *EU-MIDIS 01. Data in Focus Report: the Roma* (FRA, Vienna, 2009), at <http://fra.europa.eu/fraWebsite/attachments/EU-MIDIS_ROMA_EN.pdf>; UNDP, *Avoiding the Dependency Trap: The Roma in Central and Eastern Europe* (Bratislava, 2004), at <http://europeandcis.undp.org/>; UNICEF, *Towards Roma Inclusion: A Review of Roma Education Initiatives in Central and South-Eastern Europe* (2009), at <http://www.unicef.org/ceecis/ROMA_PAPER_FINAL_LAST.pdf>; and José Manuel Fresno, *What Works for Roma Inclusion in the EU: Policies and Model Approaches* (Publications Office of the

Minority Governance in and beyond Europe, ISBN 978-90-04-27648-2. pp. 199-222.

institutions has now at least made the issue hard to ignore: exclusion and poverty, as well as the processes of discrimination and stereotyping that exacerbate it continue to be a reality for many Roma; thus, reports stress, these persisting problems should worry policy-makers on all institutional levels.[3]

Bringing the issues facing the Roma to the attention of EU policy-makers has of course been only one of the goals set by advocacy groups. The more important ambition has been to rely on the EU's power to bring about a large-scale domestic political and socioeconomic change that would effectively improve the position of Romani communities throughout Europe and create more inclusive societies. The sorts of domestic policies that have now been put in place to achieve this goal, and the pace at which they have been implemented, vary across European states. The results are diverse as well. We have arrived at a moment in which a better insight is needed into the factors influencing these policies and determining their successes and failures.

This article will neither tackle the issue of influence directly, nor assess the success of these policies. Rather, more modestly, the goal of this article is to help lay the foundations of such an analysis by offering a contextualized exploration of the current landscape of institutions and policies of relevance to the Roma on the level of the EU. I believe a comparative examination of domestic success and failure can only be performed properly on the basis of a thorough understanding of this quickly shifting landscape of institutions and policies and of the political environment in which they have been adopted.

This article analyzes the recent developments on the level of the European institutions from five different, yet related perspectives. In the first section, I outline a number of key evolutions within the EU that have had particular consequences for the ways in which the situation of the Roma is addressed. These are ongoing processes of EU policy-making and institutional change that have been driven by the overall dynamics of European integration, such as the EU's pursuit to promote fundamental rights standards, the EU enlargement process, and the evolving European social inclusion agenda. In the second section, I consider a number of important events that have clearly spurred the EU's policy-making on the Roma over the last few years. I highlight in particular the recent upsurge of intra-EU migration, the troubling responses of certain states to the east-west

---

EU, Luxembourg, 2011). Recent reporting by internationally active Roma civil society organisations include ERGO, *The Black and White Book: Roma Inclusion in South Eastern Europe in Practice* (2009), at <http://www.ergonetwork.org/media/userfiles/media/egro/Black%20&%20White.pdf>; and Bernard Rorke, *Review of EU Framework National Roma Integration Strategies (NRIS)* (Open Society Foundations, 2012), at <http://www.romadecade.org/files/downloads/General%20Resources/roma-integration-strategies-20120221.pdf>.

3 The term "Roma" is here used in accordance with the way in which EU documents define it. So, the term is stretched to its broadest meaning so as to include communities who rely on a variety of other designations (such as Sinti, Khale, Romungre, Gypsies, Travellers, Gens de Voyage and so forth) but are yet considered to be part of the target group for the policies discussed herein.

mobility of Roma, and the rise of anti-Roma rhetoric and behaviour. In the third section, I focus on a series of recent EU initiatives and methods meant to facilitate Romani participation in EU policy-making and to stimulate the input of a variety of stakeholders in the debate about what Europe should do. In the fourth section, I explore some of the financial means that the EU has put forward in its attempt to persuade member states to increase their efforts for the inclusion of Roma. To conclude, in the fifth section, I focus on the political dynamics of the EU's growing concern for the Roma and the unintended consequences these dynamics may produce.

II. Key Evolutions within the EU and their Implications for the Roma

A. The EU's Fundamental Rights Agenda

The first development within the EU that warrants highlighting is the growing importance of the EU's fundamental rights agenda. Fundamental rights may not have been part of the initial institutional set-up of the EEC, but, as is argued by Smismans, "several interwoven discourses on fundamental rights developed which assigned, retrospectively, such rights as inherent in the European project and based them on a common European heritage."[4] The result is mainly visible in a number of legal shifts. The Maastricht Treaty (1992) and the Treaty of Amsterdam (1997) enabled European institutions to take measures to combat discrimination based on ethnic origin, including discrimination against the Roma. In addition, in 2000, the European Council of Nice proclaimed the EU Charter of Fundamental Rights, which, even though it had no formal legal status within Union law at the time, had a profound influence on the institutions.[5] The adoption of the Racial Equality Directive 2000/43/EC in June 2000 was another significant step; it prohibits racial discrimination in the areas of employment, education, social security, healthcare and access to goods and services in all EU member states. This directive was clearly the result of a particular set of political circumstances. It was adopted in a quick manner thanks to decisive political will among the member states prompted at that time by a widespread urge to respond forcefully to the inclusion of the Freedom Party in the Austrian government. Since 2000, the political context seems to have made such legal breakthroughs less likely: European Commission officials have pointed out that it would be harder now to find unanimous support for new legislation proposals in the field of anti-discrimination.[6] The Racial Equality Directive is of considerable importance for

4 Stijn Smismans, "The European Union's Fundamental Rights Myth", 48(1) *JCMS* (2010), 45-66.

5 EU Network of Independent Experts on Fundamental Rights. *Commentary of the Charter of Fundamental Rights of the EU* (Brussels, 2006), 15.

6 Melanie Ram and Peter Vermeersch, "The Roma", in Bernd Rechel (ed.), *Minority rights in Central and Eastern Europe* (Routledge, London, 2009), 61-73, at 72.

the Roma; it has given victims of discrimination the right of redress, and it mandates member states to designate a special independent institution that promotes equal treatment and provides independent assistance to victims of discrimination in pursuing complaints. Responding to this new context, many EU countries have improved their anti-discrimination legislation, and victims of discrimination, including Roma, now have better access to justice, and enjoy, at least in theory, increased victim protection against discrimination.[7] The legal landscape of the EU has further developed with the coming into force of the Lisbon Treaty in December 2009, which made the Charter of Fundamental Rights an integral part of EU law.

With the establishment of a stronger fundamental rights core within the EU came additional possibilities for monitoring by independent actors. NGOs could, more effectively than before, rely on the context of European institutions and legal arrangements when drawing up their reports. Moreover, some EU member states committed themselves to cooperation with non-EU member states and international NGOs in the field of inclusion of Roma in the context of the Decade for Roma Inclusion (2005-10). Additional reporting could also be performed by independent advisory bodies to the EU, in particular by the EU Agency for Fundamental Rights (FRA), which in cooperation with EU institutions, the Council of Europe and other international organisations has devoted specific attention to the case of the Roma.[8]

B. The Enlargement Process

Monitoring by independent organizations has also happened in the context of a parallel large-scale EU development that needs to be highlighted here: the enlargement process. In the context of its enlargement to Central Europe, the EU demanded from candidate member states a number of profound institutional changes and guarantees, and these requirements are still in place for current candidates in South-Eastern Europe. In response to those demands, the candidate countries have been increasingly prepared to adopt newly emerging European legal standards on minority protection and anti-discrimination.[9] The attention for the Roma in the context of the EU enlargement process dates from the 1990s. By including the requirement of minority protection in the Copenhagen criteria of 1993, the EU aspired to set the moral standard in this field and to seek compliance from its neighbours to the East. EU demands to the Central European countries regarding the Roma were primarily outlined in the Commission's 1997 Opinion on each country's application for membership and the subsequent annual

7 See, for example, the analysis Sina van den Bogaert, "Roma Segregation in Education: Direct or Indirect Discrimination: An Analysis of the Parallels between Council Directive 2000/43/EC and recent ECtHR Case Law or Roma Educational Matters", 71(4) *Heidelberg Journal of International Law* (2011), 719-753.

8 See, at <http://fra.europa.eu/fraWebsite/roma/roma_en.htm>.

9 Ram and Vermeersch, *op.cit.* note 6.

Regular Reports from 1998 to 2003. In addition, Accession Partnership documents in 1999 and 2001 emphasized priority areas for attention. For Romania and Bulgaria, there was an additional Accession Partnership in 2003, an additional Regular Report in 2004, and subsequent monitoring reports in 2005 and 2006. For all countries, these documents were supplemented by periodic statements and commissioned studies of the European Commission, the European Council, and the European Parliament, which became more numerous over time.[10] As a result, pressure increased, but lack of reciprocal commitments from the EU also led to a rather inconsistent enlargement policy.[11] The EU's conditions on minority protection appeared to be open to various interpretations and created uncertainty over which commitments exactly candidate member states needed to make to safeguard their accession;[12] for this and other reasons, membership conditionality remained rather ineffective.[13] Moreover, in the case of the Roma, adopting new policies and institutions has been far easier than fixing problems on the ground, many of which turned out to be not easy to resolve and require measures that could be unpopular among the wider electorate. Moreover, while political will to improve the lives of the Roma has been present at the national level, implementation has often been confronted with impediments at the local level.[14] Empirical research shows that both in 'old' and 'new' EU member states, problems with local policy implementation persist[15] despite the pressure that was exerted during the accession phase. There are currently no strong and effective responses to the practice of some local policy-makers of portraying Romani citizens systematically as a burden on the local economy, rather than as a group that deserves economic support as equal citizens.

C. The EU's Social Inclusion Agenda

The third development that warrants highlighting is the growing importance of the EU's social inclusion agenda, which has received particular attention in recent times as the economic crisis and severe issues of inequality among and within member states seriously threaten the EU's latest grand ambitions for economic

10 *Ibid.*, 68.

11 Philip Alston and Joseph H H Weiler, "An 'ever closer union' in need of a human rights policy: the European Union and human rights", 2000, at <http://centers.law.nyu.edu/jeanmonnet/archive/papers/99/990101.html>, p. 13.

12 Peter Vermeersch, "Ethnic Mobilisation and the Political Conditionality of European Union Accession: The Case of the Roma in Slovakia," 28(1) *JEMS* (2002), 83-101.

13 Bernard Steunenberg and Antoaneta Dimitrova, "Compliance in the EU Enlargement Process: The Limits of Conditionality," 11 *EiOP* (2007).

14 Ram and Vermeersch, *op.cit.* note 6.

15 Eva Sobotka and Peter Vermeersch, "Governing Human Rights and Roma Inclusion: Can the EU be a Catalyst for Local Social Change?", 34(3) *HRQ* (2012), 800-822.

advancement, the Europe 2020 goals.[16] Since 2000, efforts to tackle poverty and social exclusion in the EU have benefitted from the Open Method of Coordination (OMC), a 'soft' process in which states and European institutions collaborate on shared concerns in a voluntary manner. Three policy themes have dominated the Social OMC: active inclusion, which covers employment activation, minimum income and access to services; child poverty and well-being; and homelessness and housing exclusion. More recently, the social inclusion of migrants and ethnic minorities (especially the Roma) and the impact of the financial and economic crisis have come more to the fore.[17] Ongoing developments in the sphere of the EU's social inclusion agenda have reinforced particular initiatives on the Roma. For example, the Belgian Presidency of the Council of the EU in the second half of 2010 chose to focus on the issue of the early childhood development of the Roma, not only because general attention to Roma was on the rise but also because the issue of 'combating child poverty' had become a leading theme for the OMC and for the European Platform against Poverty and Social Exclusion. The subsequent Belgian report emphasized that there was 'a political window of opportunity to tackle the issue of Romani poverty through the perspective of early childhood services'.[18] Underpinning this choice was the observation that the topic of the living conditions of Romani children, although clearly quite alarming (with serious concerns about nutrition, health and early development), had remained to a large extent outside the general poverty debate. Moreover, the topic fit nicely in with the broader Belgian focus on child poverty. The work that was performed in the context of this platform meeting yielded a number of important conclusions, among them the proposal to promote the use of the Europe 2020 Strategy to mainstream the issue of inclusion of Roma into the broader policies on poverty and social exclusion. In particular, member states were recommended to present National Strategies for the Inclusion of Roma as part of their National Reform Programmes or to translate the headline targets into national and regional targets that address marginalised children. The Platform against Poverty and Social Exclusion was also recommended to devote special attention to Roma.[19]

16 See at, <http://ec.europa.eu/europe2020/index_en.htm>.

17 Hugh Frazer and Eric Marlier, "Social inclusion in the European Union: Where do We Stand, Where are We Going?" *Development and Transition* (June 2010), 5-7.

18 UNICEF, OSE and the Belgian Federal Planning Service for Social Integration, "Early Childhood Development and the Inclusion of Roma Families", discussion paper prepared on behalf of the Belgian Presidency of the Council of the European Union (2011), 5.

19 Danielle Dierckx and Peter Vermeersch, "The Social Affairs Agenda of the Belgian Presidency: High Ambitions and Mixed Achievement", in Steven Van Hecke and Peter Bursens (eds.), *Readjusting the Council Presidency: Belgian Leadership in the EU* (Academic and Scientific Publishers, Brussels, 2011), 153-168.

III. Key Trends and Events that have Prompted Responses from the EU

There are two recent sociopolitical trends to which EU institutions, often in concert with other European agencies, have felt a need to respond: certain radical policies of Western European member states directed toward Romani immigrants from the Eastern and South-Eastern parts of the EU, including ethnically targeted expulsion campaigns; and the rise of anti-Roma rhetoric in mainstream politics, accompanied sometimes by rising levels of violence against Roma perpetrated by extremist groups.

A. Migration and Mobility

Regarding migration, two popular assumptions persist: that Romani migration from east to west is massive; and that Roma are culturally and inherently inclined toward mobility. The latter idea is inherited from romantic portrayals of travelling Gypsies in popular culture, or perhaps, as Lucassen, Willems and Cottaar have argued, the result of a categorization practice by authorities and academics in the eighteenth and nineteenth century who sought to unify all sorts of itinerant groups under the single label of 'Gypsy'.[20] Both popular assumptions are faulty. Especially in Central and Eastern Europe Roma are usually not nomadic; as Matras wrote, "On the whole, the extraordinary feature of Romani migration is that so many Roma are prepared to take the risks of migrating *despite their lack of nomadic traditions*."[21] In addition, the extent of Romani migration is often exaggerated, which may be caused by a number of other factors: lack of precise official numbers, for example, and arguably also the high visibility, the relatively high level of internal cohesion, and the severe poverty of the Romani communities in question.

The example of the Belgian city of Ghent is instructive. Official figures provided by the city authorities show a strong increase of registered labour-seeking citizens from Bulgaria since 2004 (from 392 in 2004 to 5630 in 2011),[22] many of whom are assumed to be Roma. The overall number of migrants from the new EU member states in early 2012 was 3.6%, of which Bulgarian citizens were about 60%. These numbers are relatively small when compared with the presence of the total number of foreign citizens and Belgian citizens of foreign descent in Ghent

---

20 Leo Lucassen, Wim Willems and Annemarie Cottaar, *Gypsies and Other Itinerant Groups: A Socio-historical Approach* (Macmillan, London, 1998); Huub van Baar, *The European Roma: Minority Representation, Memory and the Limits of Transnational Governmentality* (F&N Eigen Beheer, Amsterdam, 2011), 87.

21 Yaron Matras, "Romani Migrations in the Post-Communist Era: Their Historical and Political Significance," 13(2) *Cambridge Review of International Affairs* (2000), 32. (Emphasis in the original).

22 Integratiedienst Gent, "Cijfermaterial IEM bevolking" (Gent, 2012).

(about 17.5% of the total population in 2010)[23] and certainly when compared with the size of other communities of migrants, with or without Belgian citizenship, or of migrant descent, in other Belgian urban centres. The increase between 2004 and 2011 of immigrants from the new EU member states in Ghent, however, has been highly noticeable because they often concern socioeconomically vulnerable groups: they live concentrated in particular neighbourhoods, often in detrimental circumstances, have limited access to the regular job market, and are therefore often visible in the streets during regular working hours. On the level of the municipality, extra policy initiatives have been taken to address these groups (partly on the basis of assistance through designated mediators and partly through attempts to control and stem further immigration). This extra policy attention was accompanied by rather extensive media attention and public debate, but it did not often lead to sober analysis: news headlines as well as politicians commenting on this case repeatedly spoke of a 'rush', an 'influx', or even 'a plague'.[24]

Similar developments could be observed in other European countries. In March 2011, the Netherlands counted about 125,000 working (but not all registered) labour immigrants from Central and Eastern Europe, of which the bulk (108,000) were Polish.[25] Although the number of Roma from Bulgaria and Romania constituted only a tiny portion of that overall figure, they are consistently talked about as if they are a vast group that will 'overrun' the West. Metaphors such as these are highly problematic: rather than offering a more or less realistic idea of the size of current Romani mobility, which may subsequently be used as the basis for a clearheaded discussion about adequate policies, they construct a dramatic illusionary image which, in turn, can easily be exploited for political purposes. An ostentatious example of such politics was the initiative of the radical Dutch Freedom Party (PVV) of Geert Wilders in February 2012 to launch an internet hotline calling on people to report complaints caused by the 'massive labour migration' of citizens from Central and Eastern Europe, in particular Poles, Romanians and Bulgarians. Although the website is not explicitly aimed at Roma, it has clearly induced and mobilized anti-Roma sentiment, a development that has been highlighted by several alarmed observers.[26]

---

23 Integratiedienst Gent, "Beleidsplan etnisch-culturele diversiteit 2012-2014 – bijlage 1: onderzoek en cijfers" (Gent, 2012), at <http://www.gent.be/docs/Departement%20bevolking%20en%20Welzijn/Integratiedienst/Beleidsplannen/Onderzoek%20en%20cijfers_ECD_2012-2014.pdf>.

24 References to these types of media responses are to be found, e.g., in Pascal Debruyne, et. al, "Welterusten, meneer de burgemeester!", *De Wereld Morgen*, 6 December 2010, at <http://www.dewereldmorgen.be/artikels/2010/12/06/welterusten-meneer-de-burgemeester>.

25 Official data are available at <http://www.cbs.nl/nl-NL/menu/themas/arbeid-sociale-zekerheid/publicaties/artikelen/archief/2011/2011-3423-wm.htm>.

26 See, for example, the remarks by Thomas Hammarberg in his position as Commissioner for Human Rights of the Council of Europe, quoted in Leonoor Kuijk, "PVV lokt Roma-klachten uit", *Trouw*, 28 February 2012.

National politicians and mainstream media in the receiving member states have mostly regarded the east-west mobility of Roma within the EU as a threat to their own fragile labour markets and social security systems, not as what it arguably could also be, that is, an opportunity to resolve some of the structural problems in those markets. Even if the Roma in question are young, inventive, active and willing to seek a job, they are seldom seen as a potential resource.

In some cases, notably in Italy and in France, the government responded by introducing targeted expulsion and migration control strategies.[27] In the summer and fall of 2010, it was the French case that reached international headlines. Responding to riots after a police shooting in July 2010, President Nicolas Sarkozy called an emergency ministerial meeting at which it was decided to shut down a large number of irregular Romani dwellings and single out Bulgarian and Romanian Roma for an expulsion campaign that would bring them back to their countries of origin, even if only temporarily. The 2010 crackdown was highly conspicuous because of its emphasis on security, its focus on foreigners (which from the perspective of the Roma in question must have seemed odd: the initial incidents did not involve Bulgarian or Romanian Roma but Gens du Voyage, that is, French citizens who cannot be expelled) and its overtones of ethnic discrimination. But the fact is that it was not a policy that came out of the blue. France had been sending Romanian and Bulgarian citizens home even before 2010. In 2009, the French government had already deported about 9,000 Roma to Romania and Bulgaria, and also other Western European countries (such as, Italy, Germany, Sweden, Denmark, Finland, and the United Kingdom) have for a number of years pursued targeted return campaigns. Mobility may not have yet become the Roma's preferred escape route from marginality, but expulsion has clearly become the preferred policy response to Romani migration.

Several EU actors and institutions responded forcefully to the highly publicized campaigns. As van Baar documents in detail, in a resolution adopted on 9 September, the European Parliament condemned the French policy and urged the French authorities to stop the expulsions immediately.[28] The European Commission responded through Viviane Reding, Commissioner for Justice, Fundamental Rights and Citizenship, who was in particular alarmed by the leaked memo of the French interior ministry that was distributed to local civil servants and urged French police officials to focus their efforts on migrants of Romani background.[29] Reding first threatened to bring France before the European Court of Justice for violating anti-discrimination laws but later, after the Commission

27 Peter Vermeersch, "Roma and Mobility in the European Union", in Kati Pietarinen (ed.), *Roma and Traveller Inclusion in Europe*, (Green European Foundation, Brussels, 2011), 91-97.

28 Huub van Baar, "Europe's Romaphobia: Problematization, Securitization, Nomadization", 29(2) *Environment and Planning D: Society and Space* (2011), 203-212.

29 Kim Willsher, "Orders to Police on Roma Expulsions from France Leaked", *The Guardian*, 13 September 2010.

received assurance from France that it did not single out Roma, refrained from pursuing an infringement procedure.[30]

B. Anti-Roma Politics and Behaviour

EU actors and institutions are not only spurred by domestic state policies that target Romani migrants in the countries of arrival, but also, over the last few years, they have been faced with alarming statistics of hate speech and hate crime against the Roma, both in the home countries and in the countries of arrival. Clearly, the Roma have become a more explicit target—not only discursively—of rising rightwing populism and violence.[31] Although anti-Gypsyism has a long history in Europe, today, Roma are more explicitly targeted than before as adversaries of the 'national' population in various places.

In Hungary, for example, the Roma are now widely depicted as cultural deviants and seen as an identifiable and essentially 'foreign' threat to the Hungarian economy and way of life. To some extent, anti-Roma rhetoric in Hungary now seems to eclipse anti-Semitism and resonates powerfully with anti-immigrant rhetoric in Western Europe. The trope of 'Gypsy criminality' is not entirely new—under the socialist regime, it functioned for a while as an administrative category that reified ethnic differentiation and ratified social inequality—but its resurgence today is accompanied by a new politics of nationalism. The main political exponent of this radical nationalism, Jobbik Magyarországért (Movement for a better Hungary) combines old concerns with new-style campaigning. It "promotes and perpetuates the cult of Trianon (the treaty ending World War I which 'dismembered' Hungary), licking past wounds to justify future territorial claims, whilst aggressively pushing a law and order agenda at home aimed at the supposed offenders of law and order, the Roma".[32] In the April 2010 parliamentary elections, the party gained almost 17% of the vote. Moreover, the law and order rhetoric inflated public anxieties and created an atmosphere of permissiveness toward those who propagate extremist measures to assuages those fears, be they politicians who advocate zero tolerance policies against 'the ethnic other' or private 'security' forces who claim to have the right to protect 'their' people against 'the Gypsies' with violent means. The now outlawed Magyar Gárda (Hungarian Guard), Jobbik's paramilitary wing, helped establish the idea that a 'fight against Gypsy crimes' is needed to save the nation. By joining force, even if only symbolically, with the Magyar Gárda, Jobbik managed to appoint itself to the role of civic security provider in locations in which 'Hungarians' are allegedly threatened by

30 van Baar, *op.cit.* note 28.

31 Mabel Berezin, *Illiberal Politics in Neoliberal Times: Culture, Security and Populism in the New Europe* (Cambridge University Press, Cambridge, 2009); Jon E. Fox and Peter Vermeersch, "Backdoor Nationalism," 51(2) *European Journal of Sociology* (2010), 325-357; Michael Stewart (ed.), *"The Gypsy Menace": Populism and the New Anti-Gypsy Politics* (Hurst & Co, London, 2012).

32 Fox and Vermeersch, *ibid.*, at 346.

'Gypsy criminality'. The party has also presented itself as the sole force resisting the Roma's so-called 'systematic usurpation' of the social security system.

In September 2011, Thomas Hammarberg, the Council of Europe's Commissioner for Human Rights, argued that "The consequences of anti-Roma rhetoric by politicians should not be underestimated. Their words can be understood as encouraging violent action against the Roma, such as mob violence and pogroms".[33] Political rhetoric for power is clearly one of the elements contributing to the sad succession of incidents that have plagued Hungary over the last few years. Between January 2008 and July 2010, observers registered at least 48 violent attacks against Roma, including nine fatalities (two of them minors). Dozens of Roma have been injured, 10 of whom have suffered life-threatening harm.[34]

Particularly worrying is the fact that the trend is not limited to Hungary. In other countries too, including states with autochthonous Romani populations (such as Slovakia) and countries in which Roma are more likely to be immigrants (such as Italy), such attacks have happened. Sometimes they bear the stamp of an organized movement; at other times they appear to be individual incidents.

IV. EU Policy on Roma and Specific Initiatives on Romani Participation

EU responses to this state of affairs have come in several forms. In the European Parliament, for example, over the last few years—2005, 2006 and 2008—new resolutions were adopted that concern the Roma.[35] In the resolution of January 2008, the European Parliament urged the European Commission to take heed of the conclusions of the European Council of December 2007 and to "develop a European Framework Strategy on Roma Inclusion aimed at providing policy coherence at EU level" (point six of the resolution).

Not only have European resolutions been voted, but also new European institutions and traditions have been established. These latter initiatives show an increased willingness on the part of the EU to take the issue of Romani participation seriously (or at the very least, participation of those who try to speak on behalf of Roma). The European Council of December 2007 gave its full symbolic support to the European Commission for the organisation of a series of 'European Roma Summits', of which the first one was held in September 2008 in Brussels and the second one in April 2010 in Córdoba. These highly visible meetings gathered approximately 400 representatives of EU institutions, national governments, regional and local public authorities and civil society organisations. Follow-up

33 Thomas Hammarberg, "Anti-Roma Rhetoric Underpins Obstacles to Roma Inclusion", speech at the Summit of Mayors on Roma, *Building mutual trust at the grass-roots Plenary Panel – Roma inclusion: what obstacles?* (2011), at <https://wcd.coe.int/ViewDoc.jsp?id=1835197>.

34 Stewart, *op.cit.* note 31, at xiv.

35 European Parliament resolutions P6_TA(2005)0151; P6_TA(2006)0244 (2005/2164 (INI)); P6_TA(2008)0035.

summits were organised in cooperation with the three Presidencies in office from 2010 (Spain, Belgium, and Hungary). The "Council conclusions on advancing Roma Inclusion" from June 2010 confirmed the consolidation of this new initiative.

These summits have functioned mainly as deliberative and advisory boards; they have brought together a broad range of stakeholders and have had the ambition to increase political awareness about the situation of Roma, especially among high-level national policy-makers. Yet they have also led to specific outcomes. The first Roma Summit, for example, led to the creation of a European Platform for Roma Inclusion. This is a platform for regular meetings between member state representatives, Romani activists, policy-makers and experts led by the Council presidency and aimed at the identification of best practices and the stimulation of cooperation and exchanges of experience on successful inclusion policies. The talks have led to several outcomes, one of which is a document called the "10 Common Basic Principles for Roma inclusion" (resulting from the Platform meeting in Prague on 24 April 2009, in the framework of the Czech Presidency of the EU). These principles form a guideline for policy measures and try to reach a delicate balance between, on the one hand, advocating special measures to support Roma and, on the other hand, a mainstreaming approach (the document describes it as "explicit but not exclusive targeting"). The suggestions are primarily meant to mobilize national governments, but close collaboration with the European Commission is also set as a goal. Clearly, the actors involved in this process have also tried to find another balance, one between giving responsibility to the EU for the issue of the Roma without taking responsibility away from the member states.

In April 2011, the European Commission adopted a Communication (COM(2011) 173) which confirmed this general direction. It called for an "active dialogue with the Roma", both at the national and the EU level, and it demanded a clear policy commitment from the EU member states. The latter were urged to draw up "national Roma integration strategies", a process that, in the end, must allow countries to not only compare ideas, practices and commitments, but also to create new possibilities for more robust monitoring by independent agencies and civil society actors. The European Commission has devoted a website to what has now become known as the "EU Framework for national Roma integration strategies", where the various national strategies can be consulted.[36] On 22 March 2012, the European Commission organized an Extraordinary EU Platform for Roma inclusion in Brussels, which gave all stake-holders involved an opportunity to express their views on the submitted national strategies and to discuss issues surrounding their future implementation. At the occasion, European Commissioner Reding urged the audience to be positive and to consider the achievements since 2008, which she called spectacular. Yet, she also admitted that "there is still a lot of room for improvement, in particular when it comes to securing sufficient funding for Roma inclusion and putting monitoring mechanisms in place. Fighting

36 At <http://ec.europa.eu/justice/discrimination/roma/national-strategies/index_en.htm>.

discrimination in education, employment, housing and health would also need to be better addressed, with a clearer focus on Roma women and children in particular. Most important: although we see many nice words in the national strategies, concrete deliverables, quantified targets and clear, ambitious deadlines for action are missing."[37]

V. EU Means to Address Local Issues

Although within different EU institutions the situation of the Roma is now clearly regarded as a significant public policy concern, such attention has not yet produced the much needed social change. While some EU-funded projects are no doubt successful (some are, for example, discussed in the 2010 report "Improving the Tools for the Social Inclusion and Non-Discrimination of the Roma in the EU", written for the European Commission),[38] on the whole, poverty, exclusion and discrimination persist; in some places the situation is even worse than ever before. Some authors have claimed that the EU institutions are themselves at least in part responsible for this lack of positive news.[39] They have argued that the financial commitments have remained too modest, the European Commission acts too formalistically, the EU strategies are much too dependent on the political will of other actors, and that the lack of an overall policy for the Roma sometimes leads to contradictory policies on the ground.[40] Yet, one should also continue to highlight the role of domestic and local political elites and authorities who are, and should remain, the main actors responsible for effectuating local social change.[41] The longer they wait to seize the institutional opportunities that have emerged at the European level to develop policies that effectively discourage discrimination and foster greater socioeconomic equality, the harder it will be for the EU to have an impact on local developments.

What have been the most recent building blocks of this European opportunity structure? The European Commission claims that a number of instruments and mechanisms that are meant to support more generally defined population

37 Viviane Reding, "Are National Governments Ready to Live up their Commitments?", Extraordinary meeting of the European Platform for Roma Inclusion (Brussels, 22 March 2012), SPEECH/12/215, at <http://europa.eu/rapid/pressReleasesAction.do?reference=SPEECH/12/215>.

38 Will Guy, André Liebich and Elena Marushiakova, "Improving the Tools for the Social Inclusion and Non-Discrimination of the Roma in the EU, European Commission", (European Commission, Brussels, 2010), at <http://ec.europa.eu/justice/discrimination/files/roma_report2010_en.pdf>.

39 See, e.g., Valeriu Nicolae, "Systemic Reform is Urgently Needed for the Roma", *Open Democracy*, 14 March 2012, at <http://www.opendemocracy.net/valeriu-nicolae/systemic-reform-is-urgently-needed-for-roma>.

40 Iskra Uzunova, "Roma Integration in Europe: Why Minority Rights are Failing", 27(1) *Arizona Journal of International and Comparative Law* (2010), 283-323.

41 Sobotka and Vermeersch, *op.cit.* note 15.

groups can be of specific use for the Roma. These include, for example, the Youth in Action Programme (a financial programme aimed at inspiring active citizenship, solidarity and tolerance among young Europeans) and the Second Programme of Community Action in the Field of Health. Somewhat more specifically directed at the primary concerns of many Romani communities is the EU's PROGRESS programme, which focuses on employment and social solidarity and can also be used to finance anti-discrimination campaigns. However, the main instruments on which the EU now counts for enticing national governments and local actors to engage in addressing the problem facing Roma are the structural funds.

To reduce inequalities within the EU (between regions and between member states) and to secure the social dimension of economic growth, the EU has traditionally relied on, respectively, regional policy and social policy instruments.[42] The EU structural funds (European Social Fund and the European Regional Development Fund) and the European Agricultural Fund for Rural Development are the main EU funding mechanisms supporting the socioeconomic integration of Roma. More particularly, the European Commission has recently emphasized the potential importance of the European Social Fund (ESF; including the Community Initiative EQUAL) and the European Regional and Development Fund (ERDF).

The EU's strategy is two-pronged. On the one hand, it wants to push governments into relying on existing funding schemes to address the issues facing Roma; the Communication of the European Commission of April 2010 stressed the choice for this strategy as the Commission found out that "Member states currently do not make yet sufficient use of available EU funds to address the needs of the Roma".[43] Suggestions were made in the Communication about how exactly national states should increase their efforts to make use of these available funding mechanisms and connect them directly to their national Roma integration strategies. On the other hand, the EU's funding schemes have been adjusted in such way that they can better serve the specific purpose of Roma inclusion.[44] This is, for example, quite apparent in the case of the European Regional Development Fund (ERDF). Regulation No. 437/2010 of the European Parliament and of the Council of 19 May 2010 amended Article 7(2) of Regulation (EC) No. 1080/2006 on the ERDF as regards the eligibility of housing interventions in favour of mar-

42 Mary Daly, "Assessing the EU approach to poverty and social exclusion in the last decade", in Eric Marlier, David Natali and Rudi Van Dam (eds.), *Europe 2020: Towards a More Social EU?* (Peter Lang, Brussels, 2010), 139-157; Gabriele Tondl, "EU Regional Policy", in Michael Artis and Norman Lee (eds.), *The Economics of the European Union* (Oxford University Press, Oxford, 2001), 180-211.

43 European Commission, "Communication from the Commission to the European Parliament, the Council, the European Economic and Social Committee and the Committee of the Regions: An EU Framework for National Roma Integration Strategies up to 2020", (2010) COM/2011/0173 final, at <http://eur-lex.europa.eu/LexUriServ/LexUriServ.do?uri=CELEX:52011DC0173:en:NOT>.

44 For more details see Sobotka and Vermeersch, *op.cit.* note 15.

ginalised communities. A decision of the Council of the EU now allows the extension of financial support from the ERDF for housing interventions for extremely poor and marginalised communities. Under the previously existing ERDF rules, housing interventions were only allowed in the context of integrated urban development and for the renovation of existing houses as part of an urban development plan. This meant that housing estates of the middle class could be renovated through the use of these funds, but not the housing in isolated or rural areas in which poor and marginalized populations live. This excluded many of the poorest communities. The change of regulation is not simply administrative; it builds on the underlying logic that funding regulations can have an impact on the economic integration of communities and counter processes of social exclusion. Those who have worked toward the implementation of this change hope that the ERDF has now been designed in such a way that it can serve as a community organizing tool.[45]

Yet, important challenges remain. It remains open to debate whether changes such as these—the introduction of *ex ante* conditionality in the structural funds, and more generally, European measures aimed at shaping domestic and local policies—are at this point elaborated and convincing enough to persuade member states and local governments to take the matter more seriously. Moreover, sustainability continues to be a key concern: it is still rather unclear how current opportunities should lead to lasting impact. Short-term funding might seem useful in alleviating certain pressing problems, but if the newly set-up structures for solving these problems do not survive long after the project, they might cause more distress and perhaps increase opposition to the Roma. As the 2010 PROGRESS report argues, "long-term funding programmes are needed to achieve sustainable progress. Otherwise initiatives for Roma inclusion will be vulnerable to budgetary pressures."[46] Certain examples, such as the Coexistence Village in Ostrava in the Czech Republic, where since 1997 a local NGO has tried to improve housing conditions and reduce poverty by placing responsibility in the hands of the poorest residents, demonstrate how useful and important it is to build long-term non-project-based relationships across Romani and non-Romani communities.[47] There is arguably a growing need to invest in the new spaces for citizens' participation that have emerged and now operate, either formally or informally, on the local, regional, national or European level and which may serve as a means for connecting marginalised and disadvantaged communities with mainstream society or mainstream political decision-making institutions and processes.

45 Peter Vermeersch, "Improving Access to Housing for Roma: Good Local Practices, Funding, and Legislation: Conference Report" (FRA, Open Society Fund Prague, Decade for Roma Inclusion Secretariat, Prague, 2011).

46 Guy, Liebich and Marushiakova, *op.cit.* note 38, at 37.

47 For more about the NGO in question, see <http://www.ohchr.org/EN/NewsEvents/Pages/IndianHRfightstoendRomadiscrimination.aspx> and <http://www.vzajemnesouziti.estranky.cz>.

Moreover, a narrow focus on project-based funding might unduly raise expectations about the potential of well-defined projects to change the reality of exclusion and discrimination. Something more than the projects alone is needed—a change of mindset among local power-holders and local communities. The European Council conclusions of 24 May 2011 show that there is at least a growing European awareness of the problem.[48] They include a call upon the Commission and the member states to find a way in which the various available EU funds can "work together in a more integrated and flexible manner in the future, providing an appropriate framework for integrated, long-term actions for advancing Roma inclusion". To achieve this long-term goal, some new ideas will be needed about how to develop such a framework of integration.

Apart from sustainability, there is also the concern of continuing or even rising discrimination. A broad group of civil society organizations fear that the EU's actions in the field of promoting social inclusion might not leave enough room for strengthening the fight against anti-Gypsyism. A document distributed by the European Roma Policy Coalition and the Decade of Roma Inclusion Secretariat at the occasion of the Extraordinary Meeting of the EU Platform for Roma Inclusion in Brussels on 22 March 2012 voiced the concern of about 50 Roma civil society representatives that achieving social inclusion requires sustained attention to discrimination. It argued that the National Roma Integration Strategies "cannot succeed without clear action to combat anti-Gypsyism, as this is one of the causes of exclusion that the strategies are designed to address."[49]

VI. By Way of Conclusion: The Political Dynamics of the EU's Focus on Roma

Although the current EU approach is not so much aimed at promoting the status of the Roma as a transnational European minority or constructing new European social policies targeted only at the Roma, it is clear that the EU has tried to increase its impact on domestic social policies aimed at the social inclusion of the Roma and at finding the right methods to improve their quality. In particular, it wants to promote existing financial mechanisms to persuade national governments of member states to devise and implement better social policies for their own population as a whole, including the Roma. During the course of the process, the new EU mechanisms meant to create some form of stake-holder involvement must also encourage the inclusion of the Roma's voice in domestic decision-making processes. In addition, the EU continues to rely on membership conditionality to influence policies in acceding member states.

48 Council of the EU, "An EU Framework for National Roma Integration Strategies up to 2020: Council Conclusions, 10658/11" (2011), at <http://register.consilium.europa.eu/pdf/en/11/st10/st10658.en11.pdf>.

49 European Roma Policy Coalition and Decade of Roma Inclusion Secretariat, "Document prepared at the Preparatory Meeting of Civil Society Representatives" (Brussels, 21 March 2012).

Even if this multi-dimensional effort is today far from completed and the results are still underway, one could assume that the European Commission has, at least in theory, the power and the money to change the situation on the ground—more perhaps than any other governmental structures beyond the level of the national state in Europe. However, as I have argued before,[50] we have to be careful not to ignore the risks related to what should perhaps be called the 'Europeanisation' of inclusion policies for Roma.

First, the enlargement conditionality policy of the EU—the policy that made EU membership conditional on a better protection of minorities, including the Roma—has clearly proved to have its limits. Such conditionality may have been influential in bringing attention to the Roma and in getting programmes and reforms adopted by governments in the acceding countries, but implementation has seriously lagged behind. In the end, the Central European countries were admitted to the EU while substantial problems remained. It is important that the problems connected to the conditionality strategy are kept in mind when devising policies toward the current candidate member states.

The second problem is that Europeanisation might give domestic governments an opportunity to evade their own responsibility. If NGOs claim that the Roma are a European minority, domestic politicians and governments can easily argue—and some of them have indeed argued—that the EU or other international institutions have a special responsibility for the Roma. Even when European institutions take special initiatives aimed at the Roma, they should make clear that national governments remain ultimately responsible for the protection of their own citizens. The Roma should not solely be regarded as Europeans but also as citizens of their own states. The process of Europeanisation risks the reinforcement the harmful and stereotypical idea that the Roma belong everywhere and thus nowhere. Analysis of debates in the European Parliament, for example, demonstrates that domestic politicians, even well-intended ones, might help to reinforce the idea that national policies are of less importance for the Roma than European ones because the problems facing the Roma are, as international documents time and again emphasize, 'European' in nature and thus extend the boundaries of the nation-states.[51] A 'European' interpretation of the problems facing the Roma might be problematic if it leads to a transfer of responsibilities for Roma inclusion to the level of the EU.

Third, the Europeanisation of the Romani issue might leave us with the impression that the situation of the Roma is very similar across Europe, and that formula-like solutions can be implemented. This is not the case. For example, it is clear from reports written for the European Commission that much variation

50 Peter Vermeersch, "Roma Inclusion: Can International Institutions Play a Role?" 15 *Development and Transition* (2010), 7-10.

51 Peter Vermeersch, "Reframing the Roma: EU Initiatives and the Politics of Reinterpretation", 38(8) *JEMS* (2012), 1195-1212.

exists, even if some key common areas for policy improvement can be defined, and that variation should be taken into account by policy-makers.[52]

Finally, European initiatives meant to remedy the problems that face the Roma should be implemented carefully to avoid the reinforcement of boundaries between the Roma and other population groups. If European support is not monitored well it might easily be interpreted as support uniquely for the Roma, rather than for society as a whole. The way funding mechanisms are structured and framed will be of crucial importance. As the 2010 report by Guy, Liebich and Marushiakova shows,

> funding that comes exclusively from outside a country (be it from the EU, bilateral or private donors) can address transitory problems or concrete infrastructure needs, but is otherwise unlikely to produce sustainable results. National financial support can be important to demonstrate political will and as a way of overcoming local opposition. But local financial support is important to underpin success. Such support, even if small, can demonstrate political will at the local level and the active role of local non-Roma communities as stakeholders.[53]

Roma inclusion strategies may now find the financial and symbolic support of the EU, but they also need the active involvement of local majority populations.[54] The views of "the community as a whole" will have to be taken into account not only in the context of the evaluation of the impact of measures, but also in the context of planning those measures. Deliberative processes, such as collaborative planning (meetings during which Romani and non-Romani inhabitants have a chance to legitimize each other's contribution to municipal plans), can be useful. Although the Roma will and should remain the focus of the main policy responses to the problems affecting this population, the results of the policy responses will be more effective when they are constructed on the basis of meaningful input from all parts of a local community, including other groups. There is a need to find mechanisms of social policy and human rights protection that promote the image of policy initiatives as beneficial for the Roma and non-Roma alike. Current initiatives are too often interpreted or portrayed as bringing resources to Roma that might otherwise have gone to non-Roma, while in fact they are lose-lose policies: the resources directed to the Roma have often been insufficient to bring any significant or lasting changes to Roma's daily lives. To avoid a backlash and at the same time create tangible socioeconomic change within Romani communities, it will be crucial to move from lose-lose to win-win policies so that the full support of the local governing elites and local majority populations can be garnered. Without such support, even the most promising initiatives on paper may not lead to lasting positive results on the ground.

---

52 Fresno, *op.cit.* note 2.

53 Guy, Liebich and Marushiakova, *op.cit.* note 38, at 36.

54 For a more elaborate argumentation of this issue, see Sobotka and Vermeersch, *op.cit.* note 15.

Index

K

L

M

N

O

P

R

S

T

U

www.ingramcontent.com/pod-product-compliance
Lightning Source LLC
Chambersburg PA
CBHW031323230926
51848CB00001B/67
* 9 7 8 9 0 0 4 2 7 6 4 8 2 *